Wisdom, Knowledge, and Spirituality in Self-defense

Wisdom, Knowledge, and Spirituality in Self-defense

A Rhetorical Exegetical Study of 1 Corinthians 1–6

SETH KISSI

Foreword by Ernest van Eck

WIPF & STOCK · Eugene, Oregon

WISDOM, KNOWLEDGE, AND SPIRITUALITY IN SELF-DEFENSE
A Rhetorical Exegetical Study of 1 Corinthians 1–6

Copyright © 2019 Seth Kissi. All rights reserved. Except for brief quotations in critical publications or reviews, no part of this book may be reproduced in any manner without prior written permission from the publisher. Write: Permissions, Wipf and Stock Publishers, 199 W. 8th Ave., Suite 3, Eugene, OR 97401.

Wipf & Stock
An Imprint of Wipf and Stock Publishers
199 W. 8th Ave., Suite 3
Eugene, OR 97401

www.wipfandstock.com

PAPERBACK ISBN: 978-1-5326-6230-0
HARDCOVER ISBN: 978-1-5326-6231-7
EBOOK ISBN: 978-1-5326-6232-4

Manufactured in the U.S.A.   02/12/19

I dedicate this book to my lovely wife, Mavis, my children—Akos, Paa Kay, Nana Ama, and Nana Yaw—and to all my nonbiological children—Abena, Kwadwo, Maako, Akua, Adwoa, Maabena, Azongma, and Kwakupong.

Contents

Foreword by Ernest van Eck | ix
Preface | xi
Acknowledgements | xv

CHAPTER 1
Introduction | 1

CHAPTER 2
Salutation, Thanksgiving, and Schism | 24

CHAPTER 3
Paul's Rated Image and Determinants of a Spiritual Person | 52

CHAPTER 4
Counter Assessment, Correction, and Exhortation | 71

CHAPTER 5
Correction of Wrong Perception and Further Judgment | 90

CHAPTER 6
Sexual Immorality as Evidence of Lack of Sound Knowledge and Spirituality | 119

CHAPTER 7
Lawsuits among the Corinthians—A Sign of Spiritual Degeneracy | 132

CHAPTER 8
Concluding Remarks on 1 Corinthians 1–6 | 151

Glossary | 157
Bibliography | 161
Index | 165

Foreword

OFTEN SOME OF THE most embarrassing characteristics of the modern-day church are the tension, strife, rivalry, and unhealthy competition among leaders and members that negatively effect the church. Normally, not many leaders—because they are subjectively involved—are able to respond appropriately to these challenges. However, if one, from a more objective point of view, understands why tension, strife, rivalry, and unhealthy competition surface at times, how they develop, and how they have been handled in the past, it puts one in a better position to handle these kinds of problems competently in today's church. This, Seth Kissi argues, is what his book offers.

And indeed it does. Kissi convincingly argues that 1 Corinthians was written at a time when three significant developments had taken place. The Corinthians, first, had evaluated their teachers by the impression they had of their oratory style. Second, some of the members of the believing community had come to rely on some doctrinal persuasions that promoted unhealthy relationships among them. Also, as a third development, some started to question Paul's authority over the church to the point where some members saw themselves as more spiritual than Paul, and therefore started to challenge his views. As a result, the members of the believing community aligned themselves with their favorite teachers (Paul, Apollos, or Cephas), around whom they built factions. In this regard, the Corinthians' assessment of Paul was unfavorable, and as a result, Apollos was championed.

This situation, Kissi argues, determines the tone of 1 Corinthians, and specifically 1 Corinthians 1–6. First Corinthians 1–6 is Paul's self-defense in which his foolishness becomes the foolishness of God which is wiser than men, and his weakness becomes the weakness of God that is stronger than men, a self-defense in which he has the mind of Christ which makes all other judgments directed against him null and void. It is because his readers lack sound wisdom, knowledge, and spirituality that they have

Foreword

misjudged him; they are babes in Christ and unable to appreciate spiritual truth meant for the mature.

Using rhetorical criticism as his approach, Kissi indicates that this evaluation of the Corinthians by Paul finds expression in repetitive parallels in 1 Corinthians 1–6, which tend to give overelaborations and overemphasis. Paul deliberately breaks down every "solid food" and turns it into "milk" in order to feed his "children" who have failed the test of maturity. This analysis is masterfully done, and will be a worthwhile read for anyone interested in the Corinthian correspondence.

Christianity is currently thriving on the African continent. But there is one problem: in many cases, Scripture is misinterpreted and misapplied. This leads to a similar situation as in the Corinthian community with regard to different doctrinal persuasions, unhealthy relationships, and some considering themselves to be more spiritual than others. So often Scripture is used to gain power and influence others to gain even more power.

Paul, Kissi argues, challenged these problems in his first correspondence to the believing community in Corinth. Kissi, however, and importantly, also goes further. His book successfully helps students, biblical exegetes, and ordinary Christians to understand 1 Corinthians 1–6 in such a way that it can be used effectively to challenge the same kind of problems in modern-day church and society.

Ernest van Eck
Department of New Testament and Related Literature,
University of Pretoria
29 August 2018

Preface

THIS BOOK IS THE product of my longstanding interest in 1 Corinthians, and a desire to add to other efforts meant to make the readers of 1 Corinthians appreciate its message in context. It is done with the conviction that when people understand God's word, they will be in the position to apply it appropriately to their own situation and that of others. There is already a growing concern about how Scripture is misinterpreted and misapplied in our Ghanaian and African contexts where Christianity appears to be thriving. This development calls for attempts to help students, biblical exegetes, and ordinary Christians understand God's word well enough to use it effectively so as to positively impact our society. The book is therefore an attempt to meet such a need, and is therefore designed to help both academics and nonacademics read and understand it.

The Greek words used are presented in such a way that makes it possible for one who has no knowledge of Greek to read this book meaningfully. The meanings of the Greek words are discernible in either the preceding or subsequent discussions. In most cases, the Greek words are presented in parentheses after their English translation. When need be, they come before their English meaning in brackets. At other times, the Greek comes in parentheses not after its translation, but after statements that capture the essence of the Greek words. For instance, "If they knew that they as saints would judge the world (οὐκ οἴδατε ὅτι οἱ ἅγιοι τὸν κόσμον κρινοῦσιν), they would not take their matters to unbelievers for settlement." The Greek simply says, "Do you not know that the saints will judge the world?" The preceding statement captures the essence and not the literal translation of the Greek. These imply there is no one way in which Greek words are presented in the book. Yet it is possible to make full sense of the book by bracketing or skipping the Greek words in reading. One last thing on the use of Greek

Preface

words: when Greek words begin a sentence, where applicable, small letters are used in line with the practice in the Greek New Testament.

As with the Greek language, rhetorical terms are usually presented with statements and comments that make their meaning or essence or both apparent. In addition, a glossary of the rhetorical terms used in the book has been provided in an appendix. Direct scriptural quotations are usually taken from the ESV. When other translations are used, they are indicated. Where it is considered more appropriate, my own rendering of the Greek text is used in the comments.

The rhetorical exegetical approach for the study came in handy for the reason that it had been my favorite way of interpreting Scripture. I have found the approach very useful for understanding New Testament epistles, and this study is an expression of my determination to use it in another major study following my doctoral work. Social scientific criticism, used in my doctoral study, is a useful approach for appreciating the social dimensions of the biblical text in the world in which it was written, helping one to understand how the biblical text is both a product of, and a response to, its social context. Rhetorical study, on the other hand, helps one to appreciate how the writer seeks to persuade his readers in order to achieve a particular end with respect to the readers' current circumstances.

Comments on the significance of Paul's argument are mostly incorporated into the rhetorical exegetical discussion. In a few instances, however, they are presented separately under the subheading "Comment." This happens when the comments are quite considerable in volume. The words "judge," "assess," and "evaluate" are used interchangeably for the Greek verb ἀνακρίνω in the discussion of 1 Corinthians 1:10—4:21, where all three senses are present.

The best way to read this book is to begin from the introductory and concluding chapters. The chapters in between them should be read successively from beginning to the end. These intervening chapters deal with Paul's arguments which are carefully and logically developed. This sequence helps one to follow the coherence of Paul's thought, and the consistency of his arguments, as well as the twists he incorporates to give new directions to his argument. This notwithstanding, where necessary one can read any of the intervening chapters without first reading the preceding ones. An attempt has been made to present each chapter in such a way that encapsulates its place within the broad rhetorical subunit.

Preface

The entire epistle of 1 Corinthians is regarded as a rhetorical unit expressing Paul's desire to work for the perfection of his readers, his tendency to judge the readers notwithstanding. In this light, the various arguments related to particular subjects are described as rhetorical subunits in this book. The parts of these subunits are treated as rhetorical divisions. It is hoped that as one reads this book, the manner in which Paul seeks to persuade his audience will open the eyes of one's understanding to appreciate 1 Corinthians better than before.

Seth Kissi
Trinity Theological Seminary, Legon, Acccra, Ghana
August 2018

Acknowledgements

SOME PEOPLE COME INTO one's life as a blessing in some specific ways. Professor Ernest van Eck of the Theology Department of the University of Pretoria is one such person to me. Upon hearing that I was writing this book, he sent me a very insightful book authored by Stephen J. Patterson. This book significantly enriched my discussion of the background to the issues addressed in 1 Corinthians. I also take this advantage to register my profound gratitude to Ernest for his exceptional commitment and devotion to me, and indeed, to all his students. As a student under his supervision during my doctoral studies, I was amazed by his prompt response to my work and the interest he took in it. Driving personally from Pretoria to pick me at the airport in Johannesburg anytime I visited the University, and driving me back to the port when returning, are some of his gestures that are beyond my imagination. I might sound hyperbolic if I should give more details of the things he did that have left lasting impressions on me.

I should also like to thank Professor John David K. Ekem of Trinity Theological Seminary, Legon, for his academic mentorship and supervision of my BD and MTh works. I always remember his words, "They have not said it all; we also have a contribution to make." This simple statement has been a great inspiration to me in my research and publication endeavors. The privilege of publishing a Greek textbook with him, entitled *Essentials of Biblical Greek Morphology with an Introductory Syntax*, is for me an act that baptized me into academic publishing. I am also grateful to Prof. B. Y. Quarshie, Rector of Akrofi-Christaller Institute of Theology, Mission and Culture, Akropong, for teaching me exegesis in Romans and 1 Corinthians. His insistence on understanding the Epistles without reference to another biblical text has been immense in its impact on me. I remember Professor J. O. Y. Mante, whose words challenged me to intensify my learning of the

Acknowledgements

Greek language in preparation for my Master of Theology course of study. The impact of this on my learning of Greek was enormous.

Deserving special mention is Dr. Frances Gench of Union Presbyterian Seminary, Richmond, Virginia. Her gifts of academic resources (among which is my favorite book for teaching introduction to the New Testament—Mark Allan Powell's *Introducing the New Testament*) have contributed in no small way to the building of my academic career.

I reserve great appreciation, love, and gratitude to my lovely wife, Mavis. The inconvenience she endured from the writing of this book which took place mainly in the house, and in our bedroom, is a lot. It is with love that I appreciate her understanding, love, and support. To God, who alone is worthy, be all the praise and glory for the grace to undertake this work.

Chapter 1

Introduction

TENSION, STRIFE, DIVISION, RIVALRY, and unhealthy competition among leaders and members afflict the church from time to time. Yet not many leaders are able to respond appropriately to these challenges. Notwithstanding the fact that no church wants bad press concerning these challenges, failure to handle them properly worsens such situations. Understanding how such developments come about and evaluating how they have been handled in the past put one in a better position to handle such matters competently in today's church. This is what this book offers. The Corinthians' perception and treatment of Paul and Apollos as reflected in the words of Paul, who felt poorly rated by members of his congregation, provide us with essential sociocultural dynamics from which we can learn. Understanding Paul's feelings about the situation also prepares one for some of the unfortunate realities of ministry. By appreciating the developments that resulted in the situation as reflected in 1 Corinthians, one comes to terms with the negative effects of some attitudes of church leaders and members, making the need for guarding against these attitudes imperative.

The book demonstrates the beauty, elegance, and force of Paul's rhetoric. Some puzzles in 1 Corinthians 1–6 are resolved, giving fresh insight into spiritual truths with respect to Paul's pronouncements. By setting the events in 1 Corinthians against the right background, this book helps the reader to appreciate how the attitude of the Corinthians toward teachers of wisdom and inspired men in their city influenced the problematic attitude of the believers toward their church leaders. To what extent did Paul's attempt to defend himself influence the tone of his arguments? How are the readers rated in terms of the very bases on which they had judged Paul? How do Paul's arguments reveal his emotions regarding how the Corinthians treated him? These and many more questions of practical relevance for today's church are answered in this study.

Several rhetorical studies have focused on 1 Corinthians. Most of these studies are preoccupied with the identification of the rhetorical devices used and the points made with those devices. They, however, present aspects of Paul's writings belonging to the same rhetorical unit as though they were disjointed and unrelated. The situation is not better in commentaries that employ other approaches to the study of Paul's writings. In a number of instances, Paul is presented as digressing from his address of a particular issue. I contend that Paul is a very consistent writer. It takes a little patience for one to appreciate the coherence of his writings. What this rhetorical critical approach brings to the interpretation of 1 Corinthians 1–6 is the demonstration of coherency within the first two rhetorical subunits and how this enhances understanding of the subunits. The insistence of the approach on following the development of the writer's thought, step by step, and identifying how each division relates to the other (and/or gives support and meaning to the writer's view) makes this coherence evident.

Among others, the attention given to the Greek text contributes immensely to the clarification of a number of issues on which other scholars have held different views that create difficulties in understanding Paul. Three examples should suffice here:

(1) Almost all existing commentaries on 1 Corinthians 2:1–3 fail to recognize the nexus between the image of one "in weakness and in fear and much trembling" that Paul paints of himself in 1 Corinthians 2:3 on the one hand, and his resolution to preach nothing but Christ and him crucified in the preceding two verses on the other hand (1 Cor 2:1–2). The failure to recognize this nexus is due to lack of attention not only to the flow of the argument, but also to the verb, ἐγενόμην (I became) in 1 Corinthians 2:3.

(2) There is a prevailing tendency to present the judgment Paul speaks about in 1 Corinthians 3:5–15 as applicable to Paul and Apollos and other workers in the Corinthian church. This interpretation fails to recognize three things from Paul's argument: (i) The distinct roles Paul assigns to himself (as the planter [ἐφύτευσα] and sole layer of the foundation [ἔθηκα]) on the one hand, and the roles he assigns to

Apollos (as one who waters [ἐπότισεν] as well as the builder upon the foundation [ἐποικοδομεῖ] Paul laid) on the other hand; (ii) the fact that Paul does not find anything wrong with his work which he did as a "wise" or "skillful" (σοφὸς) layer of the foundation, but raises caution about the work of the builder on the foundation; and (iii) the fact that Paul applies all the argument in the rhetorical subunit to himself and Apollos.

(3) Attempts to interpret literally Paul's injunction that the sexually immoral man be handed over to Satan has led to difficulties in interpretation in existing commentaries. A careful look at Paul's argument, however, shows that it cannot be another way of expressing the judgment of excommunication. Indeed, it is a sarcastic depiction of the very thing the immoral man had done. He had given his body to Satan in sexual immorality, confident that he was going to obtain the salvation of his spirit.

On the rhetorical devices Paul used and their significance, not much attention has been given in rhetorical studies to how they reveal Paul's intent of demonstrating that his readers were infants in Christ who were worthy only of milk. Not much focus is given to how these devices reflect his tendency to prove that the readers are unspiritual (1 Cor 3:1) and lack sound knowledge and wisdom. The uniqueness of the rhetorical devices he employs in 1 Corinthians 1–6 as compared with his other writings is indicative of how the Corinthians' own rating of Paul influenced him in his response. It is in respect of considerations like these that this study makes a contribution to the rhetorical study of 1 Corinthians.

RHETORICAL CRITICISM

Rhetorical criticism assumes that the author had a purpose for writing the biblical text. In seeking to achieve this purpose, the author makes some points, comes to some conclusions, passes some judgments, praises and blames some actions, and urges his readers to take some particular course of action. All these are done not without supporting arguments for the writer's stance. Rhetorical criticism is therefore not only interested in the point being made by the author of the biblical text, but also the supporting arguments with which the author seeks to persuade his readers to accept his position on the related issues.

Wisdom, Knowledge, and Spirituality in Self-defense

Andries Snyman has identified three approaches to rhetorical analysis of Paul's letters. Firstly, there are those that analyze Paul's letters by applying specific rhetorical models, usually of the Greco-Roman type. They endeavor to show that Paul's letters fit the typical rhetorical structure of *exordium, narratio, partitio, refutatio,* confirmatio, *and peroratio*. Others in this group follow a similar structure with a few differences.[1] The second approach tends to limit rhetoric to only "a few rhetorical techniques (such as rhetorical question) and to some stylistic devices (such as chiasms, parallelisms and alliteration)."[2] The third approach frees itself from the restrictions of any specific and limited rhetorical models in order to examine all the strategies employed in the text to determine how the author seeks to persuade his audience.[3] This approach provides more creative and innovative ways of analyzing the rhetoric of Paul's letters. The development of the third approach and its flexibility is the result of criticism against attempts to force Paul's letters to fit some particular ancient rhetorical structure.

While some think Paul wrote in the style of Hellenistic rhetoric, many scholars have pointed out how he fails as a rhetorician in his letters.[4] Concerning 1 Corinthians 1–4, Matthew Malcolm maintains, "I consider that Paul responds to this pastorally conceived problem by making use of certain conventional rhetorical motifs and techniques at a micro-rhetorical level, but without utilizing a conventional Greco-Roman macro-rhetorical arrangement."[5] Since Paul claims to have an aversion to the wisdom of word, it might be illogical and a forced exercise to make his letters fit a particular model of rhetorical structure. No doubt such attempts have produced different results for the same letter of Paul. For example, whether or not 1 Corithians 1:10 is the *propositio* has been a debate.[6] Another example is

---

1. Erickson presents six parts of what he considers to be a typical rhetorical structure of letters: *Opening, exordium, propositio, confirmatio, refutatio,* and *closing* (Erickson, *Beginner's Guide*, 126). Hardison, for his part, provides seven parts: *exordium, narration, proposition, partition, confirmation, refutation,* and *peroration*. He holds that the first four (*exordium, narration, proposition, and partition*) are usually brief and are part of the *exordium*, and based on the speaker's discretion, one or another of them could be omitted (Hardison, *Poetics and Praxis*, 65).
2. Snyman, "1 Corinthians 1:18–31," 130.
3. Snyman, "First Corinthians 1:18–31," 130.
4. Mihaila, *Paul-Apollos Relationship*, 165–68.
5. Malcolm, *Paul and the Rhetoric*, 3.
6. Malcolm, *Paul and the Rhetoric*, 138–39.

the disagreement over which part of 1 Corinthians 1:18–31 is the *probatio*.[7] Issues like these have led to this third (flexible) rhetorical approach to Paul's writings. In support of this approach, Alice Simutowe argues:

> In concurring with Morrison (2004:18), I argue that NT rhetorical criticism should not limit itself to the patterns of ancient Greco-Roman rhetoric, even though Greco-Roman rhetoric may be useful. Rather, the insights of modern as well as traditional Jewish rhetorical criticism may also be used to gain an understanding of how a text attempts to meet its rhetorical situation. Our basic question remains the same: How does this text try to persuade the audience? What is it trying to say, and how does it go about saying it? We use any tool, whether ancient or modern to help us understand how the text functions.[8]

All these speak to how diverse and creative rhetorical study of Scripture has become.

THE APPROACH OF THIS STUDY

This study leans toward the third (flexible) rhetorical approach. It must be admitted that rhetorical studies come with different emphases. A different focus is bound to produce results of its own. John Paul Heil, following the third approach, has considered the rhetoric of 1 Corinthians in reference to its use of Old Testament Scriptures. The rhetorical structure of the quotation as used by Paul, is analyzed freely using Greco-Roman rhetorical categories, modern rhetorical terms, as well as Jewish methods of exegesis like *gezera shava*, which for him have rhetorical effects.[9] It is in Paul's use of the Old Testament Scriptures that Heil determines the rhetorical units of the text. Snyman sought to prove that "Tolmie's proposal for a text-centered rhetorical analysis of Paul's letters"[10] is a credible option for rhetorical study. His work was therefore preoccupied with the identifiable types of arguments and the rhetorical techniques Paul employed for persuading his audience.

Following the third (flexible) approach, this study analyzes Paul's rhetoric as preoccupied with proving that the Corinthian believers were babes

---

7. Snyman, "First Corinthians 1:18–31," 132–33.
8. Simutowe, "Rhetorical Exegetical Study," 68.
9. Heil, *Rhetorical Role of Scripture*.
10. Snyman, "1 Corinthians 1:18–31," 142.

Wisdom, Knowledge, and Spirituality in Self-defense

in Christ and unable to appreciate spiritual truth meant for the mature. This finds expression in repetitive parallels, which tend to give overelaborations and overemphases. Paul deliberately breaks down every "solid food" and turns it into "milk" in order to feed his "children" who have failed the test of maturity. What made Paul take to this path? The Corinthians had assessed and evaluated him against other workers, particularly Apollos, and their verdict was unfavorable for Paul (1 Cor 4:3; 9:3). As portrayed by Paul, the Corinthians were misinformed or misled on many matters by the kind of knowledge and wisdom by which they operated. However, because of their judgmental attitude toward Paul, he not only concerns himself with correcting the Corinthians, but is also obsessed with evaluating and rating them. Nowhere in Paul's writing did Paul ever become so keen on evaluating and rating his readers as one finds in 1 Corinthians. Not even in Galatians, where he virtually insults the readers in his perplexity (Gal 3:1; 4:20), did Paul do what he did in 1 Corinthians. A quick scan through 1 Corinthians reveals (1) how Paul feels judged,[11] (2) how keen he was on assessing and evaluating his readers,[12] and (3) how he consequently finds

---

11. The following verses give some indication that Paul felt judged by the Corinthians:
    - "But with me it is a very small thing that I should be judged by you or by any human court. In fact, I do not even judge myself" (1 Cor 4:3).
    - "This is my defense to those who would examine me" (1 Cor 9:3).

In the following sarcastic depiction of his image in the eyes of the Corinthians, Paul uses the first-person plural as his way of talking primarily of himself:
    - "For I think that God has exhibited us apostles as last of all, like men sentenced to death, because we have become a spectacle to the world, to angels, and to men. We are fools for Christ's sake, but you are wise in Christ. We are weak, but you are strong. You are held in honor, but we in disrepute" (1 Cor 4:9-10).
    - "We have become, and are still, like the scum of the world, the refuse of all things" (1 Cor 4:13).

12. The following indicate that Paul was keen on rating and judging his readers:
    - "But I, brothers, could not address you as spiritual people, but as people of the flesh, as infants in Christ . . . for you are still of the flesh" (1 Cor 3:1-3a).
    - "Let no one deceive himself. If anyone among you thinks that he is wise in this age, let him become a fool that he may become wise" (1 Cor 3:18).
    - "Some are arrogant, as though I were not coming to you. But I will come to you soon, if the Lord wills, and I will find out not the talk of these arrogant people but their power" (1 Cor 4:18-19).
    - "I have already pronounced judgment on the one who did such a thing. When you are assembled in the name of the Lord Jesus and my spirit is present, with the power of our Lord Jesus, you are to deliver this man to Satan for the destruction of the flesh, so that his spirit may be saved in the day of the Lord" (1

fault with their wisdom and knowledge.[13] Fee argues that the fact that Paul

>   Cor 5:3b–5).
> - "Your boasting is not good. Do you not know that a little leaven leavens the whole lump" (1 Cor 5:6)?
> - "For what have I to do with judging outsiders? Is it not those inside the church whom you are to judge? God judges those outside. 'Purge the evil person from among you'" (1 Cor 5:12–13).
> - "To have lawsuits at all with one another is already a defeat for you. Why not rather suffer wrong? Why not rather be defrauded?" (1 Cor 6:7).
> - "I say this to your shame. Can it be that there is no one among you wise enough to settle a dispute between the brothers" (1 Cor 6:5)?
>
> Paul even makes mockery of their bloated self-image:
> - "Already you have all you want! Already you have become rich! Without us you have become kings! And would that you did reign, so that we might share the rule with you" (1 Cor 4:8)!
>
> These and others, including the way he modifies the maxims on the basis of which they misbehave, show how in seeking to correct his readers, Paul gets obsessed with rating and judging them.
>
> 13. It is clear from the following passages that Paul raises doubts about the knowledge of the Corinthians and the prudence of their actions:
> - "Is Christ divided? Was Paul crucified for you? Or were you baptized in the name of Paul? I thank God that I baptized none of you except Crispus and Gaius, so that no one may say that you were baptized in my name" (1 Cor 1:13–15).
> - "What then is Apollos? What is Paul? Servants through whom you believed, as the Lord assigned to each" (1 Cor 3:5).
> - "Do you not know that you are God's temple and that God's Spirit dwells in you? If anyone destroys God's temple, God will destroy him. For God's temple is holy, and you are that temple" (1 Cor 3:16–17).
> - "Let no one deceive himself. If anyone among you thinks that he is wise in this age, let him become a fool that he may become wise" (1 Cor 3:18).
> - "This is how one should regard us, as servants of Christ and stewards of the mysteries of God" (1 Cor 4:1).
> - "What do you have that you did not receive? If then you received it, why do you boast as if you did not receive it" (1 Cor 4:7b)?
> - "I have applied all these things to myself and Apollos for your benefit, brothers, that none of you may be puffed up in favor of one against another" (1 Cor 4:6).
> - "And you are arrogant! Ought you not rather to mourn" (1 Cor 5:2a)?
> - "Do you not know that a little leaven leavens the whole lump" (1 Cor 5:6b)?
> - "Or do you not know that the saints will judge the world? And if the world is to be judged by you, are you incompetent to try trivial cases" (1 Cor 6:2)?
> - "Do you not know that we are to judge angels? How much more, then, matters pertaining to this life" (1 Cor 6:3)!

Wisdom, Knowledge, and Spirituality in Self-defense

uses the expression "Do you not know that...?" ten times in 1 Corinthians with only one occurrence outside 1 Corinthians (Rom 6:16), "says much about his feelings toward the Corinthians and their behavior."[14] The foregoing holds enough bases for a rhetorical study that focuses on how Paul was preoccupied with evaluating and rating his readers. Despite the presence of abundant evidence of Paul's tendency toward the rating of his readers, this aspect of 1 Corinthians is hardly analyzed in rhetorical studies.

THE CONTEXT OF FIRST CORINTHIANS

The City

Over a long period of time, political and socioeconomic developments that involved occupation by Phoenicians and conquests by Greeks, Macedonians, and Romans gave birth to the city of Corinth we meet in the New Testament. The old city of Corinth was destroyed by Rome in 146 BCE. Ceasar rebuilt it in 44 BCE and later made it the capital of the Roman province of Achaia. By the Roman period, it had become an important center and the capital of the Achaia region because it hosted two important seaports that facilitated trade, commerce, and sea travel.[15] Corinth had a

---

- "I say this to your shame. Can it be that there is no one among you wise enough to settle a dispute between the brothers" (1 Cor 6:5)?
- "Or do you not know that the unrighteous will not inherit the kingdom of God? Do not be deceived: neither the sexually immoral, nor idolaters, nor adulterers, nor men who practice homosexuality, nor thieves, nor the greedy, nor drunkards, nor revilers, nor swindlers will inherit the kingdom of God" (1 Cor 6:9–10).
- "Do you not know that your bodies are members of Christ? Shall I then take the members of Christ and make them members of a prostitute? Never" (1 Cor 6:15)!
- "Or do you not know that he who is joined to a prostitute becomes one body with her? For, as it is written, "The two will become one flesh" (1 Cor 6:16).
- "Or do you not know that your body is a temple of the Holy Spirit within you, whom you have from God? You are not your own" (1 Cor 6:19).
- Moreover, the Corinthians have failed to understand the instruction in his previous letter that they should not associate with the sexually immoral (1 Cor 5:9–10).

14. Fee, *First Epistle to the Corinthians*, 146.
15. Harmening, *Mystery at Corinth*, 59.

strategic location on an isthmus of about 6.5 kilometers, lying between the Gulf of Corinth and the port city of Lecheum to the west, and the Saronic Gulf and the port city of Cenchrea to the east. It was on a narrow piece of land that joined the southern part of Greece (the Peloponnese) to the northern part of Greece, lying between Athens and Sparta. A lot of people and goods from many directions passed through Corinth due to the advantage its geographical location afforded. It offered an alternative inland route across the isthmus instead of the risky and longer sea route around it. Many captains found it safer and faster to carry their ships over land across the Corinthian isthmus on rollers. This made Corinth a very important port city. The wealth of the city was mainly due to the Isthmus of Corinth and the convenience it offered to merchants and sea travelers.[16]

As is usual with such important commercial centers, Corinth became cosmopolitan in many respects. It embraced not only people from many ethnic backgrounds, but also religious and philosophical backgrounds. Its population included Greeks, Romans, Jews, and others from the Near Eastern regions. William Harmening indicates that the city had a large number of diaspora Jews who had moved to Corinth after the Edict of Claudius in 49 CE.[17] Raymond Collins surveys a number of works in which the kind of wisdom the Corinthians relied on is believed to be influenced variously by Jewish wisdom tradition (including that of Hellenistic Judaism of the type of Philo of Alexandria), Jewish apocalyptic and philosophical thoughts, as well as inceptive forms of gnostic ideas.[18] Oh-Young Kwon mentions the influence in Corinth of rhetoricians and orators such as Cicero, whose "excellent eloquence" was admired by many who traveled to Corinth.[19] John Drane holds that mystics from the east were part of the population in Corinth.[20]

The ethnic diversity of the city also meant that, religiously, Corinth was diverse. While the presence of Jews, and later the Jesus movement, introduced their respective religions into the city, the worship of Roman and Greek gods had long been present in the city. The famous temple to the goddess of love, Aphrodite, is said to have hosted a thousand temple prostitutes in the city. While public prostitution was part of the pagan religion,

16. Grant, *Paul in the Roman World*, 16.
17. Harmening, *Mystery at Corinth*, 60.
18. Collins, *First Corinthians*, 96–97.
19. Kwon, *First Corinthians 1–4*, 38.
20. Drane, *Introducing the New Testament*, 322.

these prostitutes also became clients for people in the night. The city was noted for its immoral life to the extent that "to behave like a Corinthian (*korinthiazestai*) meant to indulge in immoral acts of sex and drunkenness. Craig Keener observes that sexual immorality and food dedicated to idols were regular parts of pagan religious activities, and both were usually part of banquets.[21] In terms of sports, Corinth was the host city for one of the two athletic festivals—the isthmian games, the other being the Olympic games.[22] Carl Holladay notes that the church in Corinth reflected the diversity of ethnicity, world views, and attitudes of the larger community.[23]

The Occasion for the Letter

Paul wrote 1 Corinthians in response to reports he had received concerning some disturbing developments in the church. Some members of Cleo's household had given him a report about division in the church (1 Cor 1:11). The church in Corinth, like many other churches in the first century, met in the homes of prominent members of the church. The house of Chloe was likely one of the various meeting places of the Corinthian church.[24] The issue of incest in the church was another problem that must have reached Paul as a report (1 Cor 5:1). In addition to these reports, the church had written a letter requesting that Paul address a number of issues of concern to them (1 Cor 7:1; 8:1; 12:1). It is possible that it was during their visit to Paul in Ephesus that Stephanas, Fortunatus, and Achaicus sent the letter in question to Paul (1 Cor 16:17). Paul picks the issues one after the other and responds to them with such introductory statements as "Now concerning . . ." (Περὶ δὲ . . .) as in 1 Corinthians 8:1, 12:1, and 16:1. Other subjects are introduced slightly differently, as in 1 Corinthians 11:2, 11:17, and 15:1.

The Rhetorical Situation

First Corinthians was written at a time when three significant developments, all of which determined the tone of the letter, had taken place. First,

21. Keener, *1–2 Corinthians*, 9.

22. It is said that the city of Corinth no longer hosted the Isthmian games after 146 BCE, after which time Sikyon took over until 44 BCE when Corinth regained charge of it. See Jaśelsner, "Cultural Memory, Religious Practice," 112.

23. Holladay, *Critical Introduction*, 307.

24. Phillips, *Exploring 1 Corinthians*, 12.

the Corinthians had evaluated their teachers by the impression they had of the teachers' style of delivery and the persuasive power of their proclamation. This led to a situation in which the Corinthians aligned themselves with their favorite teachers around whom they built factions. Second, the believers had come to rely on some doctrinal persuasions that in part promoted unhealthy conduct and attitudes among them. And finally, Paul's authority over the church was dwindling to the point where some members, who saw themselves as more spiritual than him, challenged his views. Each of these three factors deserve some details.

Evaluation and Alignment to Teachers

On their evaluation and alignment to their favorite teachers, as well as the resulting division in the church,[25] Keener makes the following observation:

> Recent scholarship has challenged older reconstructions based on "mirror-reading," but some of the situation, at least, seems fairly clear. In the past, many suggested different "parties" in the Corinthian church (1 Cor 1:12) with diverging theologies (those who argued for Gnosticism in Corinth particularly favored this view). Today, scholars are more apt to emphasize divisions over favorite teachers and their styles.[26]

This division over favorite teachers makes sense in light of two different developments: one is about the work of philosophers and inspired men in the general scene of Corinth, and the other is about specific developments related to the work of Apollos in Corinth.

---

25. While allegiance to teachers brought about some division in the church, it appears other factors also contributed to the problem as witnessed in other parts of 1 Corinthians apart from 1 Corinthians 1–4. There were those who saw themselves as possessors of knowledge who did not respect other members who did not possess their knowledge. The possessors of knowledge did not care about how their actions affected members who did not share their knowledge, especially in the issue of food offered to idols. In their abuse of the Lord's Supper, it appears some social and economic classes showed up. Those who had something to bring (usually the rich and the free) felt more comfortable eating early in their meetings so that by the time those who had nothing to bring (the poor, usually slaves) came, there was nothing for them to eat.

26. Keener, *1–2 Corinthians*, 8.

Wisdom, Knowledge, and Spirituality in Self-defense

Of Philosophers and Inspired Men

Anthony Thiselton's review of some scholarly works leads to an important conclusion. He maintains that Corinth was influenced by a kind of rhetoric that was more concerned with winning admirers than it was with the teaching of truth that was synonymous with Rome due to the works of its classical rhetoricians.[27] Henry Nguyen observes that during the time of Epictetus, outstanding orators like the Sophists used philosophy for purposes other than teaching truth, with their preoccupation being on "eloquence, mannerisms, and visual appearance" that could attract an audience.[28] Keener intimates,

> Like politicians, philosophers and orators competed for attention; more practically they vied for pupils and their fees. Students evaluated speakers; chose those they favored; and vigorously advocated their schools' interests against those of other schools (Suetonius *Tib.* 11.3; Philostratus *Vit. Soph.* 1.8.490), including in Corinth (cf. Dio Chrysostom *Or.* 8.9).[29]

What emerges from the observations above is the active attempts by teachers not only to persuade their hearers, but also to win their loyalty and patronage. In this respect, Thiselton notes that in granting fame to rhetoricians, the judgment of the audience was "manipulated and shaped by sophistic rhetoricians" whose strategies were seductive.[30] Scholars who think like this argue that these developments set the stage for the situation Paul addressed in 1 Corinthians. The Corinthians are understood to be behaving toward their teachers in the same manner as they did to the teachers of philosophy.

In his doctoral thesis, Timothy Brookins discusses recent scholarly works on the background to the Corinthian problem of division to demonstrate that the Corinthians were evaluating their teachers by the same token as their secular counterparts.[31] The situation was such that the evaluation of speakers' rhetoric and active defense of preferred teachers was a normal

---

27. Thiselton, *1 Corinthians*, 15.
28. Nguyen, *Christian Identity in Corinth*, 97.
29. Keener, *1–2 Corinthians*, 25.
30. Thiselton, *1 Corinthians*, 16.
31. Brookins, "Wise Man among the Corinthians," 19.

part of students' life.³² Commenting on the situation that arose after Paul had left Corinth, Keener notes,

> Although Paul may lack "opponents" in First Corinthians, some Corinthians do wish to "evaluate" or "examine" him (1 Cor 9:3), a matter to which he is sensitive (2:14–15; 4:3). Although neither Paul nor Apollos encouraged division (cf. 1 Cor 16:12), informal "schools" apparently formed around them in Paul's, and probably Apollos' absence.³³

Keener argues, "Apollos' spoken rhetoric was superior to Paul's (though Paul's argumentation in his letters was skillful: 2 Cor 10:10)."³⁴ There was a complex background that involved some connection between wisdom, knowledge, oratory, and inspired men, a background which was partly responsible for the Corinthians' rating of their leaders. This background had some implications. This meant that, an impressive speaker would be regarded as a dispenser of knowledge and wisdom, while an inspired speaker would be expected to speak persuasively. Wisdom and knowledge would also be associated with spirituality. Gordon Fee is right in holding that in the church in Corinth, wisdom suggested "superior spirituality."³⁵ Matthew Malcolm states, "In terms of background, I concur with Chrysostom that the problems arise from a situation in which current leaders were being undermined and pushed aside as a result of the believers' preference for polished oratory."³⁶

The interplay of rhetoric, oratory, wisdom, knowledge, inspiration, and spirituality was fluid and complex in the Corinthian church, with a similarly complex background in the city and beyond. Ecstatic utterances, as may have been practiced by the Corinthians, were common in the pagan religions. Adherents considered the "mysterious ejaculations and rapt utterances" as "inspired utterances" and a sharing in the divine being.³⁷ Associated with spirit possession in pagan religions were ecstasy, revelations, miracles, and utterances of unfamiliar words revealed by the spirits.³⁸ The association of superior wisdom and knowledge with the divine,

---

32. Keener, *1–2 Corinthians*, 9.
33. Keener, *1–2 Corinthians*, 9.
34. Keener, *1–2 Corinthians*, 9.
35. Fee, *First Epistle to the Corinthians*, 237.
36. Malcolm, *Paul and the Rhetoric*, 3.
37. House, "Tongues and the Mystery Religions," 142.
38. House, "Tongues and the Mystery Religions," 140–42.

Wisdom, Knowledge, and Spirituality in Self-defense

as was later known among the gnostics, meant that what was uttered by inspiration was highly prized as spiritual. Earle Ellis discusses the wisdom and knowledge Paul deals with in 1 Corinthians and finds the Old Testament and apocalyptic Judaism lying in the background.[39] He intimates that the association of wisdom and knowledge with the "pneumatics"[40] in the Corinthian church has affinity with the prophets and wise men of Jewish literature through whom God gave knowledge and wisdom to his people. It is believed that the interest and emphasis on persuasion and its association with wisdom and spirituality explain the rhetoric with which Paul wrote 1 Corinthians. Keener thinks Paul ends up putting more rhetoric in his letter than was usually permitted. In the words of Keener, he seemed to be saying "If it is rhetoric you want, I am able to offer it—for what, if anything, it is truly worth."[41]

The rhetorical tone of 1 Corinthians gives the impression that all the readers were against Paul, which was not the case. The tone only indicates that in 1 Corinthians, Paul was primarily addressing those who stood against him. That is to say, it is mainly the conduct of such people that attracted Paul's response in 1 Corinthians. This is one of the keys to understanding Paul's argument in 1 Corinthians.

The Nature of Apollos's Teaching in Corinth

Before dealing with the nature of Apollos's teaching in Corinth, it will be helpful to make a few observations about the specific problem of the division. Commenting on the competition among the teachers that resulted in the division in the Corinthian church, Eric Anum argues to the effect that one preacher presented the gospel to satisfy his cultural taste, while discrediting the variant adaptation of the message which was to the cultural taste of another preacher.[42] He maintains, "Opposing views were being met with rejection and resistance."[43] Given Apollos's Alexandrian background, John Drane argues that as "an eloquent man well versed in the scriptures," Apollos may have given an interpretation of Scripture similar to what was practiced by Philo of Alexandria in which what prophets like Moses said

---

39. Ellis, "'Wisdom' and 'Knowledge' in Corinthians," 82–94.
40. These are people who considered themselves as spiritual.
41. Keener, *1–2 Corinthians*, 29.
42. Anum, "Division and Reconciliation," 11.
43. Anum, "Division and Reconciliation," 12.

were presented as anticipating what Greek philosophers later taught. He maintains that if this is what happened, then Apollos would have had a lot of admirers.[44]

On the Hellenistic Jewish tradition Apollos inherited, Stephen Patterson gives insightful revelation about the influence of traditions within the collections of wisdom sayings (including those of Jesus) prior to the writing of the canonical Gospels. On the general scene, Patterson writes,

> Collecting the sayings of a famous person was quite a common activity in the ancient world. And it meant something. It meant that this person was a teacher, a sage, and more. He or she was a messenger from God. Wisdom, insight, prophetic sayings of public critique were all gifts from on high shared through God's chosen sages and prophets.[45]

The discovery of the Gospel of Thomas, in addition to the collection of the sayings of Jesus by Papias and the Q source (the source of Jesus' sayings in Matthew and Luke), meant for Patterson that the collection of the sayings of Jesus was a popular practice at the very early stages of the development of Christianity (prior to the writing of the Gospels). His analysis of the reconstructed Q and the Gospel of Thomas led him to the conclusion that for believers in Christ (mainly Jews) living at a time and place such as Edessa, the place where the Gospel of Thomas was initially used, the sayings of Jesus were more important than his death (see Matt 7:24–25; Luke 6:47–48). This is because the absence of persecution and suffering in that part of the world did not call for the kind of reflection on the significance of Jesus' death, as it happened in the Roman provinces where persecution was the order of the day. For such people, Patterson maintains, "At a time when many wonder about the wisdom of martyrdom, the glorification of suffering, or even the logic of vicarious death, it will be helpful to realize that this was not the only way that early followers of Jesus found meaning in his life. Many found meaning primarily in his sayings."[46]

Apollos's teaching ministry in Corinth can be appreciated within this development of interest in the sayings of Jesus and others like John the Baptist. Patterson has reconstructed the problem Paul found in Apollos's

---

44. Drane, *Introducing the New Testament*, 323.

45. Patterson, *Lost Way*, 16. Patterson intimates that "Greek and Roman philosophical schools also collected sayings and anecdotes of their great teachers like Epictetus, Epicurus or Diogenes" (*Lost Way*, 111).

46. Patterson, *Lost Way*, 17.

Wisdom, Knowledge, and Spirituality in Self-defense

teaching against the Alexandrian Hellenistic Jewish tradition and traditions in the early collection of the sayings of Jesus. This deserves some extensive attention here. He argues to the effect that Apollos's favorite teacher was John the Baptist, whom Apollos considered the teacher of Jesus. Apollos is said to have spoken and taught "accurately the things concerning Jesus, though he knew only the baptism of John" (Acts 18:25). Gleaning from Acts, Patterson concludes that Priscilla and Aquila did not succeed in correcting Apollos concerning his teaching about Jesus, contrary to what Acts says (Acts 18:26). This accounts for why Apollos baptized his converts in Ephesus only with John's baptism. Indeed, Paul was surprised to learn this about Apollos's converts (considered disciples of Christ) when he visited Ephesus (Acts 19:1–6). Paul's reaction was to explain to the disciples that John was only preparing his hearers to believe in Jesus (a precursor to Jesus). So it was Paul who actually baptized the so-called "disciples" of Christ in the name of Jesus after they had believed his message about Jesus. Patterson concludes, "In spite of their [Priscilla and Aquila] efforts, Apollos was still baptizing people as John had taught. Jesus, after all, had been baptized by John. If it was good enough for Jesus, Apollos must have thought, who were Priscilla and Aquila to dispute its adequacy?"[47] Against this background, Patterson surmises that "much of what Paul says in this letter (First Corinthians) is to roll back the effects of Apollos's teaching," given the fact that Paul was in the position to know what Apollos taught.[48]

On the content of his teaching, Patterson considers Apollos as a wisdom teacher who taught the "wisdom of words" (1 Cor 1:18–20). Describing it as "worldly" (1 Cor 1:20) meant that Paul must have found it reflecting "the sophistication and subtlety of the Jewish Platonism of Alexandria" where Apollos came from.[49] Prominent in this teaching would be the concept of the human person as comprising the flesh (*sarx*), the soul (*psychē*), and spirit (*pneuma*) (see 1 Cor 2:14—3:4). Apollos would have taught that "when the spirit reigns, it pours forth in spiritual gifts like ecstatic speech and prophecy (see 1 Cor 12–14)," and that "the spirit is from God," and "just knowing this could lift one above whatever lowly station one began in and produce such pride that someone like Paul could mistake it for 'boasting' (see 1:26–31)." Such teaching could be required of baptismal candidates

---

47. Patterson, *Lost Way*, 219.
48. Patterson, *Lost Way*, 221.
49. Patterson, *Lost Way*, 221.

to be baptized by Apollos in the order of John's baptism, which Jesus had received too.[50]

Apollos would have considered the Spirit coming upon Jesus at his baptism (Matt 3:13–17; Luke 1:9–11; John 1:32–34) as the time when Jesus became a son in line with the declaration of the voice that spoke from heaven. Understood in terms of Jesus's own baptismal experience, the baptism of the Corinthians by Apollos would also mean the believers had experienced "the reality of immortal life [in becoming children of God at baptism], so that any idea of a future resurrection of the dead was superfluous (see 1 Cor 15:12)."[51] This could explain why they would not expect a future resurrection (1 Cor 15), hence, "already they were fulfilled, already they were rich, already they were 'reigning'" (see 1 Cor 4:8).[52] For the believers baptized by Apollos, therefore, the kingdom of God had already come; it was not to be expected in the future.

Patterson establishes the presence of such teachings in Q and the Gospel of Thomas and reckons that Apollos's wisdom theology "must have been taking shape among those who collected and cherished the wisdom of Jesus of Nazareth (and John the Baptist)"[53] before the written Gospels.[54] He demonstrates with texts from the reconstructed Q in which Jesus is presented along with John the Baptist as equals, prophets of wisdom sayings. Patterson argues that it was possible for the believers to believe in two prophets of wisdom—John the Baptist and Jesus—who both suffered "the fate of all of Wisdom prophets."[55] This is in line with the tradition that portrayed John and Jesus as children of Wisdom in Q and the Gospel of Thomas, where all that mattered was believing and keeping the word of wisdom.[56]

Following the unfolding understanding here, "Apollos was a follower first of John, not Jesus."[57] Patterson demonstrates from Luke and Q how the baptism of John by his followers continued along with the ministry of Jesus up to some twenty years after the death of both (John and Jesus). In practice, therefore, the portrayal of John as the precursor to Jesus in the

---

50. Patterson, *Lost Way*, 221.
51. Patterson, *Lost Way*, 222.
52. Patterson, *Lost Way*, 222.
53. Patterson, *Lost Way*, 222.
54. Patterson, *Lost Way*, 222–41.
55. Patterson, *Lost Way*, 224.
56. Patterson, *Lost Way*, 224.
57. Patterson, *Lost Way*, 223.

Wisdom, Knowledge, and Spirituality in Self-defense

Gospels did not end the tradition of John, who continued to preach and make disciples (Luke 7:20–23), and whose followers continued to make converts. The friendly portrayal of Jesus and John as working for the same goal explains how Apollos could go to Ephesus "as a follower of Jesus who practiced the baptism of John" for he could honor both John and Jesus as teachers of wisdom.[58]

Given the understanding that all who were baptized had become the children of God (and a similar understanding in the Hellenistic world), what was left in terms of Christology was for Jesus and John to be considered as "messengers sent by God into the world to reveal Wisdom's ways to the children of God."[59] By regarding Jesus and John as messengers of God, it was possible to hold one above the other. By deduction, Patterson maintains that the development that led later to the insistence in the Johannine prologue that Jesus, and not John, was the Logos sent by God, reflects a situation in which teachers like Apollos may have taught that John was the messenger sent from God, a predecessor and not a precursor to Jesus. His students could have had some understanding of this that led them to curse Jesus, that is if Paul's words in 1 Corinthians 12:3 touched on anything going on among the Corinthians.[60] If Patterson takes matters too far here, one would think it reasonable at least to hold that when Paul insisted, "no one can lay a foundation other than that which is laid, which is Jesus Christ" (1 Cor 3:11), he was certainly fighting not against another Christ foundation, but another foundation in the tradition of John and his baptism. Could this be the reason that Paul was thankful that he did not baptize many Corinthians, since that could have led them to claim that they were baptized in Paul's name (1 Cor 1:14–15)? The tone of Paul's question makes it almost certain that some baptism was being done in some other names. It is now time to conclude on the first of the factors responsible for the situation addressed in 1 Corinthians.

An attempt has been made to explain that concepts related to wisdom, knowledge, inspiration, oratory, and persuasion underpin the situation one encounters in Paul's first Letter to the Corinthians. Traditions within Hellenistic and Jewish religions and philosophy produced a situation which shaped, in part, a number of things, including the message Apollos preached in Corinth, the Corinthians' attitude to that message, and the Corinthians'

---

58. Patterson, *Lost Way*, 225.
59. Patterson, *Lost Way*, 231.
60. Patterson, *Lost Way*, 233.

Introduction

attitude toward Paul and his message. This situation should also provide the background against which Paul's argument in 1 Corinthians should be considered. It is now time to turn attention to the second factor accounting for the Corinthian situation.

The Corinthians' Love for Wisdom, Knowledge, and Sense of Inspiration

The Corinthians' love for knowledge, wisdom, and oratory, and the association of these with spirituality, led to a situation in which knowledge became the guiding principle for almost everything they did. In many instances, they would quote the maxims from which they drew inspiration for their actions. It is ironic that, inspired as these words of knowledge were thought to be, they misled the Corinthians in a number of ways and thus gave Paul cause to write 1 Corinthians. In a number of instances, we find Paul arguing against their kind of knowledge or its wrongful application, showing that the Corinthians lacked sound knowledge.[61]

Whether in their immoral sexual practice or lawsuits against one another (1 Cor 5–6), the Corinthians had words of knowledge that made them see nothing wrong with what they were doing. Some of them believed that having sex was inimical to their spiritual development even in the context of marriage, and so they were denying their spouses sexual intimacy. Some were worried about the spiritual status of their children with unbelieving spouses and wondered whether they should divorce such unbelieving spouses. Some of the unmarried among them were now contemplating whether they should stay away from marriage (1 Cor 7). Those who possessed knowledge were eating food sacrificed to idols. They acted this way because they knew idols had no real existence. Moreover, they believed that there is only one God, hence how could other entities be gods too? Those who did not possess this knowledge were considered weak (1 Cor 8–10). Some of their women believed that they were released from the custom that demanded that they covered (or folded) their heads to signify that they were under the authority of their husbands (1 Cor 11). Similarly,

---

61. It has been noted that Paul would usually identify these words of wisdom (maxims) on the basis of which the Corinthians acted, and raise caveats against them to either correct or debunk them. He would then present the Corinthians with how they ought to see things and behave in the light of true knowledge. Attention has also been called to some instances in which Paul does this in Kissi, *Gifts and Spirituality*, 16–18.

Wisdom, Knowledge, and Spirituality in Self-defense

some of the women thought that liberty in Christ freed them from the traditional custom that required them to refrain from talking in public as was culturally honorable for women, and as a demonstration of humility and respect for their husbands (1 Cor 14:34–36).

Furthermore, their misconception about inspiration had led them to believe that only those who were involved in what they called "gifts" were inspired. They regarded the rest who were involved in what they termed "services" and "works" as people lacking inspiration (1 Cor 12). This led to a situation in which they had become preoccupied with exhibiting their spiritual "credentials" by displaying their gifts during their meetings. Such preoccupation made their meetings chaotic and confusing as many people prophesied or spoke in tongues at the same time, though they were supposed to be ministering to each other in turns with those gifts (1 Cor 14). There were also some whose knowledge made them believe that there was going to be no future resurrection since they were living in the reality of the resurrected life (1 Cor 15).

Paul's attempt to correct his readers saw him raising caveats against the words of wisdom on which they had come to rely. As this will show, some of these words of wisdom are presented with modification and thrown back to them.[62] In holding this position, one differs from Ellis who argues that Paul does not address his readers as opponents.[63] This, for him, rules out any possibility of addressing his readers in 1 Corinthians as he did in other letters in which his adversaries were addressed. Ellis is therefore opposed to the view that one finds Paul incorporating ideals of his opponents "that

---

62. For a list of these words of wisdom and how Paul modifies and throws them back to the Corinthians, see Kissi, *Gifts and Spirituality*, 16–18.

63. He maintains that unlike 2 Corinthians 10:13, Philippians 1 and 3, Galatians 1:1—2:5, Romans 16:17–18, and Titus 1:10–16 where Paul addresses opponents, in 1 Corinthians, Paul speaks as a father who is addressing his children (4:15). He thinks if Paul has to differ, he comes by way of concession and qualification (7:1–16; 8:1–13) or apostolic appeal (1 Cor 1:1–4; 11:13–16; 14:37; 15). He insists Apollos and Cephas are co-workers (3:6, 22–41; 9:5). On the Corinthians' judgment of Paul (4:3–5; 9:3), he argues that it should not be taken as an opposition, but as the normal practice in which one subjects a fellow *pneumatic* to the test as reflected in 1 Corinthians 2:6–16 (Ellis, "'Wisdom,' and 'Knowledge,' in Corinthians," 83). In holding a different view from Ellis, it should be pointed out that the fact that the readers, as Paul's children, treat him in such a contemptuous manner, makes him even more perplexed. Not even in 2 Corinthians did Paul threaten to come to the Corinthians with a rod as he does here (1 Cor 4:21). His unique, persistent, and repeated attack on their views and ill-conceived self-image carry the tone of one addressing his opponents whether or not the readers actually are his opponents.

Introduction

are modified and redirected against them in First Corinthians."[64] While Ellis's analysis is impressive, he fails to recognize the presence of Paul's clear references to readers' views, which come with antithetical clauses that seek to question the validity of their views in the manner in which they apply them. It is clear at least from 1 Corinthians 9:3 that Paul did not shy away from defending himself against those who sat in judgment of him. How then does he respond to his accusers without dealing with their views? In this sense, while one may not describe the readers as Paul's adversaries, his manner of responding to them is similar to how he responded to those Ellis calls his "adversaries" at least in one way—by picking up their views, modifying them and throwing it back at them. One agrees with Fee, who maintains that, "'Everything is permissible for me' is almost certainly a Corinthian theological slogan. This is confirmed by the way Paul cites it again in 10:23; in both cases he qualifies it so sharply as to negate it—at least as a theological absolute."[65] In these ways, Paul casts a slur on the wisdom and knowledge underlying the actions of the Corinthians, or at least on the wisdom in the application of their knowledge. We should now look at the third of the factors that explain the situation addressed in 1 Corinthians.

Paul's Declining Authority

Paul's authority over the church had dwindled, partly due to the effect of the first two factors. Apollos came to Corinth after Paul's departure from that city. With Apollos in Corinth, Paul was not the only one who had God's word for the Corinthians. What would happen in a situation where Apollos was more appealing to the Corinthians than Paul? What would happen if Apollos's teaching varied from that of Paul? Again, what would happen if the Corinthians had cause to rate Apollos as more powerful or spiritual than Paul based on the qualities they associated with spirituality? All of these conditions could have accounted for the waning of Paul's authority in the Corinthian church. On Paul's dwindling authority, Mark Finney writes,

> for the factionalism was undermining his apostolic credibility, with some of the Corinthians now openly rejecting his authority. . . . Paul's initial honor status was likely to have been unquestionably high. He was, after all, founder and leader of the community, and appears to have exuded both apostolic authority and a level of

64. Ellis, "'Wisdom' and 'Knowledge,' in Corinthians," 83.
65. Fee, *First Epistle to the Corinthians*, 251.

Wisdom, Knowledge, and Spirituality in Self-defense

charismatic power . . . But now, such authority appears to be neither unlimited nor widely recognized. It was restricted primarily by those in Jerusalem, by personal inadequacies on his own part, and later by other so-called *super apostles* who came to Corinth after him (2 Cor 11:5). Following his departure from the province the recognition of his authority was, it seems, increasingly undermined and was certainly rejected by those who were in competition with him. Hence, Paul's letter attempts not only to bring harmony to a fractured community, but also to improve his honor standing and re-assert his authority.[66]

Ronald Charles holds a similar view on the challenging state of Paul's authority in Corinth. He writes,

Reading Paul's ethical teaching in terms of an authoritative discourse does not place Paul himself above or outside the complex power relations operating within the church. Paul's rhetoric demonstrates his awareness of the precariousness of his authority in relation to competing ideas and discourses put forward by different members of the church at Corinth.[67]

With their self-understanding in light of Apollos's teaching as painted by Patterson, it is not surprising that some of the Corinthians who saw themselves as prophets or spiritual contested some of the teachings of Paul. Paul was aware of this as evidenced by 1 Corinthians 14:37–38, where he warned such people who had the tendency of rejecting his instructions. He also was not silent over those who had become arrogant toward him (1 Cor 4:18). He even threatened to come to them and find out their power beside their talk (1 Cor 4:19–20). He was even prepared to come to such members with a rod (1 Cor 4:21).

While those rating him (1 Cor 4:3) considered themselves as people who had arrived, they regarded Paul in a way that assigned to him such a negative image as Paul plays back to them in 1 Corinthians 4:9–13; as one sentenced to death, a spectacle to the world, a fool, weak, and held in disrepute, etc. The judgment Paul suffered at the hands of the readers produced in Paul the tendency to evaluate and rate the believers also. It was not enough for Paul to correct and educate them as children; it was also necessary for him to make pronouncements on how he saw them too. He therefore not only sought to inform them where they were misinformed,

---

66. Finney, "Honor, Rhetoric and Factionalism," 2.
67. Charles, "Report of 1 Corinthians 5," 150.

or point out their mistakes where they were mistaken, but he was equally concerned with evaluating and rating (judging) them. Before insisting they did not qualify to judge him (1 Cor 4:5), he had made statements that rated them as unqualified for that purpose. His statement in 1 Corinthians 3:1 in which he describes the Corinthians as unspiritual, fleshly, and infants in Christ is instructive on this. Paul's argument in 1 Corinthians 1–6, and indeed in the entire epistle, should be considered, at least in part, as a response to his accusers who had sat in judgment of him. His persistent questioning of the validity of their knowledge is a sentiment that flows from his feeling of being judged by them as he tries to put them right. To appreciate all this, one should patiently follow Paul's argument in the following study.

Chapter 2

Salutation, Thanksgiving, and Schism

RHETORICAL DIVISION OF 1 CORINTHIANS 1-6

SCHOLARS ARE UNANIMOUS ON 1 Corinthians 1–4 as the first rhetorical subunit of the letter.[1] The division of this subunit, however, has been varied due to differences in the focus of the rhetorical approaches. The division in this study, with its focus on Paul's self-defense, differs from that of other New Testament scholars in the rhetorical study of 1 Corinthians 1–4.[2]

In speeches, the classical rhetorical structure of exordium, narratio, partitio, refutatio, confirmatio, and peroratio stand out more clearly than in pastoral letters. Even in such speeches, not all the parts are considered necessary in all cases. As has been remarked by Matsen, Rollinson, and Sousa, "Deliberative oratory does not always require an exordium, such as

---

1. Many refer to it as a rhetorical unit; however, in this book, the whole of the letter is taken as a rhetorical unit, and hence the unit within the letter that deals with a particular subject is considered a subunit.

2. Malcolm proposes the following rhetorical divisions within the first subunit aside from the salutational introduction: (1) 1:10—2:25; (2) 2:6—3:4; (3) 3:5—4:5; and (4) 4:6–21 (Malcolm, *Paul and the Rhetoric,* 49). Mihaila follows the same division (*Paul-Apollos Relationship,* vii). Looking at Paul's use of cultic imagery as a means of dealing with the identity crisis of the Corinthians, Hogeterp identifies 1 Corinthians 3:9–17 as a separate rhetorical unit within the subunit differing from the two writers above (*Paul and God's Temple,* 311). In the light of the role of Old Testament quotations in Paul's arguments, Heil has the following rhetorical divisions of the first subunit: 1 Corinthians 1:18–31, 2:6-16, 3:18–23. This division is based on his analysis of the impact Paul's use of Scripture has on his audience (Heil, *Rhetorical Role of Scripture,* 10, 11).

is necessary in forensic speeches, since he who asks an orator for his opinion is naturally well disposed to him."[3] The treatment of several themes in pastoral letters makes their rhetorical structure complex. So while there may be a statement of an overriding rhetorical purpose for the letter in the opening part, the different sections of the letter dealing with specific issues may require their own divisions as rhetorical subunits. In some cases, aspects of the rhetorical subunit may be identified as exordium or *narratio* or *confirmatio* or *refutatio* or *peroratio*. These parts, however, do not always stand out clearly in each subunit of a pastoral letter.

THE SALUTATION

First Corinthians 1:1–3

> 1 Παῦλος κλητὸς ἀπόστολος Χριστοῦ Ἰησοῦ διὰ θελήματος θεοῦ καὶ Σωσθένης ὁ ἀδελφὸς 2 τῇ ἐκκλησίᾳ τοῦ θεοῦ τῇ οὔσῃ ἐν Κορίνθῳ, ἡγιασμένοις ἐν Χριστῷ Ἰησοῦ, κλητοῖς ἁγίοις, σὺν πᾶσιν τοῖς ἐπικαλουμένοις τὸ ὄνομα τοῦ κυρίου ἡμῶν Ἰησοῦ Χριστοῦ ἐν παντὶ τόπῳ, αὐτῶν καὶ ἡμῶν. 3 χάρις ὑμῖν καὶ εἰρήνη ἀπὸ θεοῦ πατρὸς ἡμῶν καὶ κυρίου Ἰησοῦ Χριστοῦ.[4]

> 1 Paul, called as an apostle of Christ Jesus by God's will, and Sosthenes our brother: 2 To God's church at Corinth, to those who are sanctified in Christ Jesus and called as saints, with all those in every place who call on the name of Jesus Christ our Lord—both their Lord and ours. 3 Grace to you and peace from God our Father and the Lord Jesus Christ.[5]

The salutation of 1 Corinthians 1:1–3 is an important part of the exordium. Paul makes very important statements in this division that must be understood and held through our reading of the entire letter. In the salutation, he identifies himself not only as Paul, but also as a called apostle of Christ Jesus (κλητὸς ἀπόστολος Χριστοῦ Ἰησοῦ).[6] Rhetorically,

---

3. Matsen et al., *Readings from Classical Rhetoric*, 218.

4. The Greek text used in this book is taken from Nestle-Aland Greek New Testament, 28th edition.

5. Unless otherwise indicated, all Scriptures in English are from the ESV.

6. κλητὸς ἀπόστολος (*klētos apostolos*) should be understood in terms of one called into the office of an apostle. The adjective κλητὸς (*klētos*), one called, appointed, or elected, qualifies "apostle" to underscore the fact that Paul was one called by God and made an apostle. In this sense, the rendering of κλητὸς ἀπόστολος as "called . . . to be an apostle" by

Wisdom, Knowledge, and Spirituality in Self-defense

identifying himself as a called apostle is a way of establishing his credibility as the basis on which what he says should be taken seriously. The statement of his apostleship here should also be rightly seen as an expression of Paul's sentimental response to those who questioned the authenticity of his apostleship. In the same salutation, he indicates that he sends this letter with Sosthenes, a Christian brother.

Still in the salutation, Paul identifies the recipients as the church of God in Corinth with the present participle (οὔσῃ [being]) emphasising its present existence in the city of Corinth. By qualifying the church with "of God" (τοῦ θεοῦ), Paul is holding up the quality of the product of his work as a genuine apostle who brought the Corinthians to faith. This position is legitimate if considered against the contention against his apostleship in which the readers, as a product of his labor, became one of his greatest defenses (1 Cor 9:1–2; cf. 2 Cor 3:1–6). The unfavorable assessment and judgment of Paul by the Corinthians (1 Cor 4:3–5; 9:3), and his defense in this letter (as will be shown), gives more legitimacy to this view. If, however, it is presumed to be too early to set the contest of Paul's apostleship against the background of 1 Corinthians, and if it is assumed that the qualifying genitive "of God" is used not to hold up the quality of his congregation in defending the genuineness of his apostleship, it should still be pointed out that the expression appears to be used predominantly by Paul. It is also significant that the developments that led to the serious contest of his apostleship in 2 Corinthians had begun by the time 1 Corinthians was written. As intimated in chapter 1, his authority was declining as the Corinthians sat in judgment of him (1 Cor 4:3; 9:3; cf. 1 Cor 4:18, 19; 5:2). Some who considered themselves spiritual and prophets also had the tendency to reject his instructions (1 Cor 14:37–38).

Apart from Acts 20:28, where "the church of God" (τῇ ἐκκλησίᾳ τοῦ θεοῦ) is used, all the occurrences of the phrase are from Paul's letters (1 Cor 1:2; 10:32; 11:22; 15:9; 2 Cor 1:1; Gal 1:13; 1 Tim 3:5, 15). The same expression is present in 1 Thessalonians 1:1 with a slight variation as "the church of the Thessalonians in God the Father and the Lord Jesus Christ (cf. 2 Thess 1:1). It can be argued that the use of "the church of God" (τῇ ἐκκλησίᾳ τοῦ θεοῦ) almost exclusively by Paul should indicate something about the apostle's intention for using this expression. In the first place, even the only

---

the ESV, ASV, KJV, and NLT should not make one lose sight of the fact that Paul identifies himself with an adjective that designates him as a called person in no ambiguous term. The use of κλητός (*klētos*) here is therefore attributive, attributing Christ's calling and appointment to Paul's apostleship.

occurrence of the expression outside Paul's writing in Acts is found on the lips of Paul as he urges the elders from Ephesus, with whom he had labored, to care for the church of God—that is, the church in Ephesus—in the expected event that he would be executed. Apart from these uses of "the church of God" associated with Paul, in all other instances where the local church is qualified in the New Testament, it is the city or the house in which the churches are located that qualifies them. We read of the church in Jerusalem (Acts 8:22), the church at Antioch (Acts 13:1), the church in Cenchreae (Rom 16:1), and the church in Babylon (1 Pet 5:13). All the seven churches to whom letters were addressed in Revelation are identified by the names of their cities—Ephesus (2:1), Smyrna (2:8), Pergamum (2:12), Thyatira (2:18), Sardis (3:1), Philadelphia (3:7), and Laodicea (3:14). Those identified by the homes of meeting include the church in the home of Priscilla and Aquila (Rom 16:3–5), the church in the home of Nympha (Col 4:15), and the church in the home of Philemon (Phlm 1:1–2). It can be said that identifying the church with the city or the home of meeting was the usual way of referring to a church in the New Testament. Even where Paul mentions the church of God, he also adds the city. The fact that Paul does something more than the others in qualifying the churches in which he labored as "of God" should be of interest to curious minds. My opinion is that Paul uses the expression to point to the quality of the product of his work as evidence of the genuineness of his apostleship. As a true apostle of the risen Lord, his labor produces nothing less than "the church of God."

Apart from being the church of God, the believers are those who have been sanctified in Christ (ἡγιασμένοις ἐν Χριστῷ Ἰησοῦ). The perfect participle "having been sanctified" (ἡγιασμένοις) presents the recipients in a very definite and unambiguous term. They are not yet to be sanctified, but have been sanctified. The effect of the perfect tense lies in the present state of the sanctification. The same definiteness is found in their identification as people *called* and *holy*. The use of the adjective κλητοῖς (called) and the noun ἁγίοις (holy, saint) establishes this definiteness. That is to say, the believers are people *called*, *elected*, or *appointed* as *holy* (*elected* and *holy*). Both their election and their being holy should be understood as the work of God in them (divine initiative). The expression "called holy" or "called as holy"[7] (κλητοῖς ἁγίοις) removes the notion of "not-yet-holy" some readers

---

7. The HCSB renders it as "called saints" with the NASB rendering it "saints by calling." In many English versions, the rendering of κλητοῖς ἁγίοις is problematic. The use of verbal forms in place of the Greek adjective is the main difficulty in the English. This speaks to morphological as well as syntactical differences between biblical Greek and the

have of the rendering of the phrase in the ASV, ESV, and KJV as "called to be saints" or "called to be holy." The rendering of the expression as "called as saints" by HSCB is better in light of the discussion here. Considered as the product of his labor in Christ, the readers, described in the qualities ascribed to them, adds to Paul's credibility as an apostle. This fits perfectly into the purpose of the exordium where a speaker not only establishes his or her credibility, but also a rapport with the readers.

Anyone familiar with the issues Paul is about to address in 1 Corinthians might wonder why Paul described the believers as people who presently are sanctified, elected by God and holy. Such wondering would not be out of place if one considers that Paul is displeased with their envy, strife, and division, acts which in part made him describe them as fleshly and babes in Christ (1 Cor 3:1–3). They were the very people who had either committed or condoned the sexual immorality that would hardly be found among unbelievers (1 Cor 5–6). How about their lawsuits against fellow believers (1 Cor 6)? Indeed, throughout the whole epistle, Paul had to contend with many unacceptable forms of conduct and attitudes of the recipients. So why does he describe them in terms that give the impression that they were flawless? Surely saints and holy people do not behave the way the Corinthian believers were behaving—this is true! But for Paul, describing them in such flawless words is necessary. It is crucial for the purpose of his argument throughout the letter. Such ways of describing his audience are characteristic of his appeal to his readers for the desired ethical behavior. While offering him the basis on which he calls his readers to order, in 1 Corinthians, it also becomes the standard against which he assesses and rates the readers who had also rated (judged) him.

In almost all his appeal to his readers for right conduct, the use of the *indicative* and the *imperative* is almost consistently at work. In the indicative, Paul establishes (indicates) what God has done in the life of the believer that makes possible, urgent, and meaningful the ethical life he calls on the believer to live. His call on them to live the required life is therefore the imperative that arises from the indicative. In the indicative, Paul points out the potential and capacity in believers to be (or to do) what they are expected to be (or to do) based on what God has achieved for them in Christ. The imperative calls on them to be (or to do) what they are now capable of being (or doing). If the indicative says, "You are a child of God,"

English language. It therefore takes some discussion and explanations to make sense of the expression in English.

the imperative says, "therefore be (become) the child of God that you are." That is to say, "You are a child of God, therefore live as a child of God." In the same vein, if the indicative says, "You are holy," the imperative says, "therefore be (become) the holy person that you are." In other words, "You are holy, therefore live as a holy person."

It is therefore important that Paul first reminds the readers that they have been sanctified in order for him to justifiably urge them to live as people who have been sanctified. Similarly, he needed to remind them that they were God's elected people and holy (saints) so that his call on them to live as such throughout his letter would make sense. It does not make sense to call on the pig to behave as a sheep. It only makes sense to expect the sheep to behave like a sheep or urge it to behave as such. One behaves according to one's nature as it was generally held in the Mediterranean society. For Paul therefore, the believers could only be called upon to behave according to whom God had made them. He could only call upon them to live as saints only because they had been made saints. In this light, one can argue that Paul meant everything he said in the description of his readers in the salutation. The use of the perfect participle "sanctified" (ἡγιασμένοις) with its present effect (that they still are sanctified people) was very purposeful and deliberate. The same can be said of the use of the adjective κλητοῖς (called) and the noun ἁγίοις (saints) to show that his readers are God's chosen ones and holy. It is only in the truth of their status (resulting from God's work in Christ) that the believers have the strength, power, and motivation to live as God wants them to. Pointing out who they are in Christ is as important as calling on them to live as such.

Now, in reminding the Corinthians of who they are in Christ, Paul indicates that they are not the only beneficiaries of God's sanctification, election, and holiness. The believers share these with all who call upon the name of the Lord (σὺν πᾶσιν τοῖς ἐπικαλουμένοις τὸ ὄνομα τοῦ κυρίου). The expression "in every place" (ἐν παντὶ τόπῳ) along with "all who call on the name of Jesus Christ" should not lead one to the conclusion that the letter was addressed to both the Corinthian believers and all those who call upon the name of the Lord everywhere. Whereas the dative κλητοῖς ἁγίοις indicates an indirect object (personal interest) to be translated as "to those called holy," the dative of πᾶσιν τοῖς ἐπικαλουμένοις does not express indirect object. This dative is the result of the preceding preposition, σὺν (with). This implies that it is the three preceding divine acts of sanctification (ἡγιασμένοις), being called (κλητοῖς), and being made holy (ἁγίοις) that

Wisdom, Knowledge, and Spirituality in Self-defense

the readers share with all who call upon the name of the Lord everywhere. Whereas the message of the letter has relevance for all people everywhere, it should be recognized that Paul was dealing with issues which were specific to the Corinthian church. It should also be noted that unlike other epistles in which Paul gives clear instructions for the letters to be read in other churches, 1 Corinthians has no such instructions. In Colossians 4:6, for example, Paul instructs the Colossian church to pass the letter on to the church of the Laodiceans, and for the Colossians, in turn, to read the letter he wrote to the Laodiceans.

Paul ends the salutation with greetings of grace (χάρις) and peace (εἰρήνη). He follows the structure of letter writing of his time in greeting his audience here. However, as Mark Powell observes, Paul substitutes grace and peace for the "greeting" one finds in letters of his day. Powell observes that as a Jew and a Christian, Paul combines both the greeting of peace from his Jewish tradition, and grace from his Christian tradition; and he is the first known New Testament writer to have done this.[8]

The rhetorical function of the salutation, as part of the exordium, is quite critical for Paul's argument. Apart from its function of establishing a rapport with the audience, it also establishes the basic indicative on the basis of which all the succeeding imperatives in the entire argument of 1 Corinthians are presented. For instance, in the indicative established for the Corinthians to stay away from the list of immoral acts in 1 Corinthians 6:9–11, Paul calls the readers' attention to three divine acts[9] which recall the basic indicative in the exordium that they are holy and sanctified people. The repetition of the three divine acts as the indicative in 1 Corinthians 6:11 is repetitive and superfluous. Having provided the basic indicative in the salutation means that all the imperatives in the succeeding arguments are premised on the indicative in the salutation.

THE THANKSGIVING

1 Corinthians 1:4–9

> 4 Εὐχαριστῶ τῷ θεῷ μου πάντοτε περὶ ὑμῶν ἐπὶ τῇ χάριτι τοῦ θεοῦ τῇ δοθείσῃ ὑμῖν ἐν Χριστῷ Ἰησοῦ, 5 ὅτι ἐν παντὶ ἐπλουτίσθητε ἐν αὐτῷ, ἐν παντὶ λόγῳ καὶ πάσῃ γνώσει, 6 καθὼς τὸ μαρτύριον τοῦ Χριστοῦ

---

8. Powell, *Introducing the New Testament*, 220.

9. "And such were some of you. But you were washed, you were sanctified, you were justified in the name of the Lord Jesus Christ and by the Spirit of our God" (1 Cor 6:11).

ἐβεβαιώθη ἐν ὑμῖν, 7 ὥστε ὑμᾶς μὴ ὑστερεῖσθαι ἐν μηδενὶ χαρίσματι ἀπεκδεχομένους τὴν ἀποκάλυψιν τοῦ κυρίου ἡμῶν Ἰησοῦ Χριστοῦ. 8 ὃς καὶ βεβαιώσει ὑμᾶς ἕως τέλους ἀνεγκλήτους ἐν τῇ ἡμέρᾳ τοῦ κυρίου ἡμῶν Ἰησοῦ [Χριστοῦ]. 9 πιστὸς ὁ θεός, δι᾽ οὗ ἐκλήθητε εἰς κοινωνίαν τοῦ υἱοῦ αὐτοῦ Ἰησοῦ Χριστοῦ τοῦ κυρίου ἡμῶν.

4 I give thanks to my God always for you because of the grace of God that was given you in Christ Jesus, 5 that in every way you were enriched in him in all speech and all knowledge—6 even as the testimony about Christ was confirmed among you—7 so that you are not lacking in any gift, as you wait for the revealing of our Lord Jesus Christ, 8 who will sustain you to the end, guiltless in the day of our Lord Jesus Christ. 9 God is faithful, by whom you were called into the fellowship of his Son, Jesus Christ our Lord.

In a letter, the thanksgiving functions as part of the exordium. Paul mentions specific things about the believers for which he is always grateful to God. What a note on which to start the address of so many disturbing issues about the recipients! There can be no other powerful way of establishing rapport than the expression of gratitude for a people. The things for which he gives thanks are summed up in the words "because of (lit. upon) the grace of God that was given to you [pl.] in Christ Jesus" (ἐπὶ τῇ χάριτι τοῦ θεοῦ τῇ δοθείσῃ ὑμῖν ἐν Χριστῷ Ἰησοῦ, 1 Cor 1:4). The following verse (1 Cor 1:5) should be considered as *enumeratio*, giving further details of the preceding verse (1 Cor 1:4). Being "enriched in him in all speech and all knowledge" (ὅτι ἐν παντὶ ἐπλουτίσθητε ἐν αὐτῷ, ἐν παντὶ λόγῳ καὶ πάσῃ γνώσει, 1 Cor 1:15) is the *amplification* of the grace of God that was given to the Corinthians in Christ Jesus (1 Cor 1:4). The grace given to the Corinthians is therefore synonymous with their being enriched in all speech (utterance) and knowledge. The effect is that they do not lack even one gift[10] (μὴ ὑστερεῖσθαι ἐν μηδενὶ χαρίσματι) as they wait for the coming of the Lord (1 Cor 1:6).

Of all the grace the Corinthians have received, why does Paul point out only speech and knowledge for thanksgiving? This is an important question for the rhetorical consideration of the thanksgiving. But before attending to this question, we should note a few things. In the first place, he claims the recipients were enriched in the areas of speech and knowledge just as the mystery of Christ was confirmed in them (καθὼς τὸ μαρτύριον τοῦ Χριστοῦ

---

10. The Greek says they are not left behind in any gift (μὴ ὑστερεῖσθαι ἐν μηδενὶ χαρίσματι).

Wisdom, Knowledge, and Spirituality in Self-defense

ἐβεβαιώθη ἐν ὑμῖν). It is clear concerning the period that the gifts were seen as confirmation of the gospel the apostles proclaimed. HCSB is therefore right in translating the phrase "In this way, the testimony about Christ was confirmed among you." This speaks to two likely situations. In the first place, it could reflect the importance of the gifts to the believers. The gifts would mean for them the activity of the Spirit, which would confirm everything they had been taught to believe about themselves as God's chosen people and the eschatological blessings awaiting them. Secondly, the essence of gifts can be considered against the background of the questioning of Paul's apostleship, which at this time had not became so pronounced as in 2 Corinthians, but which certainly showed significant signs (cf. 1 Cor 9:1–3; 14:37–38). In his response to those who contested his apostleship, the quality of his work was one of his major defenses (1 Cor 9:2; cf. 2 Cor 10:8, 13–14; 12:13). Thus, if we consider the gifts Paul gives thanks for in light of his claim that they were confirmations of the mystery of Christ, then Paul must be pointing to the genuineness of the readers' conversion to emphasize the quality of his work as a true apostle.

The question of why Paul gives thanks for only the gifts of utterance and knowledge can also be considered in this light. Throughout 1 Corinthians, almost all the problems Paul addressed were caused either by the wrong use of the gift of utterance or the misapplication of the gift of knowledge. Only two examples will be cited here since they will not be encountered in the succeeding chapters, where examples relating to sexual immorality and lawsuits are discussed. The first example has to do with the misuse of knowledge in relation to eating food offered to idols, a misuse of knowledge which thrived on certain maxims. The self-image of those who claimed they possessed such knowledge is reflected in their maxim quoted in 1 Corinthians 8:1 ("all of us possess knowledge" [πάντες γνῶσιν ἔχομεν]). In relation to this particular problem, two maxims are identified: (1) "We know that an idol is nothing in the world" (οἴδαμεν ὅτι οὐδὲν εἴδωλον ἐν κόσμῳ [1 Cor 8:4]) and (2) "There is no God but one" (ὅτι οὐδεὶς θεὸς εἰ μὴ εἷς [1 Cor 8:4]). The second example is about the misuse of the gifts of utterance (1 Cor 12–14). In the application of his teaching on the subject, only the gifts of tongues and prophecy were given specific remedial instructions (1 Cor 14).

Now, if the Corinthians' operation of these gifts was the cause of the problems addressed in this letter, why then did Paul give thanks for them? It appears by giving thanks, Paul was affirming that the gifts are good for the body of Christ. The problem was the misuse of the gifts which produced results contrary to the intended purpose of the gifts. With his gratitude for the gifts, his correction of their misuse should be appreciated and accepted as meant for the good of the readers. It is particularly against the Corinthians' love and boasting of the gifts of knowledge that Paul highlights the *irony* of their lack of knowledge and understanding as demonstrated in their questionable conducts. The *ironic* nexus between their gifts and their conduct can be described in the words of Peter Naylor who holds that "enriched" represents a bit of light *sarcasm* that recognizes the Corinthians' capacities, rather than their spirituality.[11]

The concluding words of the thanksgiving are insightful. These words are forward looking, expressing hope for the blamelessness of the readers—a hope for which Paul works hard in writing 1 Corinthians. Not discouraged by their misconduct and unacceptable behavior, Paul affirms that God will sustain them to the end in his faithfulness (βεβαιώσει ὑμᾶς ἕως τέλους) as guiltless people (ἀνεγκλήτους [1 Cor 1:8–9]). The heart of Paul as a pastor who will not give up on his congregants is evident here. In the midst of the problems, he has hope that they will be made blameless, and it is God who will accomplish this. The fact that God will accomplish this does not make him lose sight of his own role in making the believers perfect. First Corinthians is therefore to be seen as Paul's attempt to deal with the blameworthy state of the readers. The reason for Paul's confidence in their becoming blameless is found in God's faithfulness (1 Cor 1:9). Paul insists that God, who called them into the fellowship of his Son, is faithful (πιστὸς ὁ θεός, δι' οὗ ἐκλήθητε εἰς κοινωνίαν τοῦ υἱοῦ αὐτοῦ). The relationship between what God has done (the indicative) and what they ought to do on the basis of the divine initiative (the imperative) is clear. God's calling and their fellowship in his Son Jesus Christ are the divine initiatives that make possible their becoming blameless at the coming of the Lord (1 Cor 1:9). Paul is convinced that the fellowship of the believers exists for the purpose of perfecting the believers. This is evident in the role he plays as a member of this fellowship toward the perfection of the readers in writing 1 Corinthians. Paul, in this light, is seen to be thanking God not only for the gifts of utterance and knowledge, but also, perhaps more importantly, for the faithfulness of God in working out perfection in the recipients within the fellowship of his Son Jesus Christ.

---

11. Naylor, *Study Commentary on 1 Corinthians*, 31.

In its rhetorical function as part of the exordium, the thanksgiving establishes another indicative that points to God's gifts as that which confirm the testimony of Christ among the readers. Again, the prayer of thanksgiving previews what is to be expected in the rest of the letter (in the case of Pauline Epistles). As Ben Witherington and Darlene Hyatt note, the exordium also includes thanksgiving for the very causes of the problems addressed in the Epistles.[12] If this is anything to go by, then it is expected that the ensuing discourses would deal with their misuse of the gifts of knowledge and utterance in order to make them blameless at the coming of the Lord.

THE SCHISM AND ITS CAUSE—DIFFERENT APPROACHES TO THE GOSPEL

1 Corinthians 1:10–17

> 10 Παρακαλῶ δὲ ὑμᾶς, ἀδελφοί, διὰ τοῦ ὀνόματος τοῦ κυρίου ἡμῶν Ἰησοῦ Χριστοῦ, ἵνα τὸ αὐτὸ λέγητε πάντες καὶ μὴ ᾖ ἐν ὑμῖν σχίσματα, ἦτε δὲ κατηρτισμένοι ἐν τῷ αὐτῷ νοῒ καὶ ἐν τῇ αὐτῇ γνώμῃ. 11 ἐδηλώθη γάρ μοι περὶ ὑμῶν, ἀδελφοί μου, ὑπὸ τῶν Χλόης ὅτι ἔριδες ἐν ὑμῖν εἰσιν. 12 λέγω δὲ τοῦτο ὅτι ἕκαστος ὑμῶν λέγει· ἐγὼ μέν εἰμι Παύλου, ἐγὼ δὲ Ἀπολλῶ, ἐγὼ δὲ Κηφᾶ, ἐγὼ δὲ Χριστοῦ. 13 μεμέρισται ὁ Χριστός; μὴ Παῦλος ἐσταυρώθη ὑπὲρ ὑμῶν, ἢ εἰς τὸ ὄνομα Παύλου ἐβαπτίσθητε; 14 εὐχαριστῶ [τῷ θεῷ] ὅτι οὐδένα ὑμῶν ἐβάπτισα εἰ μὴ Κρίσπον καὶ Γάϊον, 15 ἵνα μή τις εἴπῃ ὅτι εἰς τὸ ἐμὸν ὄνομα ἐβαπτίσθητε. 16 ἐβάπτισα δὲ καὶ τὸν Στεφανᾶ οἶκον, λοιπὸν οὐκ οἶδα εἴ τινα ἄλλον ἐβάπτισα. 17 οὐ γὰρ ἀπέστειλέν με Χριστὸς βαπτίζειν ἀλλὰ εὐαγγελίζεσθαι, οὐκ ἐν σοφίᾳ λόγου, ἵνα μὴ κενωθῇ ὁ σταυρὸς τοῦ Χριστοῦ.

> 10 I appeal to you, brothers, by the name of our Lord Jesus Christ, that all of you agree, and that there be no divisions among you, but that you be united in the same mind and the same judgment. 11 For it has been reported to me by Chloe's people that there is quarreling among you, my brothers. 12 What I mean is that each one of you says, "I follow Paul," or "I follow Apollos," or "I follow Cephas," or "I follow Christ." 13 Is Christ divided? Was Paul crucified for you? Or were you baptized in the name of Paul? 14 I thank God that I baptized none of you except Crispus and Gaius, 15 so that no one may say that you were baptized in my name. 16

---

12. Witherington and Hyatt, *Paul's Letter to the Romans*, 40.

(I did baptize also the household of Stephanas. Beyond that, I do not know whether I baptized anyone else.) 17 For Christ did not send me to baptize but to preach the gospel, and not with words of eloquent wisdom, lest the cross of Christ be emptied of its power.

It is in 1 Corinthians 1:10–11 that Paul states the problem to be addressed in the first rhetorical subunit, hence the exordium for that subunit. First Corinthians 1:12–16 is an enumeratio that gives details of the facts about the problem as one finds in the *narratio*. The entire rhetorical subunit lacks a typical partitio which indicates how the author is going to carry out his argument. However, the partitio need not be stated in actual speeches exactly as learned in theories, nor is it always necessary. First Corinthians 1:17, nonetheless, indicates Paul's perspective on the issue, a perspective which also finds expression in the rest of the argument in the subunit. For Paul, the whole problem is a manifestation of their reliance on wisdom of word that empties the cross of its power (1 Cor 1:17). This makes the statement in 1 Corinthians 1:17 a topical statement that expresses the thesis of Paul's argument in the rest of this rhetorical subunit.

Paul introduces the problem of division by first stating his objective for addressing the issue. This comes in the form of an appeal (Παρακαλῶ δὲ ὑμᾶς). His aim is for all of the readers to agree in what they say (τὸ αὐτὸ λέγητε πάντες) and that there should be no division among them (μὴ ᾖ ἐν ὑμῖν σχίσματα). They should also be united (κατηρτισμένοι) in the same mind (ἐν τῷ αὐτῷ νοΐ) and the same opinion (ἐν τῇ αὐτῇ γνώμῃ). The statement of the objective comes in the form of an appeal "by the name of our Lord Jesus Christ." Paul appeals to the most significant and most honored figure of the church (at least in his view) in order to build *ethos* as a mode of appeal. Here, it is not just the mention of his name that is relevant, but more importantly, his will as represented in the appeal. The name in which the appeal is made is meant to stress the importance of the appeal. Appeal to people in the name of a deity was common in speeches of orators, philosophers, moralists, and politicians.[13]

The statement of the objective also gives important indications about the basis of the division. Firstly, it is in what they say—they are currently saying different things resulting in their division. Secondly, it is in their minds—they have different minds. Finally, it is in their opinion. In 1 Corinthians 1:11, Paul reveals his source of the information on the division—from

---

13. Keener, *1–2 Corinthians*, 23.

Wisdom, Knowledge, and Spirituality in Self-defense

the household of Chloe. He also indicates that the division involves strife (ἔριδες).

The seriousness of the problem of division and strife among the believers does not only lie in the priority it receives in the letter, but also in the elegant rhetoric by which it is presented. The apostle first announces the problem ("there is strife among you [ὅτι ἔριδες ἐν ὑμῖν εἰσιν]). The phrase "What I mean is that" (λέγω δὲ τοῦτο ὅτι) introduces the narratio that gives account of what has happened and the nature of the problem. With this phrase, Paul introduces the narratio with *distinctio*, which clarifies the division just named in unequivocal terms in an enumeratio, by which details of the division and strife are given. He insists that he is talking about a situation in which each of the believers claims to belong to one of four figures—Paul, Apollos, Cephas, or Christ. It is interesting that the distinctio *and* enumeratio of the narratio involves *anaphora* in which the initial pattern ἐγὼ μέν gives way to the repetition of ἐγὼ δέ three times in succession:

ἐγὼ μέν εἰμι Παύλου,

ἐγὼ δὲ Ἀπολλῶ,

ἐγὼ δὲ Κηφᾶ,

ἐγὼ δὲ Χριστοῦ. (1 Cor 1:12)

Thus, it gives us "I, on my part, belong to Paul, and I belong to Apollos, and I belong to Cephas, and I belong to Christ." It must be stated that ἐγὼ δέ (and I) has the same effect as ἐγὼ μέν (I, on my part). Each of the four clauses ends in a genitive. These certainly were meant to call loud attention to the enumeratio that confronts the Corinthians with their attitude expressed in the problem of division. The division is built around significant personalities in the church with members holding allegiance to one of such personalities. The strife therefore exists between groups built around these persons. As Conzelmann observes, "each" (ἕκαστος) does not necessarily imply every member of the church was involved in the parties mentioned here. At the same time, the nature of these groups is hard to determine in spite of the many attempts made to describe it.[14]

In 1 Corinthians 1:13, Paul engages three *rhetorical questions* to build *logos* as a mode of appeal in which the readers are to appreciate the misjudgment and serious implications of their actions in their division: μεμέρισται ὁ Χριστός; μὴ Παῦλος ἐσταυρώθη ὑπὲρ ὑμῶν, ἢ εἰς τὸ ὄνομα Παύλου

---

14. Conzelmann, *Commentary on the First Epistle*, 33–34.

ἐβαπτίσθητε; The first question points to Christ and what the division does to him (his body): *Is Christ divided?* The second and third questions have to do with Paul. They point to the fact that Paul cannot be compared to Christ when it comes to what Christ has done for the believers: *Was it Paul who was crucified for you? Or were you baptized in Paul's name?*

While these three questions may be considered rhetorically as representing some opposing views in terms of absurdity (*reductio ad absurdum*) as Keener holds,[15] the rhetorical effect is deductive. Rhetorically, they express the assumptions taken for granted or implied by their claims and allegiance to their respective leaders. What Paul says about himself here, at face value, may be applicable to the other leaders (Apollos and Cephas) at this point of the argument. All three questions emphasize the Corinthians' lack of appreciation of the implications of their division. We see in the first question that for Paul, the division in the church amounted to dividing Christ. The believers had broken up their fellowship in Christ in which they stand united as one body of Christ.

Questions 2 and 3, while giving further elaboration to the serious implications of their division, also expose the folly and poverty of the believers' understanding. In these two questions, Paul is indirectly confronting them with the truth that the one who deserves their allegiance is Christ. Christ is the one who was crucified for them, and it is he in whose name they were baptized, that is, if some of them had not been baptized in another name. But if Apollos baptized his converts in Corinth as he had done in Ephesus, with John's baptism, then Paul's words must reflect the connection between such baptism and the initiates' claim that they belonged to someone else apart from Christ. Understood in this sense, Paul incorporates *ethos* (as a mode of appeal) as he indirectly calls attention to Christ who alone, in Paul's view, deserves their allegiance on account of what he has accomplished for the readers.

In establishing their mistaken view of the division (1 Cor 1:13–17), Paul employs the rhetorical device of *conduplicatio* in which he repeats the various forms of the verb βαπτίζω over successive clauses, stressing the importance of the word in his argument. Whereas in the first instance the verb occurs at the end of the question, in the second instance it is somewhere in the middle of the clause. The same verb occurs at the end of the third clause, and first in the fourth, and at the end of the fifth clause and the final sentence:

---

15. Keener, *1–2 Corinthians*, 26.

> ἢ εἰς τὸ ὄνομα Παύλου ἐβαπτίσθητε;
> εὐχαριστῶ [τῷ θεῷ] ὅτι οὐδένα ὑμῶν ἐβάπτισα εἰ μὴ Κρίσπον καὶ Γάϊον,
> ἵνα μή τις εἴπῃ ὅτι εἰς τὸ ἐμὸν ὄνομα ἐβαπτίσθητε.
> ἐβάπτισα δὲ καὶ τὸν Στεφανᾶ οἶκον,
> λοιπὸν οὐκ οἶδα εἴ τινα ἄλλον ἐβάπτισα.
> οὐ γὰρ ἀπέστειλέν με Χριστὸς βαπτίζειν (1 Cor 1:13–17)

The occurrence of ἐβαπτίσθητε at the end of the third clause and ἐβάπτισα at the beginning of the next clause is an instance of *anadiplosis*. By both conduplicatio and anadiplosis, Paul calls attention to the aspect of ministry in which he did not do much, and to why he is thankful to God for not doing much. The fact that he did not baptize many people does away with the situation in which those baptized could have claimed that they were baptized into Paul's name (ἵνα μή τις εἴπῃ ὅτι εἰς τὸ ἐμὸν ὄνομα ἐβαπτίσθητε). Should we take Paul's words seriously, we might conclude that baptism was a factor in the schism. As we saw in the first chapter, Patterson's reconstruction of the teaching of Apollos involved baptism in the order of John the Baptist. Is this Paul's way of making allusion to the problem created by baptism done in the name of another person other than Christ? Does he suggest that such baptism led to the division among the Corinthians? Whichever the case, the rhetorical question has the effect of pointing to the readers' misplaced value on their teachers, thereby shaming them and building *pathos*.

Paul indicates three important things about his ministry in the Corinthian church: (1) Christ did not send him to baptize (οὐ γὰρ ἀπέστειλέν με Χριστὸς βαπτίζειν), (2) he was sent to preach the good news (ἀλλ' εὐαγγελίζεσθαι), and (3) he was to preach the good news not with the wisdom of word (οὐκ ἐν σοφίᾳ λόγου [1 Cor 1:17]). His reason for preaching without wisdom of word is so that the cross of Christ would not be emptied of its power (ἵνα μὴ κενωθῇ ὁ σταυρὸς τοῦ Χριστοῦ). In this statement lies a claim that is going to be defended in a number of ways—that is, the claim that he preached without eloquent words (wisdom of word). Two ways emerge from the statement: (1) preaching with the wisdom of word (ἐν σοφίᾳ λόγου), and (2) preaching without the wisdom of word (οὐκ ἐν σοφίᾳ λόγου). Each of these ways yields different results according to Paul. By implication, Paul finds fault with those who preach the cross with eloquent words of wisdom. Such people have emptied the cross of its power. For Paul, the effect of the message is determined by the approach used in

Salutation, Thanksgiving, and Schism

preaching it. It is no wonder that the "how" of the preaching assumes great importance in his argument in this first rhetorical subunit.

Stephen Barton summarizes the debate on the nature of the wisdom Paul avoids in terms of content and practice. Its two sources are careful study of nature and ways of humankind on the one hand, and direct revelation through intermediary spirit beings on the other. It seeks to achieve "individual and cooperate salvation"[16] by obtaining the knowledge consistent with nature and living by it. The success of the teacher of knowledge (the sophist, philosopher, or prophet) depends on his ability to teach knowledge persuasively, yielding the result of a good number of followers and material rewards from supporters and sponsors.[17] Barton further points out the hierarchical and discriminatory nature of wisdom in two ways: "It divides those who have the upbringing, learning, and leisure to pursue it from those who do not, and it divides those who follow one sophist or sage from those who follow another."[18] It is no wonder that these tendencies were showing in the way the Corinthians were relating to their leaders.

This rhetorical division presents the exordium of the first rhetorical subunit by stating the problem it addresses. It also presents the *narratio* which explains the problem. While it lacks a typical *partitio*, its concluding topical statement (1 Cor 1:17) can be considered as such since the rest of the argument in that subunit gives expression to it. The language and tone of this rhetorical division is *deliberative* as it seeks to dissuade his readers from their division in order for them to agree with one another. His appeal for unity by the name of the Lord Jesus builds *ethos* as a mode of appeal. He employs rhetorical questions to build *logos* in which the value the readers placed on their teachers is called into question. The shameful effect of the questioning of their misplaced value on their teachers incorporates *pathos* into the argument, which is enhanced by the use of enumeratio with anaphora, conduplicatio, and anadiplosis as figures of sound.

Comment

The problem of the recipients, as Paul sees it, is basically one of perception. They just cannot recognize the difference between Paul, Apollos, and Cephas on the one hand, and Christ on the other. They are therefore behaving

16. Barton, "1 Corinthians," 1318
17. Barton, "1 Corinthians," 1318.
18. Barton, "1 Corinthians," 1318.

Wisdom, Knowledge, and Spirituality in Self-defense

toward the three leaders as they should to Christ. To a group of believers who prided themselves as possessors of knowledge, the indication of the poverty of their understanding is an indictment. Up to this point Paul has introduced neither the metaphor of the temple or building (1 Cor 3:9), nor of the body (1 Cor 3:17; cf. 10:17; 11: 29) in which their division assumes disastrous imageries. Yet the effect (or implication) of their division as "dividing Christ" carries the notion of still a disastrous effect. His later pronouncement of judgment on those whose activities divided Christ will bring to a head his portrayal of the seriousness of the problem of division among the believers (1 Cor 3:17).

Though Paul had indicated that the division was caused by differing opinions and claims, he is yet to indicate how that came about. His introduction of baptism into the discussion (1 Cor 1:14–15) appears to give a clue, which should be explored further as he advances his argument. But how does Paul come to the conclusion that Christ did not send him to baptize? Surely the Lord did not instruct him not to baptize anyone in his ministry at Corinth. If Christ had given an expressed command to this effect, Paul would not have baptized the few he did. Paul should be understood as one looking back at his earlier ministry in Corinth and bringing to mind what the Lord used him to accomplish. At the end of this reminiscence, he comes to the conclusion that the Lord did not send him to baptize; the reason being that what the Lord used him to accomplish there involved the baptism of just a few members. The question one may ask is "How important was baptism for Paul if he baptized only a few of his converts?" This is an apostle noted for his use of the sacramental language of baptism.[19] The discussion of this question, however, has no place in this current work. If any deductions are to be made from Paul's interest in the number of the believers he baptized, one may suggest that perhaps the cause of the division could be traced to the number of converts a teacher baptized. Did some of the members who claimed allegiance to other teachers do so on the basis of the fact that such teachers baptized them? Did Apollos's baptism of the Corinthians in the order of John's baptism as he did in Ephesus some twenty years after John's death[20] account for Paul's argument on baptism? While such questions are legitimate, one might want to suspend conclusive deductions until later developments in Paul's argument make matters clear.

---

19. See for instance Romans 6:3; 1 Corinthians 1:13–15; 10:2; 12:13; 15:29; Galatians 3:27.

20. Patterson, *Lost Way*, 225.

JUSTIFICATION OF PAUL'S APPROACH TO THE GOSPEL

This rhetorical division incorporates different types of rhetoric and modes of appeal to increase the rhetorical effect of the argument in defense of the gospel Paul preached.

1 Corinthians 1:18–25

> 18 Ὁ λόγος γὰρ ὁ τοῦ σταυροῦ τοῖς μὲν ἀπολλυμένοις μωρία ἐστίν, τοῖς δὲ σῳζομένοις ἡμῖν δύναμις θεοῦ ἐστιν. 19 γέγραπται γάρ. ἀπολῶ τὴν σοφίαν τῶν σοφῶν καὶ τὴν σύνεσιν τῶν συνετῶν ἀθετήσω. ποῦ σοφός; ποῦ γραμματεύς;
>
> 20 ποῦ συζητητὴς τοῦ αἰῶνος τούτου; οὐχὶ ἐμώρανεν ὁ θεὸς τὴν σοφίαν τοῦ κόσμου; 21 ἐπειδὴ γὰρ ἐν τῇ σοφίᾳ τοῦ θεοῦ οὐκ ἔγνω ὁ κόσμος διὰ τῆς σοφίας τὸν θεόν, εὐδόκησεν ὁ θεὸς διὰ τῆς μωρίας τοῦ κηρύγματος σῶσαι τοὺς πιστεύοντας. 22 ἐπειδὴ καὶ Ἰουδαῖοι σημεῖα αἰτοῦσιν καὶ Ἕλληνες σοφίαν ζητοῦσιν, 23 ἡμεῖς δὲ κηρύσσομεν Χριστὸν ἐσταυρωμένον, Ἰουδαίοις μὲν σκάνδαλον, ἔθνεσιν δὲ μωρίαν, 24 αὐτοῖς δὲ τοῖς κλητοῖς, Ἰουδαίοις τε καὶ Ἕλλησιν, Χριστὸν θεοῦ δύναμιν καὶ θεοῦ σοφίαν. 25 ὅτι τὸ μωρὸν τοῦ θεοῦ σοφώτερον τῶν ἀνθρώπων ἐστὶν καὶ τὸ ἀσθενὲς τοῦ θεοῦ ἰσχυρότερον τῶν ἀνθρώπων.

> 18 For the word of the cross is folly to those who are perishing, but to us who are being saved it is the power of God. 19 For it is written, "I will destroy the wisdom of the wise, and the discernment of the discerning I will thwart." 20 Where is the one who is wise? Where is the scribe? Where is the debater of this age? Has not God made foolish the wisdom of the world? 21 For since, in the wisdom of God, the world did not know God through wisdom, it pleased God through the folly of what we preach to save those who believe. 22 For Jews demand signs and Greeks seek wisdom, 23 but we preach Christ crucified, a stumbling block to Jews and folly to Gentiles, 24 but to those who are called, both Jews and Greeks, Christ the power of God and the wisdom of God. 25 For the foolishness of God is wiser than men, and the weakness of God is stronger than men.

First Corinthians 1:18 begins what should be regarded as the *confirmatio*, the main part of the discourse which presents logical arguments in support of Paul's position. He appeals consistently to divine acts in order to build *ethos* as a mode of appeal. What Paul says should be accepted because it is God who has made it so. In 1 Corinthians 1:18, he makes it clear that the cross is the power of God (δύναμις θεοῦ) to "us who are being saved." The paradox of the cross, however, is that while it is foolishness (μωρία) to

Wisdom, Knowledge, and Spirituality in Self-defense

others who are perishing, to those who are being saved, it is the power of God. This is presented with *epiphora* in which the same word (ἐστίν) ends two clauses: Ὁ λόγος γὰρ ὁ τοῦ σταυροῦ τοῖς μὲν ἀπολλυμένοις μωρία ἐστίν, τοῖς δὲ σῳζομένοις ἡμῖν δύναμις θεοῦ ἐστιν.

The effect of the epiphora is the attention it calls to the contrasting complements to the word of the cross—simultaneously being foolishness to those who are perishing, and the power of God to those who are being saved. In what follows (1 Cor 1:19), Paul appeals to divine initiative by means of a quotation from Isaiah 29:14, which he freely modifies and presents in a frame of *chiasm*:

A ἀπολῶ
   B τὴν σοφίαν τῶν σοφῶν
   B¹ καὶ τὴν σύνεσιν τῶν συνετῶν
A¹ ἀθετήσω (1 Cor 1:19)

Sandwiched between two verbs indicating God's destruction (A) and God's thwarting (A¹) are the wisdom of the wise (B) and the discernment of the discerning (B¹). The emphatic nature of God's action against the wisdom of the wise and the discernment of the discerning lies in the place the two verbs occupy at the beginning and the end of the chiasm. The first word to hear is " I will destroy" and the last, "I will thwart." While the object of God's first action—the wisdom of the wise (τὴν σοφίαν τῶν σοφῶν) is placed after the verb "I will destroy" (ἀπολῶ), the object of the second verb—the discernment of the discerning (τὴν σύνεσιν τῶν συνετῶν) is placed before the last verb "I will thwart" (ἀθετήσω). The effect is that τὴν σύνεσιν τῶν συνετῶν immediately sounds as "a synonymously parallel repetition" of τὴν σοφίαν τῶν σοφῶν.[21] ἀθετήσω concludes the chiasm by repeating and intensifying the verbal impact of God's action represented in the verb at the beginning of the chiasm (ἀπολῶ). The elegance of the chiasm calls attention to the importance of its message. This elegance is enhanced by the *alliteration* and *assonance* of the repetition of words beginning with the same consonant sound (σ) and words containing the same vowel sound (ω) as in the following: ἀπολῶ τὴν σοφίαν τῶν σοφῶν καὶ τὴν σύνεσιν τῶν συνετῶν ἀθετήσω.

It is with this rhetoric elegance of chiasm embellished with alliteration and assonance that Paul provides reasons for his avoidance of the wisdom

---

21. Heil, *Rhetorical Role of Scripture*, 20.

of word in his preaching. He does not preach with words of wisdom because God has destroyed and thwarted that wisdom.

In what follows, Paul provides further reasons for his avoidance of the wisdom of word in his preaching. His use of enumeratio (a figure of amplification) in which four related rhetorical questions are asked in succession, is meant to establish the finality of God's decisive action against the wisdom of this age. They are as follows:

    ποῦ σοφός;
    ποῦ γραμματεύς;
    ποῦ συζητητὴς τοῦ αἰῶνος τούτου;
    οὐχὶ ἐμώρανεν ὁ θεὸς τὴν σοφίαν τοῦ κόσμου; (1 Cor 1:20)

Whereas all four are rhetorical questions, the final one answers the three preceding questions in a manner that intensifies their rhetorical effect. Thus we have in the first three: "Where is the wise? Where is the scribe? Where is the debater of this age?" With the change from ποῦ to οὐχὶ in the fourth question, Paul puts the answer "Yes" in the mouth of his readers. "Yes, he has!" then is the answer to the question, "Has God not made foolish the wisdom of this world?" He uses *forensic* language here as he brings divine judgment upon the wisdom of this world. The anaphora in the successive repetition of ποῦ in the initial position of each of the rhetorical questions makes the argument catchy and intensive. This is Paul's way of establishing that the philosopher and the debater have come to nothing (1 Cor 1:20).

Though one might think the point is clearly made, Paul does not leave it at that. His use of enumeratio helps him to explain matters well to an audience he knows very well. They are immature in Christ and incapable of taking solid food. With double conjunctions (ἐπειδὴ γὰρ [for since]) he provides the reason for which God made foolish the wisdom of this age. God himself had evaluated (ἐν τῇ σοφίᾳ τοῦ θεοῦ) the human quest for the knowledge of the divine, and had come to the conclusion that the world did not know him through wisdom (οὐκ ἔγνω ὁ κόσμος διὰ τῆς σοφίας τὸν θεόν). It therefore pleased God (εὐδόκησεν ὁ θεὸς) that through the foolishness of the proclamation (διὰ τῆς μωρίας τοῦ κηρύγματος) those who believe should be saved (σῶσαι τοὺς πιστεύοντας) (1 Cor 1:21).

The *parallelism* with which the reasons are given sets the focus on God's actions and their outcome:

    A ἐπειδὴ γὰρ ἐν τῇ σοφίᾳ τοῦ θεοῦ
      B οὐκ ἔγνω ὁ κόσμος διὰ τῆς σοφίας τὸν θεόν,

Wisdom, Knowledge, and Spirituality in Self-defense

A^1 εὐδόκησεν ὁ θεὸς διὰ τῆς μωρίας τοῦ κηρύγματος
B^1 σῶσαι τοὺς πιστεύοντας.

In A, God assesses human attempts to know him (i.e., in God's wisdom)—*divine assessment*. In B, God comes to the conclusion that human beings cannot know him through wisdom—*failure of human wisdom*. The structure is repeated in A^1 and B^1. In A^1, God is pleased that there should be the preaching of the cross (folly) instead of human wisdom—*divine choice*. This results in the salvation of those who believe in B^1—*human response and salvation*. Here, the divine action is Paul's main argument, and with it he builds *ethos* as his mode of appeal.

Paul gives further amplification to his argument by establishing why the world did not know God through wisdom. In contrast to the folly of the message of the cross, "the Jews ask for signs (Ἰουδαῖοι σημεῖα αἰτοῦσιν) and the Greeks seek wisdom" (Ἕλληνες σοφίαν ζητοῦσιν, 1 Cor 1:22). The use, again, of double conjunction (ἐπειδὴ καὶ [and since]) is meant to create a similar effect as the one noted earlier with ἐπειδὴ γὰρ. This double conjunction indicates the certainty of the reason why the world did not know God through wisdom. The signs (σημεῖα) demanded by the Jews and the wisdom (σοφίαν) sought by the Greeks could not be found in the proclamation of the cross.

The next verse (1 Cor 1:23) contrasts the attitude of Paul to the cross, on the one hand, with the attitude of the Jews and Greeks, on the other, such that, together with the previous verse, it forms another chiasm:

A Ἰουδαῖοι σημεῖα αἰτοῦσιν καὶ Ἕλληνες σοφίαν ζητοῦσιν
B ἡμεῖς δὲ κηρύσσομεν Χριστὸν ἐσταυρωμένον
A^1 Ἰουδαίοις μὲν σκάνδαλον, ἔθνεσιν δὲ μωρίαν (1 Cor 1:22–23)

A and A^1 speak about Jews and Greeks. In A, they ask for signs and seek wisdom respectively. In A^1, the cross is a stumbling block and foolishness to the Jews and Greeks respectively. Sandwiched between the Jews and the Greeks is "we" (a *metonymy* for Paul) who proclaims Christ crucified in B. The *antithesis* of the chiasm is glaring as it contrasts the cross as worthy of proclamation for Paul (and those who believe in the message of the cross), on the one hand, and as a stumbling block and foolishness to Jews and Greeks, on the other hand. Another attitude toward the cross, which contrasts that of the Jews and the Greeks is presented in the next verse (1 Cor 1:24). This time, it is about believing Jews and Greeks. "But to those" (αὐτοῖς δὲ) introduces the contrast with the same effect as " but we" (ἡμεῖς δὲ) in the previous verse (1 Cor 1:23). For believing Jews and Greeks, Christ is the power of God (θεοῦ δύναμιν) and the wisdom of God (θεοῦ σοφίαν, 1 Cor 1:24). By giving ἡμεῖς δὲ (but we, 1 Cor 1:23) and αὐτοῖς δὲ (but to those, 1 Cor 1:24) priority in their respective clauses, Paul placed emphatic stress on the subject and object that these stand for. Thus,

ἡμεῖς δὲ κηρύσσομεν Χριστὸν ἐσταυρωμένον, Ἰουδαίοις μὲν σκάνδαλον, ⌜ἔθνεσιν δὲ μωρίαν,
αὐτοῖς δὲ τοῖς κλητοῖς, Ἰουδαίοις τε καὶ Ἕλλησιν, ⌜Χριστὸν θεοῦ δύναμιν καὶ θεοῦ σοφίαν⌝. (1 Cor 1:23–24)

If Paul were asked, "Why preach a gospel that has no attraction to your audience?" His answer would be "In it alone is the power and wisdom of God" (1 Cor 1:24).

In what follows, Paul gives further reasons for his choice of preaching the message of the cross without wisdom. There is abundant use of enumeratio for amplification. In offering more reasons in amplification, Paul argues that there is a comparative advantage to his choice because God's foolishness (τὸ μωρὸν τοῦ θεοῦ) is wiser (σοφώτερον) than human wisdom, and God's weakness (τὸ ἀσθενὲς) is stronger (ἰσχυρότερον) than human strength (1 Cor 1:25). He states this in a manner that amounts to another chiastic structure when the focus is set on the power and wisdom of God: Χριστὸν θεοῦ δύναμιν καὶ θεοῦ σοφίαν. ὅτι τὸ μωρὸν τοῦ θεοῦ σοφώτερον τῶν ἀνθρώπων ἐστὶν καὶ τὸ ἀσθενὲς τοῦ θεοῦ ἰσχυρότερον τῶν ἀνθρώπων (1 Cor 1:24c–25).

Thus we have:

A δύναμιν
 B σοφίαν
 B¹ σοφώτερον
A¹ ἰσχυρότερον

This presents us with a *power-wisdom-wiser-stronger* chiasm. The presence of the following chiastic movement in the statement is worth noting. All four—ABB¹A¹—relate to God's working in Christ as represented in the cross. In the first part (AB) we have God's power and God's wisdom. In the second part (B¹A¹) we have the comparative forms of these in the reverse order (AB) where God's wisdom is wiser than men and his power stronger (more powerful) than men.

We should not lose sight of the fact that δύναμιν, "power" (of God), is equated to ἀσθενὲς, "weakness" (of God), while σοφίαν, "wisdom" (of God) equates to μωρὸν "foolishness" (of God). Considering the wisdom of God as God's foolishness, and his power as his weakness, what emerges is parallelism which repeats similar structures for emphatic effect (1 Cor 1:25):

A σοφίαν (μωρὸν)—σοφώτερον
B δύναμιν (ἀσθενὲς)—ἰσχυρότερον

In concluding this division, it should be recapped that this introductory part of the *confirmatio* compares the wisdom of this world with that of God as represented in the preaching of the cross. With irony Paul confronts his readers with the overwhelming wisdom and power of God—that is, God's foolishness that is wiser than human wisdom and God's weakness that is stronger than human strength. The language here is forensic as it defends the wisdom of God against human wisdom. The combination of chiasm, parallelism and irony is Paul's way of establishing the surpassing nature of God's wisdom and power in the face of which the wisdom and power of this age have come to nothing.

APPEAL TO THE CALLING OF THE READERS

In furtherance to his *confirmatio*, Paul resorts to *exemplum* in which the calling of the readers is appealed to as that which demonstrates how God has treated with contempt the wisdom of this world. While the appeal to the divine calling builds *ethos,* the readers' understanding of their calling as a reality builds *logos* as it represents a fact that supports the argument.
1 Corinthians 1:26–31

> 26 Βλέπετε γὰρ τὴν κλῆσιν ὑμῶν, ἀδελφοί, ὅτι οὐ πολλοὶ σοφοὶ κατὰ σάρκα, οὐ πολλοὶ δυνατοί, οὐ πολλοὶ εὐγενεῖς. 27 ἀλλὰ τὰ μωρὰ τοῦ κόσμου ἐξελέξατο ὁ θεός, ἵνα καταισχύνῃ τοὺς σοφούς, 28 καὶ τὰ ἀσθενῆ τοῦ κόσμου ἐξελέξατο ὁ θεός, ἵνα καταισχύνῃ τὰ ἰσχυρά, καὶ τὰ ἀγενῆ τοῦ κόσμου καὶ τὰ ἐξουθενημένα ἐξελέξατο ὁ θεός, τὰ μὴ ὄντα, ἵνα τὰ ὄντα καταργήσῃ, 29 ὅπως μὴ καυχήσηται πᾶσα σὰρξ ἐνώπιον τοῦ θεοῦ. 30 ἐξ αὐτοῦ δὲ ὑμεῖς ἐστε ἐν Χριστῷ Ἰησοῦ, ὃς ἐγενήθη σοφία ἡμῖν ἀπὸ θεοῦ, δικαιοσύνη τε καὶ ἁγιασμὸς καὶ ἀπολύτρωσις, 31 ἵνα καθὼς γέγραπται· ὁ καυχώμενος ἐν κυρίῳ καυχάσθω.
>
> 26 For consider your calling, brothers: not many of you were wise according to worldly standards, not many were powerful, not many were of noble birth. 27 But God chose what is foolish in the world to shame the wise; God chose what is weak in the world to

shame the strong; 28 God chose what is low and despised in the world, even things that are not, to bring to nothing things that are, 29 so that no human being might boast in the presence of God. 30 And because of him you are in Christ Jesus, who became to us wisdom from God, righteousness and sanctification and redemption, 31 so that, as it is written, "Let the one who boasts, boast in the Lord."

To prove that God has indeed made useless the wisdom and power of the world, Paul points to three things about the readers' calling. He reminds them that at the time God called them, (1) not many of them were wise (σοφοί) from a human perspective, (2) not many of them were powerful (δυνατοί), and (3) not many were of noble birth (εὐγενεῖς). Among the few who were important by human standards, Dachollom Datiri mentions Crispus, the ruler of a synagogue (Acts 18:8), and Erastus, the city's director of public works (Rom 16:23).[22] Besides the few prominent people, none of them qualified as wise, powerful, or noble. It is observed that Paul gives a christological reformulation to the Jewish idea (and indeed to what is common to the ancient world) of the lofty being brought low as the lowly is lifted high.[23] The rhetorical structure of the foregoing statement is worthy of note:

οὐ πολλοὶ σοφοὶ κατὰ σάρκα,
οὐ πολλοὶ δυνατοί,
οὐ πολλοὶ εὐγενεῖς. (1 Cor 1:26)

Thus, "not many were wise according to the flesh, not many were powerful, not many were of noble birth." With enumeratio, Paul provides details of what he seeks to point out about them, creating anaphora with his repetition of οὐ πολλοὶ at the beginning of each clause. This makes the statement catchy. The importance of the exemplum is to be felt in the cumulative effect of the rhetorical device. In the next two verses (1 Cor 1:27–28), he continues with *commoratio* in which the divine activity among the readers is repeated in different expressions for emphasis. The irony of the expression is apparent in their contradictory tone:

ἀλλὰ τὰ μωρὰ τοῦ κόσμου ἐξελέξατο ὁ θεός, ἵνα καταισχύνῃ τοὺς σοφούς,

---

22. Datiri, "1 Corinthians," 1380.
23. Conzelmann, *Commentary on the First Epistle*, 50.

καὶ τὰ ἀσθενῆ τοῦ κόσμου ἐξελέξατο ὁ θεός, ἵνα καταισχύνῃ τὰ ἰσχυρά,
καὶ τὰ ἀγενῆ τοῦ κόσμου καὶ τὰ ἐξουθενημένα ἐξελέξατο ὁ θεός, τὰ μὴ ὄντα, ἵνα τὰ ὄντα καταργήσῃ

The parallelism in the repetition of the same structure throughout is obvious. All the three *parallels* are part of a long sentence which ends in the next verse (1 Cor 1:29). Three parallel structures of two clauses each can be identified.[24] The repetition of the following words are noteworthy: καὶ τὰ (7x), τοῦ κόσμου (3x), ἐξελέξατο ὁ θεός (3x), ἵνα (3x), καταισχύνῃ (2x) with its parallel [in function] καταργήσῃ (1x). This repetitive occurrence of words gives the argument aesthetic quality that draws attention to the point being made. The repetition of ἐξελέξατο ὁ θεός (God chose) at the end of the first clause of each of the three parallels highlights divine initiative in God's choice of the readers. This allows Paul to give priority of place to the objects of God's choice in those clauses. These objects (analogous with the recipients) are described as "the foolish things" (τὰ μωρὰ) of the world, "the weak things of the world" (τὰ ἀσθενῆ τοῦ κόσμου), "the insignificant things of the world" (τὰ ἀγενῆ τοῦ κόσμου), "the despised things" (τὰ ἐξουθενημένα), and "the things that are not" (τὰ μὴ ὄντα).

These objects have their contrasts in the final position of the second of the parallels.[25] They are "the wise" (τοὺς σοφούς), "the strong" (τὰ ἰσχυρά), and "the things that are" (τὰ ὄντα). Their final position highlights the contrast and irony of what has been used to shame and nullify them. The third clause shifts from the use of one object (in the preceding clause) to three. Two come before the verb of the divine action and one after it. However, their forms in the accusative make the three nouns the objects of the same divine activity regardless of their position in relation to the verb.[26] The use of three nouns (as objects of God's choice) in a row (in the third parallel) gives cumulative effect to the nouns, intensifying the effect of what has been used to nullify (καταργήσῃ) "the things that are" (τὰ ὄντα).

With the irony of foolish things shaming the wise and weak things shaming the strong, etc., the readers are confronted with the wisdom and

---

24. The pattern for all three is: *conjunction-accusative-genitive-aorist-nominative, conjunction-present subjunctive-accusative.*

25. Structurally, the third parallel ends with the verb καταργήσῃ. In meaning, however, ὄντα occupies the final position.

26. The third object, though placed after the verb and separated by a comma, still stands out as one of the objects of the verb by its form in the accusative.

Salutation, Thanksgiving, and Schism

strength of God in their own experience of divine election. The language of choosing one thing in order to shame the other sounds epideictic, while the nullifying of the things that are represents divine judgment on the wisdom and strength of the world, a forensic expression. With the exemplum, Paul builds *logos* by advancing reasons from the experience of the readers, and *ethos* by appealing to divine initiative. This is meant to make insignificant the wisdom of this age on which the readers have come to rely. If God's wisdom (in the message of the cross) is what has resulted in their election as God's people, then it will be self-defeating to abandon this wisdom.

In what follows, we have Paul's concluding statements that derive from his exemplum. By introducing it with "so that" (ὅπως), Paul indicates the derivative nature of the clause. The clause then represents the purpose for God's action in the irony: "so that no flesh may boast before God" (ὅπως μὴ καυχήσηται πᾶσα σὰρξ ἐνώπιον τοῦ θεοῦ). The second concluding statement is a further elaboration on the first. ἐξ αὐτοῦ (from [out of] him) with its antecedent in the preceding θεοῦ ("of God") points the readers once again to the divine initiative which has resulted in their being in Christ Jesus (ὑμεῖς ἐστε ἐν Χριστῷ Ἰησοῦ). With the relative pronoun ὅς (who), Paul refers back to Christ Jesus (Χριστῷ Ἰησοῦ), indicating who he is for the readers. This elaboration, in essence, is repetition of the point made over and over again. Four nouns complement this relative pronoun (ὅς), making Christ the one who has become (ἐγενήθη) wisdom to them (σοφία ἡμῖν) from God, righteousness (δικαιοσύνη), sanctification (καὶ ἁγιασμός), and redemption (καὶ ἀπολύτρωσις). The *polysyndeton* in the repetition of καὶ before the last two nouns is Paul's way of giving cumulative effect to these benefits from Christ (1 Cor 1:30). It is for these benefits in Christ that the next call is made to the readers.

A quotation from Jeremiah 9:23–24 which Paul modifies, becomes the *sententia* with which he captures the main sense of his argument at the end of this rhetorical division. The introduction of the quotation with "so that just as" (ἵνα καθώς) shows what Paul intends it to be for the audience. Its intent is for them to act in accordance with the quotation "Let the one who boasts, boast in the Lord" (ὁ καυχώμενος ἐν κυρίῳ καυχάσθω). The language of 1 Corinthians 1:30–31 is of deliberative rhetoric as it seeks to persuade the readers to boast in the Lord. That is to say, the Corinthians are to appreciate their benefits in Christ and be proud of the message that brought them these benefits. Conzelmann is right in holding that boasting

Wisdom, Knowledge, and Spirituality in Self-defense

in the Lord is boasting in the cross,[27] the message of which the Corinthians are now ashamed of.

This rhetorical division deals with the reasons that justify Paul's choice of approach to his preaching of the gospel (of the cross). God has brought the wisdom of this world to nothing and has decided to save people through the folly of what Paul preaches. The calling of the readers shows that God has indeed set aside the wisdom of this age in order to save all people by the message of the cross. Several reasons are advanced as he builds a *logos* mode of appeal. However, with his appeal to divine initiative he incorporates *ethos*. The praise of God's wisdom and the indication that the wisdom of this world has failed to make people know God makes the language one of epideictic rhetoric. While the language of God nullifying the wisdom of this world is forensic, that which urges the readers to boast in the Lord is deliberative. The combination of all three forms of rhetoric language increases the persuasive effect of the argument. The rhetorical strategies involve appeal to divine initiative, chiasm, enumeratio, rhetorical questions, amplification, contrast, irony, exemplum, commoratio, parallelism, and sententia. The division further employed epiphora, alliteration, assonance, anaphora, and polysyndeton to enhance the appeal of its argument.

Comment

Paul grounds his argument on the core belief and shared value of the believers—their calling and their being in Christ. He links their calling in Christ to the message he preaches, and identifies it with the benefits they have in Christ. Christ is their wisdom from God (σοφία ἡμῖν ἀπὸ θεοῦ), their righteousness (δικαιοσύνη), their sanctification (ἁγιασμός), and their redemption (ἀπολύτρωσις). Now if the message of the cross is what entails all these benefits, then the believers must have cause to be proud of it. That is to say, these benefits should provide the incentive for the believers to continue to stand by the message. This leads logically to Paul's exhortation that those who boast should boast in the Lord[28]—the Lord whose goodness brings them all the benefits. In this way, 1 Corinthians 1 ends on a strong note of appeal for the Corinthians to take a stand with the message of the

---

27. Conzelmann, *Commentary on the First Epistle*, 51.

28. This quotation from Jeremiah 9:24 is freely modified by Paul for his purpose. The Jeremiah quotation speaks of boasting because one understands and knows the Lord, and knows that the Lord shows faithful love, justice, and righteousness on the earth.

cross. Paul challenges his readers by confronting them with the question "Who is on the Lord's side, who is not ashamed of his gospel, who will take all the benefits of the cross and not shy away from identifying with it?

Chapter 3

Paul's Rated Image and Determinants of a Spiritual Person

THIS CHAPTER CONTINUES WITH the confirmatio of the first rhetorical subunit of the epistle. The first part deals with the ill-conceived image of Paul by his readers while the second part sets out qualities that define what a spiritual person is. Between the two, Paul establishes the uniqueness of the wisdom he preaches which he subsequently holds up as something that can be appreciated only by the spiritual (mature) person.

PAUL'S IMAGE AMONG THE CORINTHIANS AS SHAPED BY HIS APPROACH TO THE GOSPEL

First Corinthians 2:1–5 focuses on the impact Paul's approach to the gospel had on his image. He does not shy away from talking about how he went about his proclamation among the Corinthians. With the focus on his personal testimony about how he went about his work, he builds *ethos* as a mode of appeal in which he expects the readers to accept what he says on the basis of his credibility as the one whose work brought them to faith in Christ.

1 Corinthians 2:1–5

> 1 Κἀγὼ ἐλθὼν πρὸς ὑμᾶς, ἀδελφοί, ἦλθον οὐ καθ' ὑπεροχὴν λόγου ἢ σοφίας καταγγέλλων ὑμῖν τὸ μυστήριον τοῦ θεοῦ. 2 οὐ γὰρ ἔκρινά τι εἰδέναι ἐν ὑμῖν εἰ μὴ Ἰησοῦν Χριστὸν καὶ τοῦτον ἐσταυρωμένον. 3 κἀγὼ ἐν ἀσθενείᾳ καὶ ἐν φόβῳ καὶ ἐν τρόμῳ πολλῷ ἐγενόμην πρὸς

ὑμᾶς, 4 καὶ ὁ λόγος μου καὶ τὸ κήρυγμά μου οὐκ ἐν πειθοῖ[ς] σοφίας [λόγοις] ἀλλ' ἐν ἀποδείξει πνεύματος καὶ δυνάμεως, 5 ἵνα ἡ πίστις ὑμῶν μὴ ᾖ ἐν σοφίᾳ ἀνθρώπων ἀλλ' ἐν δυνάμει θεοῦ.

1 And I, when I came to you, brothers, did not come proclaiming to you the testimony of God with lofty speech or wisdom. 2 For I decided to know nothing among you except Jesus Christ and him crucified. 3 And I was with you in weakness and in fear and much trembling, 4 and my speech and my message were not in plausible words of wisdom, but in demonstration of the Spirit and of power, 5 so that your faith might not rest in the wisdom of men but in the power of God.

At this stage of his argument, Paul has established enough *premises* to make his approach to the proclamation of the good news appreciable. Now, the justification of his approach takes a clever slide into his defense against the rating given him by the readers.

Firstly, he reminds his readers of how he initially came (ἐλθὼν) to them with the gospel—he came (ἦλθον) proclaiming (καταγγέλλων) to them the mystery of God not with eloquent word or wisdom (ὑπεροχὴν λόγου ἢ σοφίας, 1 Cor 2:1). This was as a result of his careful decision (judgment [ἔκρινά]) to know (εἰδέναι) nothing among them except Jesus Christ and him crucified (εἰ μὴ Ἰησοῦν Χριστὸν καὶ τοῦτον ἐσταυρωμένον, 1 Cor 2:2).

The use of ἔκρινά (have judged, assessed) should imply a careful consideration and assessment of a situation by which a decision has been arrived at. The decision then becomes a judgment which one can hardly find fault with. It is possible in this situation, therefore, for one to stand firmly by such a resolution. Fee has observed, "To know nothing" does not mean that he left all other knowledge aside, but rather that he had the gospel, with its crucified Messiah, as his singular focus and passion while he was among them."[1]

How his resolution and focus on the gospel relates to the next statement in 1 Corinthians 2:3 is instructive. Lack of attention to this nexus has led to both inappropriate renderings of the verse and failure to appreciate Paul's argument. With κἀγὼ ("And I"), Paul makes an emphatic connection between his resolution and focus (Christ and him crucified), on the one hand, and what he says about himself subsequently, on the other. He delays the verb to give priority to three noun phrases that describe his state: "in weakness" (ἐν ἀσθενείᾳ), "and in fear" (καὶ ἐν φόβῳ), "and in much

---

1. Fee, *First Epistle to the Corinthians*, 92.

Wisdom, Knowledge, and Spirituality in Self-defense

trembling" (καὶ ἐν τρόμῳ πολλῷ). He then completes the clause with the verb and its object: "I became to you" (ἐγενόμην πρὸς ὑμᾶς). The clause of 1 Corinthians 2:3 should be translated with Paul's resolution and focus (in the preceding verse) in mind because of the introductory κἀγώ ("and I") which is inferential and consequential. That is, "I resolved to know nothing among you except Jesus Christ and him crucified, and I (i.e., as a result) became to you [as one] in weakness and in fear and in much trembling." Paul intends ἐγενόμην πρὸς ὑμᾶς to mean, "I became to you." That this is the case is clear from his choice of ἐγενόμην as against two verbs he had used earlier in 1 Corinthians 2:1. He chose aorist forms of ἔρχομαι (ἐλθών [participle], and ἦλθον) when he wanted to say "I came." By departing from the use of ἔρχομαι, Paul wanted his use of γίνομαι (ἐγενόμην) to be taken differently (and not as "I came"). Taken appropriately, ἐγενόμην completes the sense of the referential κἀγώ by describing (together with the noun phrases) what Paul *became* (appeared) as a result of knowing nothing among the Corinthians except Jesus Christ and him crucified. The rendering of ἐγενόμην πρὸς ὑμᾶς as "I was with you" by ESV, ASV, KJV, and NKJV, and as "I came to you" by HCSB, ISV, NIV, and NLT, weakens the role Paul intended the verb to play in his argument.

In this light, Paul's statement in 1 Corinthians 2:3 (appearing in weakness and in fear and in much trembling) should be understood as the resulting image he had among the Corinthians for sticking to a message of foolishness and weakness. How could someone carrying a message of weakness and foolishness appear wise and strong? No wonder he became to them (ἐγενόμην πρὸς ὑμᾶς) a person in weakness and in fear and in much trembling—an apt description of a person carrying a message that appears foolish and weak, and which could indeed become a stumbling block. The vital role of the description of his image in the eyes of the Corinthians in his argument is to be felt in the cumulative effect of the polysyndeton used in stating the three noun phrases (ἐν ἀσθενείᾳ καὶ ἐν φόβῳ καὶ ἐν τρόμῳ πολλῷ ἐγενόμην). The repetition of καὶ (and) in this instance is not redundant; it is meant for repetitive emphasis on his image that resulted from his resolution. For Paul therefore, his low image and rating among the Corinthians is simply due to the message he preached.

Keener is of the view that Paul's unimpressive speech may have been embarrassing to some of the Corinthians, especially the elite among them whose compatriots would judge them by the kind of teachers they entertained.² Not even the fact that some powerful religious leaders (like Moses) "were weak in delivery (Exod 4:10; cf. Jer 1:6)" could count for Paul's defense in a situation like this.³ As Keener further notes, to make matters worse, Paul's manual labor in support of his ministry would have discredited him as a wise teacher who could win patronage among the high class.⁴ The impact of all these (especially his unimpressive delivery) on his image was an important subject that needed to be addressed by Paul in his defense here. One should therefore take exception from Paul Sampley who insists that Paul's admission that, like Moses, he was unskilled in speech was consistent with what orators of his time were urged to say of themselves.⁵ The fact that the Corinthians complained about his unimpressive speech and bodily presence (2 Cor 10:10; cf. 2 Cor 10:1) makes the matter more than a mere rhetorical strategy for an orator. Moreover, Paul argues that he does not preach the gospel as an orator, which means he has no incentive for admitting what orators are told to admit in their speech. The truth is that Paul was dealing with what his readers found unimpressive about him.⁶ He does not dispute it here; however, he attributes it to his resolution to preach Jesus Christ and him crucified. Scholars' attempts to explain Paul's weakness, fear, and much trembling without any connection to his preaching Jesus Christ and him crucified is therefore not helpful. Such attempts do not make Paul's writings appear as coherent and consistent as they are.

The first part of the next verse (1 Cor 2:4a) is also expressive of the result of his resolution to know nothing except Jesus Christ and him crucified. The commoratio of this verse restates in a different way what Paul had said in 1 Cor 2:1b, as well as 1 Cor 2:2. He insists, "my speech (ὁ λόγος μου)

2. Keener, *1–2 Corinthians*, 34.
3. Keener, *1–2 Corinthians*, 34–35.
4. Keener, *1–2 Corinthians*, 46.
5. Sampley, "1 Corinthians," 818.
6. Fee finds a connection between Paul's personal weakness and his gospel (*First Epistle to the Corinthians*, 93). While it might be appropriate to admit with Fee that, "there was a genuine correspondence between Paul's own personal weaknesses and his gospel (cf. Col 1:24)," "in weakness" here should be appreciated from Paul's preceding resolve that identifies him solely with the message of the crucified Christ. He had earlier indicated that this message was the weakness of God, which though stronger than men, is unimpressive, and folly on account of the fact that it was proclaimed without persuasive words. The addition of "in fear and much trembling" (ἐν φόβῳ καὶ ἐν τρόμῳ πολλῷ) is Paul's way of casting back to the readers their view of him resulting from his weak and umpressive message.

and my proclamation (τὸ κήρυγμά μου) were not with persuasive words of wisdom (πειθοῖ[ς] σοφίας [λόγοις])." By contrast (ἀλλ'), they were accompanied by demonstration of the Spirit (ἀποδείξει πνεύματος) and of power (δυνάμεως).

The argument of 1 Corinthians 2:1–4 is represented in a *chiastic* structure. In it, Paul's resolve to proclaim the message of the cross and its effect on him are sandwiched between statements about his approach to the gospel. This is a loud way of indicating that how he appeared was due to the manner in which he proclaimed the message:

A ἦλθον οὐ καθ' ὑπεροχὴν λόγου ἢ σοφίας καταγγέλλων ὑμῖν τὸ μυστήριον τοῦ θεοῦ.
   B οὐ γὰρ ἔκρινά τι εἰδέναι ἐν ὑμῖν εἰ μὴ Ἰησοῦν Χριστὸν καὶ τοῦτον ἐσταυρωμένον.
   B¹ κἀγὼ ἐν ἀσθενείᾳ καὶ ἐν φόβῳ καὶ ἐν τρόμῳ πολλῷ ἐγενόμην πρὸς ὑμᾶς
A¹ καὶ ὁ λόγος μου καὶ τὸ κήρυγμά μου οὐκ ἐν πειθοῖ[ς] σοφίας [λόγοις] ἀλλ' ἐν ἀποδείξει πνεύματος καὶ δυνάμεως

A describes the manner of Paul's preaching (not with lofty speech or wisdom) and A¹ does the same (without persuasive words but with demonstration of the Spirit and power). B expresses Paul's resolve to stick to the message of the cross while B¹ expresses the effect of his resolve to stick to the message of the cross (showing in his appearing in weakness, in fear, and much trembling). Thus we have,

A Manner of proclamation
   B Resolve
   B¹ Effect of Resolve
A¹ Manner of proclamation

The principle, then, is the message you carry determines how you appear and what you become to your audience. One therefore agrees with Naylor, who understands Paul to be "conceding that his teaching gives the impression of being weak and foolish, both in content and in presentation."[7] Similarly, Mihaila argues that Paul "embodies the weakness of the cross."[8] It is therefore surprising that Naylor misses this connection between the message and its presenter in his comments on 1 Corinthians 2:2. He argues

7. Naylor, *Study Commentary on 1 Corinthians*, 45. See also his comment on 1 Corinthians 2:1 where Paul's message is described as "a weak, insipid thing" (*Study Commentary on 1 Corinthians*, 59).

8. Mihaila, *Paul-Apollos Relationship*, 179.

that by "weakness" Paul "alludes to his reaction to suspicious townsfolk and possibly to ill health." Here, Naylor loses sight of the nexus between the type of message he (Naylor) had described in the previous verse (1 Cor 2:2) as "a weak, insipid thing" and its effect on the image of Paul in the succeeding verse (1 Cor 2:3).[9] John MacArthur therefore got it right in recognizing that "The weakness in which Paul had come to Corinth was the weakness of the gospel which is really the power of God (1 Cor 1.25, 27)."[10] MacArthur, however, goes way back into the previous chapter to make the connection instead of the preceding two verses (1 Cor 2:1–2)." He consequently concludes with respect to "fear and much trembling," that Paul did not mean "mental timidity or physical shaking," since these are things Paul had urged believers against (Acts 13:46; 19:8; Eph 3:12; 6:19). He proposes that given the pagan and immoral nature of the city among others, Paul was fearful of what the outcome of his proclamation would be in the city, and for "his own inadequacy and sin which could weaken his ministry (cf. 1 Cor 9:16, 27)."[11]

Comment

With the foregoing in mind, it must be emphasized that the principle in Paul's argument in 1 Corinthians 2:1–3 is: the nature of the message is determined by the manner in which it is proclaimed, and the image of the preacher is shaped by the nature of the message. If the message is proclaimed with the brilliance of speech or wisdom, it appears wise and strong, but without the brilliance of speech or wisdom, it appears foolish and weak. The presenter of a wise and strong message appears wise and strong (powerful), but the presenter of a message of folly and weakness appears foolish and weak. Paul's resolution to stick to Christ and him crucified without the brilliance of speech or wisdom could therefore not make him appear wise and strong. Paul is therefore not using hyperbole here as Sampley suggests, for he was dealing with what he actually did in his ministry in Corinth and the reality of its consequential image for him.[12]

9. Naylor, *Study Commentary on 1 Corinthians*, 59.
10. MacArthur, *1 Corinthians*, 56.
11. MacArthur, *1 Corinthians*, 56.
12. On "I determined to know nothing among you except Jesus Christ and him crucified" (1 Cor 2:2), Sampley holds that "Paul uses hyperbole, an exaggeration, as a means of focusing on what is central," pointing to what brings Christians together (Sampley, "1 Corinthians," 818). The rhetorical import of this, however, is the attention drawn to the

Wisdom, Knowledge, and Spirituality in Self-defense

The dynamics of such a situation explains Paul's lot in the division. Barton explains, "In the competitive, display-oriented culture of Greco-Roman Corinth, Paul's self-confessed lack of rhetorical prowess and personal presence (cf. 2 Cor 10:10) is a damaging admission . . . Who would want to associate with someone so lacking in the expected qualities of display and domination?"[13]

To his advantage, however, Paul sets a new standard for assessment. He turns attention to "the demonstration of the Spirit and of power" with which he proclaimed his message. The shift was clever and powerful. There was general association of the spirit (the divine) with wisdom and knowledge (revealed knowledge) in nearly all the religions during the period. The demonstration (manifestations) of the spirit was invariably seen in utterances, miraculous acts, and persuasions. It is no wonder that Corinthian *pneumatics* (those who considered themselves to be spiritual) cherished gifts of utterance, wisdom, and knowledge, which Paul acknowledged in his thanksgiving (1 Cor 1:5). Their claim to knowledge (1 Cor 8:10–11; cf. 8:1b, 7) and their claim to be "prophets and spiritual" (1 Cor 14:37) are instructive on how they considered themselves as inspired and possessors of revealed knowledge (superior knowledge). With these in the background, Paul now appeals to the activity of the Spirit in him. His message was as a result of the demonstration of the Spirit and power, regardless of how it came. Indeed it was this power of his message that convicted them and resulted in their conversion when he first came to Corinth. Their own gifts of utterance and wisdom are confirmations of the power of his preaching among them. His manner of presentation should not make them lose sight of this. Much as the demonstration of the Spirit and power could refer to his performance of some miraculous acts at the initial stages of his ministry in Corinth (2 Cor 12:12), it is important to note that Paul does not make explicit reference to miracles here (a deliberate avoidance intended to fix their gaze on what matters—the cross and its effect (the power of God) in their conversion and current status as people in Christ (1 Cor 1:30; cf. 1:4).

By the time Paul wrote 2 Corinthians, his readers had come to the conclusion that his letters were more powerful than his physical appearance and speech. Paul plays this back to them: "For they say, 'His letters are weighty and strong, but his bodily presence is weak, and his speech of

---

negative view of the message in the eyes of the Corinthians, and Paul's resolve to stick to it nonetheless because of God's saving power and wisdom it.

13. Barton, "1 Corinthians," 1319.

no account'" (2 Cor 10:10). He testifies personally to the powerful effect of his messages as weapons having "divine power to destroy strongholds," which are "arguments and every lofty opinion raised against the knowledge of God." It also takes "every thought captive to obey Christ" (2 Cor 10:4–5). For Paul, the power of his message, as witnessed by the readers, is evidence of the power of the Spirit at work in him. His focus on this power is in order that the readers' faith might rest in the power of God (1 Cor 2:5). Paul's aversion to reliance on spiritual experiences without sound knowledge steeped in love, is responsible for his avoidance of explicit appeal to miracles here. We should consider his recognition that his readers lack no gift (*charisma*) in 1 Corinthians 1:7, but when he came to them he could not address them as spiritual people (1 Cor 3:1). Their resultant attitude of jealousy and strife (1 Cor 3:3) as well as the division among them (1 Cor 3:4) are pointed out as evidence of their unfortunate spiritual stage. For Paul, the demonstration of the Spirit in terms of gifts and miraculous acts is not the defining factor of spirituality. This is why he speaks of the power of God without an explicit appeal to miracles. On the contrary, he refers explicitly to the word of the cross as the power of God in this rhetorical subunit.

For Paul therefore, what many consider as spiritual manifestations are not proofs of a spiritual person. The Corinthians' overreliance on spiritual experiences prompts Paul to spiritualize the wilderness experiences of the Jews (with the cloud, the Red Sea, and the rock) in order to impress upon them that spiritual experiences are not enough to make one pleasing to God (1 Cor 10:1–5). This is because in spite of their spiritual experiences in the wilderness, many of the Jews died for failing to please the Lord (1 Cor 10:5–6). If reliance on gifts and miracles as spiritual experiences has failed to establish the readers in sound spirituality, Paul would not seek to appeal to the same failing spiritual experiences as a basis for justifying his choice of approach to the gospel. For Paul, the effect of his gospel (resulting in the conversion of the Corinthians) is proof of the demonstration of the Spirit and of power. It is indeed the power of God unto salvation for all who believe. In their conversion, he made their faith rest not on human wisdom, but on the power of God—the cross (1 Cor 2:5), the weakness of God (which is stronger than men, 1 Cor 1:25).

In arguing that his approach to the gospel was responsible for his low image among the Corinthians, Paul built an *ethos* with a personal testimonial on how he went about the proclamation of his gospel. Commoratio and chiasm are the two main rhetorical devices employed for his argument.

Wisdom, Knowledge, and Spirituality in Self-defense

While commoratio was useful for the repetitive effect needed for his infant audience, chiasm was used to emphasize the effect of his style of preaching on his image among the Corinthians. Finally, polysyndeton was used to stress the Corinthians' low perception of Paul.

THE UNIQUENESS OF THE WISDOM PAUL PREACHED

1 Corinthians 2:6–9

> 6 Σοφίαν δὲ λαλοῦμεν ἐν τοῖς τελείοις, σοφίαν δὲ οὐ τοῦ αἰῶνος τούτου οὐδὲ τῶν ἀρχόντων τοῦ αἰῶνος τούτου τῶν καταργουμένων. 7 ἀλλὰ λαλοῦμεν θεοῦ σοφίαν ἐν μυστηρίῳ τὴν ἀποκεκρυμμένην, ἣν προώρισεν ὁ θεὸς πρὸ τῶν αἰώνων εἰς δόξαν ἡμῶν, 8 ἣν οὐδεὶς τῶν ἀρχόντων τοῦ αἰῶνος τούτου ἔγνωκεν. εἰ γὰρ ἔγνωσαν, οὐκ ἂν τὸν κύριον τῆς δόξης ἐσταύρωσαν. 9 ἀλλὰ καθὼς γέγραπται.
>
> ἃ ὀφθαλμὸς οὐκ εἶδεν καὶ οὖς οὐκ ἤκουσεν καὶ ἐπὶ καρδίαν ἀνθρώπου οὐκ ἀνέβη,
> ἃ ἡτοίμασεν ὁ θεὸς τοῖς ἀγαπῶσιν αὐτόν.

> 6 Yet among the mature we do impart wisdom, although it is not a wisdom of this age or of the rulers of this age, who are doomed to pass away. 7 But we impart a secret and hidden wisdom of God, which God decreed before the ages for our glory. 8 None of the rulers of this age understood this, for if they had, they would not have crucified the Lord of glory. 9 But, as it is written, "What no eye has seen, nor ear heard, nor the heart of man imagined, what God has prepared for those who love him."

After drawing attention to his unfortunate image resulting from his preaching the crucified Christ, he insists that this message is God's special wisdom reserved for God's special people. From 1 Corinthians 2:6, Paul appears concessional in his rhetoric against wisdom. He is not against wisdom *per se*; it is the kind of wisdom that matters. If it is God's wisdom, it is good and must both be proclaimed and relied upon. With anaphora (in which the same words are repeated at the beginning of each clause) he makes this concessional statement of the wisdom he proclaims. He contrasts this wisdom with the wisdom of the world:

> σοφίαν δὲ λαλοῦμεν ἐν τοῖς τελείοις,
> σοφίαν δὲ οὐ τοῦ αἰῶνος τούτου οὐδὲ τῶν ἀρχόντων τοῦ αἰῶνος τούτου τῶν καταργουμένων.

While the first clause, introduced by σοφίαν δὲ, is concessional to Paul's earlier statement about the wisdom of the world (1 Cor 2:1), the second, with the same introductory σοφίαν δὲ, expresses the contrast between the wisdom Paul preaches and the wisdom he avoids. In both cases σοφίαν δὲ expresses antithesis. While the wisdom Paul proclaims is *antithetical to* that of this age (τοῦ αἰῶνος τούτου) and the rulers of this age (τῶν ἀρχόντων τοῦ αἰῶνος), it is also proclaimed to those who are mature and able to understand it, and not to babes.

His appeal to expressions typical of Gnosticism makes him sound selective in his proclamation of wisdom. On the surface, he appears to be proclaiming a special message (of wisdom) to a selected few—the mature (τοῖς τελείοις). But to say this of him would be overstretching his statement. There is hardly any basis for assuming that Paul's proclamation of the wisdom of God was done selectively among only the believers he considered mature (as 1 Corinthians 2:6 appears to say). He had preached this wisdom even to the babes in Corinth, the recipients. How could he conclude that he could not address them as spiritual, except after they had failed to understand what spiritual people are expected to understand?

Going by his language here and what follows, Paul is caught up in the very attitude he was trying to correct. His response to his accusers absorbs him into dividing the members of the church into "spiritual" (πνευματικός) and "unspiritual," (ψυχικὸς) "mature" (τέλειος) and "immature" (νήπιος), at least in his language here.[14] Fee contends that "much of the language of this paragraph is not common to Paul, the explanation of this phenomenon is, as before, to be found in his using *their* [the readers'] language but filling it with his own content and thus refuting theirs."[15] In essence, Paul should be understood to be arguing that it is the mature (subsequently described as those who possess God's Spirit) who are able to discern God's wisdom. His language therefore gives a different impression from his indiscriminate proclamation of the wisdom of God (the message of the cross) to all the Corinthians.

The next statement (1 Cor 2:7) is also antithetical and is set against the last part of the preceding verse (1 Cor 2:6) that speaks of the wisdom of the rulers of this age. With the contrasting ἀλλὰ (but), Paul identifies what he proclaims (using the first-person plural, λαλοῦμεν) as the wisdom of God (θεοῦ σοφίαν) in hidden mystery (ἐν μυστηρίῳ τὴν ἀποκεκρυμμένην).

14. See Fee's observation on this in Fee, *First Epistle to the Corinthians*, 99.
15. Fee, *First Epistle to the Corinthians*, 100.

Wisdom, Knowledge, and Spirituality in Self-defense

With εἰς (indicating purpose), Paul identifies "our glory" (δόξαν ἡμῶν) as the purpose for this wisdom proclaimed in hidden mystery. He maintains this is God's decision beforehand (προώρισεν), even before the ages (πρὸ τῶν αἰώνων).

With another relative pronoun, ἥν (which), Paul gives further qualification of the wisdom of God proclaimed in hidden mystery (1 Cor 2:8). None of the rulers of this age (οὐδεὶς τῶν ἀρχόντων τοῦ αἰῶνος τούτου) mentioned in the preceding verse knew it (ἔγνωκεν). His logical proof for this is that if they knew this hidden wisdom of God (εἰ γὰρ ἔγνωσαν), they would not have crucified the Lord of glory (οὐκ ἂν τὸν κύριον τῆς δόξης ἐσταύρωσαν). This *logos* appeal should be understood not only in terms of the crucifixion of the Lord, which can be reckoned as the bringing to fruition of what God had decided beforehand, but it should also be understood in terms of the rejection of the crucified Lord by the rulers of this age. It is the hidden nature of the wisdom of God (as contained in the message of the Cross) that accounts for their rejection. Following his argument this far, it is clear that the cross (folly and stumbling block) hides the wisdom of God and makes it a mystery hidden away from the wise.

The wisdom of God (proclaimed in hidden mystery) meant for our glory emphasizes, among other things, the emotive dimension of the importance that those who have this mystery should attach to it. In these two qualifications of the wisdom of God (as mystery and as meant for our glory), Paul is making a very loud statement of assessment and judgment. If the wisdom of God as a mystery is for our glory, those who have received it should value it if they are mature enough to recognize what it is. If that is not clear enough at this point, Paul now makes it clear. He employs commoratio to present this wisdom of God for our glory with a quotation from Isaiah 64:4 in which all four clauses speak about the same thing—the hidden mystery of God revealed in the message of the cross:

ἃ ὀφθαλμὸς οὐκ εἶδεν
καὶ οὖς οὐκ ἤκουσεν
καὶ ἐπὶ καρδίαν ἀνθρώπου οὐκ ἀνέβη,
ἃ ἡτοίμασεν ὁ θεὸς τοῖς ἀγαπῶσιν αὐτόν (1 Cor 2:9)

The parallel structure of this commoratio is worthy of note. The first two and the fourth are introduced with relative pronouns (ἃ, οὖς and ἃ with the second preceded by the copulative καὶ). The conjunction καὶ of the third gives the clause the effect of the relative pronoun in the second. The essence of the first three clauses is that the mystery of God's wisdom is incomparable to anything ever experienced by any eye, any ear, and any heart. The threefold expression speaks to the uniqueness and superiority of the wisdom of God proclaimed in the mystery of the cross. The final clause says it is exactly *what* (ἃ) God has prepared for those who love him (τοῖς ἀγαπῶσιν αὐτόν). Paul's purpose for presenting the wisdom of God (with this quotation) in commoratio is to impress its uniqueness and value upon his readers. This is crucial for Paul in a context in which the recipients had failed to give the message of the cross the importance it deserves as the wisdom of God.

This division establishes the superior and unique nature of the wisdom of God Paul preached as represented in the cross. The emotive significance of this argument incorporates *pathos* into the *logos* mode of appeal that advances reasons to prove that the rulers of this age did not know the wisdom of God. The tone of celebration with which the wisdom of God is presented makes this division epideictic rhetoric. Paul's claim that the rulers who rely on the wisdom of this age are doomed to come to nothing, and his insistence that they had failed to know God's wisdom, incorporates forensic language into his argument. The use of commoratio reflects Paul's treatment of his readers as infants incapable of eating solid food meant for the mature, hence ideas are restated in many different ways to help them come to terms with what is meant. Chiasm and antithesis were two important ways of establishing the difference between the wisdom of God in Paul's preaching and the wisdom of this present age which he avoids.

QUALITIES OF A SPIRITUAL PERSON

In this rhetorical division, Paul argues that it is the spiritual person who understands the wisdom of God that is proclaimed in the hidden mystery of the cross. It is a continuation of the confirmatio. He begins with a topical statement that establishes the mystery of God as revealed. He follows it up with a series of logical premises that lead to the conclusion that it takes a spiritual person to understand the mystery of God's wisdom as revealed in the proclamation of the cross.

1 Corinthians 2:10–16

> 10 ἡμῖν δὲ ἀπεκάλυψεν ὁ θεὸς διὰ τοῦ πνεύματος. τὸ γὰρ πνεῦμα πάντα ἐραυνᾷ, καὶ τὰ βάθη τοῦ θεοῦ. 11 τίς γὰρ οἶδεν ἀνθρώπων τὰ τοῦ ἀνθρώπου εἰ μὴ τὸ πνεῦμα τοῦ ἀνθρώπου τὸ ἐν αὐτῷ; οὕτως καὶ τὰ τοῦ θεοῦ οὐδεὶς ἔγνωκεν εἰ μὴ τὸ πνεῦμα τοῦ θεοῦ. 12 ἡμεῖς δὲ οὐ

> τὸ πνεῦμα τοῦ κόσμου ἐλάβομεν ἀλλὰ τὸ πνεῦμα τὸ ἐκ τοῦ θεοῦ, ἵνα εἰδῶμεν τὰ ὑπὸ τοῦ θεοῦ χαρισθέντα ἡμῖν. 13 ἃ καὶ λαλοῦμεν οὐκ ἐν διδακτοῖς ἀνθρωπίνης σοφίας λόγοις ἀλλ' ἐν διδακτοῖς πνεύματος, πνευματικοῖς πνευματικὰ συγκρίνοντες. 14 ψυχικὸς δὲ ἄνθρωπος οὐ δέχεται τὰ τοῦ πνεύματος τοῦ θεοῦ. μωρία γὰρ αὐτῷ ἐστιν καὶ οὐ δύναται γνῶναι, ὅτι πνευματικῶς ἀνακρίνεται. 16 ὁ δὲ πνευματικὸς ἀνακρίνει [τὰ] πάντα, αὐτὸς δὲ ὑπ' οὐδενὸς ἀνακρίνεται. τίς γὰρ ἔγνω νοῦν κυρίου, ὃς συμβιβάσει αὐτόν; ἡμεῖς δὲ νοῦν Χριστοῦ ἔχομεν.

> 10 these things God has revealed to us through the Spirit. For the Spirit searches everything, even the depths of God. 11 For who knows a person's thoughts except the spirit of that person, which is in him? So also no one comprehends the thoughts of God except the Spirit of God. 12 Now we have received not the spirit of the world, but the Spirit who is from God, that we might understand the things freely given us by God. 13 And we impart this in words not taught by human wisdom but taught by the Spirit, interpreting spiritual truths to those who are spiritual. 14 The natural person does not accept the things of the Spirit of God, for they are folly to him, and he is not able to understand them because they are spiritually discerned. 15 The spiritual person judges all things, but is himself to be judged by no one. 16 "For who has understood the mind of the Lord so as to instruct him?" But we have the mind of Christ.

The Spirit's role of searching and revealing the things of God in 1 Corinthians 2:10 is the overriding principle in the following argument. With ἡμῖν (us) as *metonymy,* Paul points indirectly to himself as the recipient of what God has revealed (ἀπεκάλυψεν ὁ θεὸς) through his Spirit (διὰ τοῦ πνεύματος). Some may argue that ἡμῖν (us) refers to all believers or all the teachers of the Corinthians. Whereas this is the obvious expectation, that is not what it indicates in the flow of this argument.[16] The first-person plural is used here in reference to his role as the one who preaches the mysteries of God, who first brought it to the Corinthians, who as a result comes to the conclusion that only the mature and the spiritual are able to discern

---

16. This is not the only place he uses the first-person plural as an indirect reference to himself. Among the many instances, he claims, "And we impart this in words not taught by human wisdom but taught by the Spirit, interpreting spiritual truths to those who are spiritual" (1 Cor 2:13). His use of pronouns other than the first-person singular to refer to himself is abundant (see 1 Cor 1:23; 2:6, 7, 16; 4:9, 10, 11, 12, 13, etc.). In all such instances, the one to whom the pronoun refers to should be determined within the context of the argument and not merely by the literal sense of the pronoun. All this is in line with his preference for indirect reference to people, including himself.

the wisdom of God entailed in the message of the cross—a test which the readers had failed. The importance of the initial adversative δὲ (but) is to express the contrast between the rulers of this age, who could not know the wisdom of God, and Paul, to whom God has revealed this wisdom. The second clause of the verse establishes the critical role of God's Spirit in the revelation of God's wisdom. It comes with the introductory inferential γὰρ (for) followed by the Spirit's function of searching all things (τὸ . . . πνεῦμα πάντα ἐραυνᾷ). The addition of καὶ τὰ βάθη τοῦ θεοῦ (and the depth of God) zeros in on Paul's focus and interest in the argument. He moves from the general (πάντα, "all things") to the specific point of the argument. The Spirit's searching of all things is not as important for him as his searching the depths of God in this argument. The argument is in the form of chiasm, which presents us with *God-the Spirit-the Spirit-God* pattern—ἡμῖν ⌜δὲ ἀπεκάλυψεν ὁ θεὸς διὰ τοῦ πνεύματος. τὸ γὰρ πνεῦμα πάντα ἐραυνᾷ, καὶ τὰ βάθη τοῦ θεοῦ (1 Cor 2:10):

A ὁ θεὸς
 B τοῦ πνεύματος
 B¹ τὸ . . . πνεῦμα
A¹ τοῦ θεοῦ

The ABB¹A¹ chiasm says, *God* has revealed to us through *the Spirit* and *the Spirit* searches all things, even the depth of *God*.

The next verse (1 Cor 2:11) employs γὰρ (functioning as because) to provide the first premise in support of the statement that the Spirit searches the depth of God. Paul employs a question-and-answer response: "for which man knows the [thought] of a man (τίς γὰρ οἶδεν ἀνθρώπων τὰ τοῦ ἀνθρώπου) except the spirit of the man in him (εἰ μὴ τὸ πνεῦμα τοῦ ἀνθρώπου τὸ ἐν αὐτῷ)," With this use of *hypophora* Paul does not require his infant audience to answer. He follows it up with another hypophora which moves the argument to a higher level. His use of οὕτως (in the same way) shows that the same principle is at work in the succeeding premise as in the preceding one. He argues, "in the same way, no one knows the mind of God (οὕτως καὶ τὰ τοῦ θεοῦ) except the Spirit of God (εἰ μὴ τὸ πνεῦμα τοῦ θεοῦ). Here, he resorts to *a minore ad maius* argument in which what applies to a man is also applicable to God.

In the succeeding verse (1 Cor 2:12), Paul moves the argument further by indicating the purpose for receiving God's Spirit. By saying "Now we have not received the spirit of the world (ἡμεῖς δὲ οὐ τὸ πνεῦμα τοῦ κόσμου ἐλάβομεν) but the Spirit from God (ἀλλὰ τὸ πνεῦμα τὸ ἐκ τοῦ θεοῦ)," he

Wisdom, Knowledge, and Spirituality in Self-defense

makes a point which should be understood by deduction. This should imply, "therefore we know the depth or thought of God." However, instead of such deduction (introduced by "therefore"), which is typical of syllogism, he introduces another clause with ἵνα to indicate the purpose of receiving the Spirit of God. He maintains the reason is so that we may know (ἵνα εἰδῶμεν) the things freely given to us by God (τὰ ὑπὸ τοῦ θεοῦ χαρισθέντα ἡμῖν). The slide away from the expected flow of the syllogism is an important indication of where Paul wants to take the argument. God's purpose for giving his Spirit is for the particular purpose of understanding the things God has freely given us. What God has freely given to us appears in the rhetorical subunit for the first time as the *object we receive* and *what God gives*.

The amplification of what has been freely given to us in 1 Corinthians 2:13 explains that what has been freely given is what Paul teaches. "Which also" (ἃ καὶ) is intended to make *what has been freely given* in the preceding verse the object of what is taught. His point is that he speaks of what God has freely given us, not by human wisdom (λαλοῦμεν οὐκ ἐν διδακτοῖς ἀνθρωπίνης σοφίας λόγοις), but by means that are of the Spirit (ἀλλ' ἐν διδακτοῖς πνεύματος). The spiritual things are taught by means of interpreting spiritual things by things that are spiritual (πνευματικοῖς πνευματικὰ συγκρίνοντες).

By his use of the adversative δὲ in 1 Corinthians 2:14, Paul contrasts the unspiritual person (ψυχικὸς) with the spiritual person (of the implied subject of λαλοῦμεν, [we]) who teaches the things freely given in spiritual terms (1 Cor 2:13). This unspiritual person (ψυχικὸς δὲ ἄνθρωπος) does not receive the things of the Spirit of God (οὐ δέχεται τὰ τοῦ πνεύματος τοῦ θεοῦ). The reason the unspiritual person does not receive the things of the Spirit of God is that they are foolishness to him (μωρία γὰρ αὐτῷ ἐστιν). Moreover, the unspiritual person cannot know them (καὶ οὐ δύναται γνῶναι) because the things are spiritually discerned (ὅτι πνευματικῶς ἀνακρίνεται). The enumeratio here provides important details and spells out what the unspiritual person is unable to do in contrast to what the spiritual person does (teaching the things freely given by spiritual means). The syllogism of the argument is not straightforward because of the deliberate shift in terminology. He shifts from "the hidden wisdom revealed to us" to "the things freely given to us" by the Spirit of God. This shift deliberately disturbs the flow of the syllogism to change its course. Does Paul want "the hidden wisdom revealed to us" to be a metonymy for "the things freely given to us," or does the latter refer to something different? As for the wisdom of God (the depth of God), we know what it is about—the message of the cross. We should be on the lookout for what "the things freely given to us" refers to as the argument advances.

Paul now shifts attention back to the spiritual person who interprets things by means of the Spirit (1 Cor 2:15; cf. 2:13). He keeps alternating from the spiritual person to the unspiritual person with adversative conjunctions. In contrast to the unspiritual person who cannot discern things spiritually, the spiritual person judges (discerns) all things (ὁ δὲ πνευματικὸς ἀνακρίνει [τὰ] πάντα). At the same time, no one judges him (αὐτὸς δὲ ὑπ' οὐδενὸς ἀνακρίνεται). Does this mean no one ever judges the spiritual person? Does it mean he does not value the judgment of others because he has already evaluated matters and is certain about the rightness of what he does? These should be clarified as we follow the rest of the argument.

Paul concludes this subunit with a *sentential*, a modified quotation from Isaiah 40:13 which carries the essence of his argument. In its modified form, the quotation inquires if one could know the mind of the Lord (τίς γὰρ ἔγνω νοῦν κυρίου) so as to instruct him (ὃς συμβιβάσει αὐτόν). Paul does not respond to this question in the fashion of hypophora as in the early part of this rhetorical division. He presents it as a typical rhetorical question with the assumption that his readers would supply the obvious answer—"No one can!"

The rhetorical nature of this division is instructive. First Corinthians 2:12 and 2:16 form an *inclusio*. Receiving the Spirit from God (1 Cor 2:12) and having the mind of Christ (1 Cor 2:16) point to that which makes one understand the things of God. The inclusio means that the expressed purpose for having the Spirit of God—"that we might understand the things freely given us by God" (1 Cor 2:12)—is also the purpose for having the mind of Christ (1 Cor 2:16). Back to the sententia the question goes, "For who has understood the mind of the Lord so as to instruct him" (1 Cor 2:16)? The answer should be, "No one!" The concluding statement, "But we have the mind of Christ," is indicative of where Paul wants to take the argument. It represents Paul's claim that he has the mind of Christ while still using the metonymy of the first-person plural. If Paul has the mind of Christ, it means logically that Paul understands the things freely given to us by the Spirit.

The importance of this rhetorical division is to be found in the principles it sets out for Paul's subsequent assessment of the Corinthians and his correction of their misplaced view and attitude toward their teachers.

Wisdom, Knowledge, and Spirituality in Self-defense

The loud nature of the rhetorical style lying between the two verses forming the inclusio—that is, 1 Corinthians 2:13–15 lying between 1 Corinthians 2:12–16—speaks to this importance. In the Greek there are three sentences:

ἃ καὶ λαλοῦμεν οὐκ ἐν διδακτοῖς ἀνθρωπίνης σοφίας λόγοις ἀλλ' ἐν διδακτοῖς πνεύματος, πνευματικοῖς πνευματικὰ συγκρίνοντες.

ψυχικὸς δὲ ἄνθρωπος οὐ δέχεται τὰ τοῦ πνεύματος τοῦ θεοῦ. μωρία γὰρ αὐτῷ ἐστιν καὶ οὐ δύναται γνῶναι, ὅτι πνευματικῶς ἀνακρίνεται.

ὁ δὲ πνευματικὸς ἀνακρίνει [τὰ] πάντα, αὐτὸς δὲ ὑπ' οὐδενὸς ἀνακρίνεται. (1 Cor 2:12–15)

The repetition of διδακτοῖς (taught by) in the first sentence; the repetition of πνεύματος (spiritual) in the first and second sentences; the repetition of various forms of πνευματικὸς as πνευματικὸς, πνευματικοῖς (by/with spiritual things), πνευματικῶς (spiritually) and πνευματικὰ (spiritual things) throughout the three sentences; and the repetition of ἀνακρίνεται (of the second sentence) in the forms, ἀνακρίνει and ἀνακρίνεται in the third sentence, all speak to the importance of the word —"spiritual" and "judging" (discerning) in the argument. The cacophony produced by the hard consonants of these words, coupled with the alliteration and assonance in the repetition of consonant and vowel sounds respectively in διδακτοῖς and the various forms of πνευματικὸς, have the effect of drawing attention to these key words in the argument. These emphasize the Spirit's role in the discernment (understanding) of the things of God and the things freely given to us by God.

The concluding verses for this division (1 Cor 2:15–16) brings the argument to a head in chiasm:

A ὁ δὲ πνευματικὸς ἀνακρίνει [τὰ] πάντα,
  B αὐτὸς δὲ ὑπ' οὐδενὸς ἀνακρίνεται.
  B¹ τίς γὰρ ἔγνω νοῦν κυρίου, ὃς συμβιβάσει αὐτόν;
A¹ ἡμεῖς δὲ νοῦν Χριστοῦ ἔχομεν.

A and A¹ speak of the capacity of the spiritual person for sound judgment. In A, he or she is able to judge all things. In A¹, he or she has the mind of Christ, the reason he or she is able to judge all things. B and B¹ speak about the spiritual person's freedom from other people's judgment resulting from his qualities in A and A¹. B says the spiritual person is judged by no one. B¹ says it in another way—no one can know the mind of the Lord enough to be able to instruct the spiritual person who has the mind of the

Lord. It is significant that the inability of others judging the spiritual person (B and B¹) is sandwiched between the spiritual person's credentials as one judging all things because he has the mind of Christ. The importance of this point can hardly be missed.

The one who cannot instruct the Lord is only said to *know* (ἔγνω) the mind of the Lord (B¹). The spiritual person, on the other hand, *has* (ἔχομεν) the mind of Christ. The difference between "know" and "have" is the key. The one who knows the mind of Christ cannot judge the one who has the mind of Christ. It is impossible for the one who knows the mind of Christ to *know* more than the one who *has* the mind of Christ. Those who have the mind of Christ then are placed over and above those who know the mind of Christ. By saying "we have the mind of Christ," Paul presents himself ("we") as the Lord who cannot be instructed by the one who claims to know the mind of the Lord. The Lord becomes a metonymy for Paul in this particular case. Paul is saying in other words, "I have the mind of Christ, hence no one can judge me." For Paul therefore, the Corinthians can claim to *know* the mind of the Lord, but that does not qualify them to judge Paul as one who *has* the mind of Christ. This will be given explicit application as Paul advances his argument, but just to peep into what lies ahead, this understanding explains why Paul insists "But with me it is a very small thing that I should be judged by you or by any human court" (1 Cor 4:3).

It is of utmost importance to observe the correlation between being spiritual and being able to recognize the things given freely by God. This is antithetical to being unspiritual and not being able to recognize the things freely given us by God, and hence not being willing to receive them as freely given. Spirituality is therefore defined here by one's ability to understand and recognize things freely given us by God and to receive them as such.

First Corinthians 2:10–16 therefore presents us with principles that define a spiritual person. These are meant to lay the bases on which Paul is going to assess the Corinthian believers in 1 Corinthians 3 and 4 in a series of arguments. At the same time, it is the basis on which he reassesses himself as a spiritual person against the rating of the Corinthians. This understanding calls into question Conzelmann's claim that the pneumatics described here are "a superior class" who set aside the offense of the cross in favor "of the knowledge of spirit to spirit."[17] This view of Conzelmann leads him to recognize a break in Paul's thought here. Following Bultmann, he thinks that Paul is drawn into such ideas for the purpose of argument. If

---

17. Conzelmann, *Commentary on the First Epistle*, 57.

Wisdom, Knowledge, and Spirituality in Self-defense

the language here reflects that of the Corinthian *pneumatics,* the principles here are consistent with Paul's argument. Against this view of Conzelmann, the understanding of this study points *not* to a break in Paul's thought, but the setting forth of principles that define a spiritual person, principles by which Paul is able to achieve two things—namely, presenting himself as a spiritual person who has the mind of Christ, and presenting the Corinthians as unspiritual people who cannot understand spiritual things communicated by the "spiritual Paul." Conzelmann's own conclusion should have led him to this realization. He maintained that Paul was claiming to have a wisdom foreign to his readers, and as such, a superior religious status to them.[18] It was his failure to recognize the role of the principles set out in 1 Corinthians 2:10–16 in Paul's argument that led him to conclude that there was a break in Paul's thought.

In this rhetorical division, chiasm is used to highlight the crucial role of the Spirit in one's understanding of the things of God. Paul's use of bending syllogism with hypophora enables him to establish the principles that define what a spiritual person is. His use of contrast helps him to distinguish the spiritual person from the unspiritual person. With the use of a quotation as sententia, Paul presents himself as one who has the mind of the Lord who can hardly be judged or instructed by those who do not have the mind of Christ. In doing so, metonymy enables him to use the first-person plural and "the Lord" when referring to himself. *Cacophony,* alliteration, and assonance were figures of sound that drew attention to important points of the argument.

---

18. Conzelmann, *Commentary on the First Epistle,* 71.

Chapter 4

Counter Assessment, Correction, and Exhortation

This chapter deals with Paul's assessment of the Corinthians in light of the qualities of the spiritual person outlined in the preceding arguments.

COUNTER ASSESSMENT—THE CORINTHIANS ASSESSED

This segment of 1 Corinthians 3 begins as a forensic rhetoric passing judgment on the readers. Paul employs enumeratio as he lists various conditions that portray their spiritual state. He does this in a way that shows that the Corinthians' perceptions and attitudes are in consonance with their spiritual state.

 1 Corinthians 3:1–4

> 1 Κἀγώ, ἀδελφοί, οὐκ ἠδυνήθην λαλῆσαι ὑμῖν ὡς πνευματικοῖς ἀλλ' ὡς σαρκίνοις, ὡς νηπίοις ἐν Χριστῷ. 2 γάλα ὑμᾶς ἐπότισα, οὐ βρῶμα. οὔπω γὰρ ἐδύνασθε. ἀλλ' οὐδὲ ἔτι νῦν δύνασθε, 3 ἔτι γὰρ σαρκικοί ἐστε. ὅπου γὰρ ἐν ὑμῖν ζῆλος καὶ ἔρις, οὐχὶ σαρκικοί ἐστε καὶ κατὰ ἄνθρωπον περιπατεῖτε; 4 ὅταν γὰρ λέγῃ τις, ἐγὼ μέν εἰμι Παύλου, ἕτερος δέ, ἐγὼ Ἀπολλῶ, οὐκ ἄνθρωποί ἐστε;

> 1 But I, brothers, could not address you as spiritual people, but as people of the flesh, as infants in Christ. 2 I fed you with milk, not solid food, for you were not ready for it. And even now you are not yet ready, 3 for you are still of the flesh. For while there is jealousy and strife among you, are you not of the flesh and behaving only in

a human way? 4 For when one says, "I follow Paul," and another, "I follow Apollos," are you not being merely human?

This division opens straightway with Paul's words of assessment that rates the Corinthians as unspiritual. This is because in his previous visit to them he could not address them as spiritual (οὐκ ἠδυνήθην λαλῆσαι ὑμῖν ὡς πνευματικοῖς). He employs *simile* in describing the readers' spiritual condition. In three successive uses of ὡς (as) with adjectives, Paul presents images of the readers that represent his assessment of them:

οὐκ ἠδυνήθην λαλῆσαι ὑμῖν
ὡς πνευματικοῖς ἀλλ᾽
ὡς σαρκίνοις
ὡς νηπίοις ἐν Χριστῷ

The particle οὐκ (not) in the first line negates ὡς πνευματικοῖς (as spiritual), which then becomes synonymous with ὡς σαρκίνοις (as fleshly) in the second simile. The next simile, ὡς νηπίοις ἐν Χριστῷ (as infants in Christ), should be seen in terms of enumeratio, which amplifies the two similes with additional detail. The assessment and rating of the Corinthians as infants (νηπίοις) contrasts them with the mature (τελεῖοι) to whom the wisdom of God is proclaimed (1 Cor 2:6). Similarly, their assessment as "fleshly" (σαρκίνοις) and "not spiritual" (οὐκ . . . ὡς πνευματικοῖς) brings to mind all the things said about the unspiritual person in 1 Corinthians 2. It is the judgmental tone of Paul's assessment here that makes the language forensic.

Paul advances his argument with commoratio in which he restates his assessment of his readers (1 Cor 3:2). His manner of giving amplification to his assessment of the readers is deliberately superfluous: "I fed you with milk (γάλα ὑμᾶς ἐπότισα), not solid food" (οὐ βρῶμα). Of course! Milk is not solid food; everyone knows this! Is this another way of treating his readers as babes? In any case, this superfluous amplification helps him to sound emphatic. The emphasis is intensified by the extension of their condition to the present where they are still not able to take solid food (ἀλλ᾽ οὐδὲ ἔτι νῦν δύνασθε).

Taken together, "I *fed* you" (ὑμᾶς ἐπότισα, 1 Cor 3:2) and "I could not *speak* to you" (οὐκ ἠδυνήθην λαλῆσαι ὑμῖν, 1 Cor 3:1) indicate that "milk" is used in terms of the teaching given to the readers. The use of milk (γάλα) to describe students who have failed to live up to expectation is well known in Hellenistic writings.[1] Now Paul says it was not only in the past that the

---

1. Johnson gives evidence of Hellenistic use of "solid food" for students who live

readers were not able to eat solid food, but now also they still cannot. In saying the Corinthians could only take milk as infants, Paul was actually returning the same judgment with which they had judged him. As Fee observes, "The Corinthians, enamored by wisdom and thinking of themselves as 'spiritual,' are less than enchanted with Paul's message, which they regard as mere 'milk.'"[2]

The certainty of the description of their spiritual state is given away by the amplification given to it by Paul in repetitive descriptions. "For still you are fleshly" (ἔτι γὰρ σαρκικοί ἐστε, 1 Cor 3:3) serves to reaffirm what was said in 1 Corinthians 3:1, in which the same condition received three parallel descriptions in "not as spiritual," "fleshly," and "infants." The repetitive amplification of their rating is followed by a demonstration of evidence: "for . . . there are jealousy and strife among you (ὅπου γὰρ ἐν ὑμῖν ζῆλος καὶ ἔρις)." This submission of proof of their state as unspiritual belongs to the confirmatio. The subsequent rhetorical question beginning with οὐχὶ demands the answer, "Yes, we are fleshly and walk according to human nature." The recurrence of their rating as "fleshly" as opposed to "spiritual" in the first three verses (1 Cor 3:1–3) must be purposeful. It is curious that this recurrence does not end here as more amplification of their spiritual rating continues.

First Corinthians 3:4 presents another rhetorical question which comes as a tag to their claims of allegiance to their respective teachers: "For when one says, I belong to Paul, and another, I belong to Apollos, are you not [merely] human (ὅταν γὰρ λέγῃ τις. ἐγὼ μέν εἰμι Παύλου, ἕτερος δέ. ἐγὼ Ἀπολλῶ, οὐκ ἄνθρωποί ἐστε;)?" In furtherance of his confirmatio, Paul offers up more evidence in support of his assessment of the Corinthians as being unspiritual. Keener intimates that political parties bore the names of the founders, and slogans similar to "I am of so-and-so" were typical expressions of rivalry in political, academic, and athletic experience.[3] He is of the view that the use of similar expressions by Paul here is Paul's way of presenting their division in a ridiculous way. While some hold that there was actually a group claiming to belong to Christ's party, others think

---

up to their training, and "milk" for learners who fail to live up to their training by citing ancient sources such as Epictetus *Discourses* 2.16.39; Philo, *Noah the Planter* 9: *Every Good Man Is Free* 160; and Seneca, *Letters* 88:20 (See Johnson, *Hebrews*, 156).

2. Fee, *First Epistle to the Corinthians*, 98.

3. Keener, *1–2 Corinthians*, 24.

that Christ's group was hypothetical.⁴ The fact that the precise nature of Christ's and Cephas's groups cannot be ascertained makes a definite stance on either position difficult. But that is not where the crux of the matter lies. If such groups as of Cephas and Christ did not really exist, then Paul must have used them to heighten the absurdity of their misguided behavior.

The effect of the question in 1 Corinthians 3:4 is similar to the preceding one. The statement preceding the question tag gives an indication that their division was an important factor in Paul's rating of the Corinthians. The envy and strife (ζῆλος καὶ ἔρις, 1 Cor 3:3) gives the impression that their division involved active rivalry. The appeal to the readers' character of envy and strife in support of Paul's argument is a *nonfallacious argumentum ad hominem* in the sense that their character logically supports the argument. The offering up of reasons for his rating of the Corinthians at various points in this rhetorical division makes his appeal one of *logos*.

A significant turn in Paul's argument occurs when Paul narrows the division (and strife) to Apollos and himself in 1 Corinthians 3:4, and consistently so throughout the rest of 1 Corinthians 3 and 4. Paul gives the indication that the whole issue of division and its manifestation of envy and strife were between these two parties: Paul's and Apollos's.

In this rhetorical division, Paul employs enumeration as he lists the conditions that portray the unfortunate spiritual state of the readers in an argument which employs forensic language in judging them. With the use of simile in enumeratio, he provides details of his description of their lowly spiritual state. In addition, commoratio is employed to restate Paul's assessment of the readers' spiritual condition, while with rhetorical question, he provides support for his claim that the readers are not spiritual in what is considered as nonfallacious argumentum ad hominem. The main mode of appeal is *logos*.

CORRECTION OF THE CORINTHIANS' PERCEPTIONS OF PAUL AND APOLLOS

1 Corinthians 3:5–9

> 5 Τί οὖν ἐστιν Ἀπολλῶς; τί δέ ἐστιν Παῦλος; διάκονοι δι' ὧν ἐπιστεύσατε, καὶ ἑκάστῳ ὡς ὁ κύριος ἔδωκεν. 6 ἐγὼ ἐφύτευσα, Ἀπολλῶς ἐπότισεν, ἀλλὰ ὁ θεὸς ηὔξανεν. 7 ὥστε οὔτε ὁ φυτεύων ἐστίν

---

4. Keener holds the hypothetical view of the Christ group, while Datiri holds that it actually existed. See Keener, *1–2 Corinthians*, 25; Datiri, "1 Corinthians," 1379.

τι οὔτε ὁ ποτίζων ἀλλ' ὁ αὐξάνων θεός. 8 ὁ φυτεύων δὲ καὶ ὁ ποτίζων ἕν εἰσιν, ἕκαστος δὲ τὸν ἴδιον μισθὸν λήμψεται κατὰ τὸν ἴδιον κόπον. 9 θεοῦ γάρ ἐσμεν συνεργοί, θεοῦ γεώργιον, θεοῦ οἰκοδομή ἐστε.

5 What then is Apollos? What is Paul? Servants through whom you believed, as the Lord assigned to each. 6 I planted, Apollos watered, but God gave the growth. 7 So neither he who plants nor he who waters is anything, but only God who gives the growth. 8 He who plants and he who waters are one, and each will receive his wages according to his labor. 9 For we are God's fellow workers. You are God's field, God's building.

The following two rhetorical questions are insightful with respect to the Corinthians' perceptions of Paul and Apollos. They touch on how the Corinthians perceived Paul and Apollos. Paul asks, "What then is Apollos? What is Paul (Τί οὖν ἐστιν Ἀπολλῶς; τί δέ ἐστιν Παῦλος;)?" Then the answer: "Servants through whom you believed" (διάκονοι δι' ὧν ἐπιστεύσατε). Paul finds the right answer to these questions to be crucial, and hence does not leave it to chance. His use of hypophora is just to ensure that the right answer is provided. It is important to note that the answer is qualified with "as the Lord assigned to each" (καὶ ἑκάστῳ ὡς ὁ κύριος ἔδωκεν). By this qualifier, Paul clearly sees his role as different from that of Apollos, but they stand together as God's assigned workers.

He resorts to amplification by enumeratio with which he supplies more information in order to increase the probability of his readers understanding what he means. To this end, he adds his role, that of Apollos, and that of God, in order to demonstrate who matters in the church. The parallelism of the presentation of these roles is meant to foster easy comparison and assessment:

    A ἐγὼ ἐφύτευσα (I planted)
      B Ἀπολλῶς ἐπότισεν (Apollos watered)
        C ἀλλ' ὁ θεὸς ηὔξανεν (but God granted the growth) (1 Cor 3:6)

The final position given to God's role with the adversative ἀλλ'(C) sets the Lord's role in contradistinction to the roles played by Apollos and Paul (A & B). The roles of planting (for Paul) and watering (for Apollos) as human roles are contrasted with the divine role of granting growth. Without God's role, the roles played by Paul and Apollos would come to nothing. This is Paul's way of indicating who matters in the economy. This deduction from their roles is obvious, but in line with his view of the readers as infants, he resorts to another *enumeratio* in which the right deduction is spelled out for the readers:

> ὥστε οὔτε ὁ φυτεύων ἐστίν τι
> οὔτε ὁ ποτίζων
> ἀλλ' ὁ αὐξάνων θεός (1 Cor 3:7)

Thus,

> "Neither the one who sows is anything"
> "nor the one who waters"
> "but God who gives the growth"

With ὥστε (so that), Paul provides a clear indication that what follows is the expected deduction from his preceding statement. The effect of ἀλλ' (but) in this is similar to what was seen in the preceding parallelism.

There is further amplification by way of *enumeratio*. It offers obvious *deductions*: "He who plants and he who waters are one, and each will receive his wages according to his own labor" (1 Cor 3:8). "For we are God's fellow workers" (θεοῦ γάρ ἐσμεν συνεργοί) comes in as a concluding statement on the roles of Apollos and Paul though this does not end the discussion on their roles (1 Cor 3:9).

Paul now shifts attention to the readers who are described corporately (ἐστε) via the images of God's field (θεοῦ γεώργιον) and God's building (θεοῦ οἰκοδομή). The description of Paul and Apollos as God's fellow workers and the readers as God's field and building forms the following parallelism:

> A θεοῦ γάρ ἐσμεν συνεργοί,
>   B θεοῦ γεώργιον,
>   B¹ θεοῦ οἰκοδομή ἐστε (1 Cor 3:9)

The parallelism of the three lines is intended to show how Apollos and Paul relate to God (A) on the one hand, and how the readers relate to God (B & B¹) on the other. That is to say, whereas Apollos and Paul relate to God as fellow workers (συνεργοί), the readers relate to God as God's field (γεώργιον) and God's building (οἰκοδομή). Paul's identification of Apollos and himself as "coworkers" (συνεργοί), as "one" (ἕν), and as people who are entitled to their wages (μισθὸν), should not make one press too far the innocence of either of the two in the division. Caution is therefore to be exercised in conclusions such as that of Patrick Hartin. Hartin, whose entire work focused on the relationship between Apollos and Paul, concludes,

"Paul never speaks negatively of Apollos. Instead, his words present him more as partner."[5]

While one cannot deny that Apollos and Paul were partners, to hold that "Paul never speaks negatively of Apollos" will be to overstretch Paul's statement here. Here, Paul only indicates that they were both workers of God and both were entitled to their wages according to their labor; nothing more, nothing less! A closer look at Paul's argument does not rule out the idea that Paul found fault with Apollos's style of presentation, its impact on the gospel, and how it may have contributed to the division in Corinth. We should not lose sight of Paul's statement that implies that by preaching the gospel with eloquent words or wisdom, the cross is emptied of its power (1 Cor 1:17). If Apollos's preaching was different, as has been demonstrated in Patterson's reconstruction of his message in chapter 1, then Paul's insistence that no other foundation can be laid apart from what he had laid, which is Christ (1 Cor 3:11), is instructive.[6] This caution of Paul clearly indicates that he saw the threat of another foundation other than Christ in the work of Apollos. One is right to zero in on Apollos as it is in line with Paul's own narrowing of the division to Apollos and himself (1 Cor 3:4–8; cf. 4:6).

In this short rhetorical division, rhetorical questions and hypophora are used to clarify the identity of Apollos and Paul. The importance of clarifying this identity is seen in its amplification by way of enumeratio which provides the details needed to clarify the identities of the two leaders. The use of parallelism enables Paul to set out side-by-side the roles of Apollos, himself, and God, as well as how Paul, Apollos, and the Corinthians stand in relation to God. With enumeratio, the one who is important on the basis of their roles is made explicit. The main mode of appeal is *logos* as Paul provides logical support for clarifying the identity of the two leaders.

THE JUDGMENT OF THE ONE WHO BUILDS ON THE FOUNDATION

1 Corinthians 3:10–14

10 Κατὰ τὴν χάριν τοῦ θεοῦ τὴν δοθεῖσάν μοι ὡς σοφὸς ἀρχιτέκτων
11 θεμέλιον ἔθηκα, ἄλλος δὲ ἐποικοδομεῖ. ἕκαστος δὲ βλεπέτω πῶς

---

5. Hartin, *Apollos*, 103.

6. In addition to Patterson, Phillips shows how Apollos is very likely to have favored the allegorical hermeneutics of Philo who, according to him, pressed this approach to absurdity (Phillips, *Exploring 1 Corinthians*, 68).

Wisdom, Knowledge, and Spirituality in Self-defense

ἐποικοδομεῖ. θεμέλιον γὰρ ἄλλον οὐδεὶς δύναται θεῖναι παρὰ τὸν κείμενον, ὅς ἐστιν Ἰησοῦς Χριστός. 12 εἰ δέ τις ἐποικοδομεῖ ἐπὶ τὸν θεμέλιον χρυσόν, ἄργυρον, λίθους τιμίους, ξύλα, χόρτον, καλάμην, 13 ἑκάστου τὸ ἔργον φανερὸν γενήσεται, ἡ γὰρ ἡμέρα δηλώσει, ὅτι ἐν πυρὶ ἀποκαλύπτεται. καὶ ἑκάστου τὸ ἔργον ὁποῖόν ἐστιν τὸ πῦρ [αὐτὸ] δοκιμάσει. 14 εἴ τινος τὸ ἔργον μενεῖ ὃ ἐποικοδόμησεν, μισθὸν λήμψεται. 15 εἴ τινος τὸ ἔργον κατακαήσεται, ζημιωθήσεται, αὐτὸς δὲ σωθήσεται, οὕτως δὲ ὡς διὰ πυρός.

10 According to the grace of God given to me, like a skilled master builder I laid a foundation, and someone else is building upon it. Let each one take care how he builds upon it. 11 For no one can lay a foundation other than that which is laid, which is Jesus Christ. 12 Now if anyone builds on the foundation with gold, silver, precious stones, wood, hay, straw—13 each one's work will become manifest, for the Day will disclose it, because it will be revealed by fire, and the fire will test what sort of work each one has done. 14 If the work that anyone has built on the foundation survives, he will receive a reward. 15 If anyone's work is burned up, he will suffer loss, though he himself will be saved, but only as through fire.

By taking a closer look at Paul's argument, it is not difficult to see how he features Apollos's different gospel. Of the two images used in describing the readers' relationship to God, God's building receives greater attention. With this imagery, Paul presents his role with a simile that likens him to an expert builder (σοφὸς ἀρχιτέκτων) who lays (ἔθηκα) the foundation (θεμέλιον) of God's building (the readers). Another (ἄλλος) now builds (ἐποικοδομεῖ) on the foundation. It is logically clear in the use of the singular "another" (ἄλλος) that Appollos is implied. His role is the builder upon the foundation laid by Paul, who is the sole layer of the foundation in Corinth. Here, we have the reiteration in different expression (commoratio) of their roles as "I planted" and "Apollos watered." The caution that immediately follows the statement of Apollos's role is insightful: "Let each one sees how he builds [on the foundation]" (ἕκαστος δὲ βλεπέτω πῶς ἐποικοδομεῖ). Two of the five words of the caution are conjunctions (δὲ and πῶς). δὲ is technically understood as standing first in the sentence and is used here to introduce the caution. Here it functions like "however." πῶς indicates that the caution is about a particular way (manner) of doing things. Altogether, the caution is about *how* the one builds (ἐποικοδομεῖ) upon the foundation.

It is significant that Paul uses different verbs to distinguish his role (ἔθηκα) from that of Apollos (ἐποικοδομεῖ). It is instructive therefore that the caution goes to the one who builds on the foundation (ἐποικοδομεῖ) and not the one who lays the foundation (ἔθηκα). The use of "each" (ἕκαστος) is therefore not to be taken as referring to both Apollos and Paul, nor to other workers who come after Paul. It should be taken as a rhetorical device that lessens the direct impact of Paul's reference to Apollos. Alan Tomlison is therefore right in identifying Apollos with the builder.[7] Mark Miller similarly argues, "where Paul used the singular 'another built on it,' Paul may have Apollos in mind as the one who 'watered.'"[8] The use of "another" (ἄλλος) and "each" (ἕκαστος) is simply to lessen the direct impact of the unfavorable reference to Apollos. Sampley observes that there was preference for indirect speech at the time since it avoided the confrontational impact of direct speech and the possibility of reprisal.[9]

In this light, one differs from Fee, who argues that Apollos is not mentioned in 1 Corinthians 3:10, hence "someone else" building on it cannot be a reference to him.[10] Against Fee's view, it should be pointed out that once Apollos has been clearly mentioned with respect to his role of watering what Paul planted in 1 Corinthians 3:6–9, it would be superfluous to repeat his name in connection with his corresponding role of building on the foundation Paul had laid in the succeeding verse (1 Cor 3:10). First Corin-

7. Tomlison, "1 Corinthians," 1233.

8. Miller thinks that where Paul uses the indefinite "Let everyone consider how they build on," he refers to later workers and elders who worked in the Corinthian church (Miller, *Nazarene Commentary*, 189, footnotes 7 and 8). However, if the reference is to others, it would be abrupt as Paul applies "all this" to himself and Apollos as the layer of the foundation and builder upon the foundation, respectively.

9. Sampley, "1 Corinthians," 803.

10. See Fee, *First Epistle to the Corinthians*, 138–39. Fee holds that "Paul acknowledges in 3:5–9 that Apollos's work was not in competition with his own, but that it 'watered' what he had 'sown'" (Fee, *First Epistle to the Corinthians*, 138). He contends that taking the builder upon the foundation to be Apollos defeats Paul's earlier statements that presents them as "one in a common cause" (Fee, *First Epistle to the Corinthians*, 138). In holding a different view from Fee, one should point out that Paul's argument here is simply to show how the roles of Apollos and that of himself are insignificant in the face of God's role of granting growth. The argument touches on nothing about their cooperation or rivalry. Paul's later stress on the difference between their roles and how they played them is significant. While he played his role as a "wise" person laying a foundation, his caution raised on how the role of Apollos (in building upon the foundation) is carried out (1 Cor 3:10) is a deliberate clue for his argument. Again, Fee argues that by this time both Paul and Apollos were not in Corinth and therefore could not be those responsible for sowing the kind of wisdom under attack (Fee, *First Epistle to the Corinthians*, 56, 138). It should be pointed out that nothing in Paul's argument indicates that the one(s) responsible for this wisdom which is under attack is (are) still in Corinth.

thians 3:9 identifies Paul and Apollos as the workers in both God's field and God's building (1 Cor 3:9). If Paul and Apollos are God's fellow workers in God's building, and Paul's role is the sole layer of the foundation, what role is left for Apollos (1 Cor 3:10–11)? His use of the indefinite "someone" in 1 Corinthians 3:10 is characteristic of Paul, who prefers the indirect way of address that lessens the confrontational impact of his speech. Furthermore, the fact that Paul urged Apollos to visit the Corinthians (1 Cor 16:12) does not mean Paul did not find Apollos guilty in anyway as Fee suggests.[11] Since this call for Apollos's visit represents a much later development subsequent to Apollos's work in Corinth, a number of things could have changed to account for why Paul called for his visit. This change could have involved improvement in Apollos's teaching, for example. Such a positive development could have accounted for Paul's attempt to lessen his direct caution to Apollos.

To clarify their roles and where the problem lies, Paul resorts to distinctio by restating what he means so as to remove any ambiguity. With his narrowing the discussion to Apollos and himself in the background, he rules out the possibility of Apollos's work amounting to another foundation. The indefinite "no one" (οὐδεὶς) is another indirect reference to Apollos. He defines what the foundation is made up of, namely, "Jesus Christ" (ὅς ἐστιν Ἰησοῦς Χριστός). The statement "For no one can lay a foundation other than that which is laid, which is Jesus Christ" (1 Cor 3:11) is a polemic against another teaching, which is not Christ. It also puts all other teachings (in this particular case, Apollos's) in the role of building on Paul's foundation of Christ. The expression, "apart from that which has been laid, which is Christ" (παρὰ τὸν κείμενον, ὅς ἐστιν Ἰησοῦς Χριστός) makes Apollos's teaching suspect. It reflects Paul's recognition of a teaching other than Christ. This is one of the strongest statements in support of Patterson's view that Apollos taught a different gospel, such as John's baptism in Corinth.[12] Paul will certainly see John's baptism as "other than the foundation of Christ" (1 Cor 3:11). First Corinthians 3:11 not only establishes the exclusive nature of Paul's foundation, but also of Paul's role as the sole layer of that foundation. That it was possible for Apollos to preach a different gospel from Paul's is evident in the analysis of Apollos's bibliographic information as presented by John Phillips:

---

11. Fee, *First Epistle to the Corinthians*, 55.
12. Patterson, *Lost Way*, 219–21.

Apollos, by contrast, grew up in Alexandria, which had a large Jewish community. The Jews of Alexandria enjoyed a considerable amount of self-government. Some even held influential posts in the city administration. Philo's brother, Alexander, was not only chief customs officer, he was fabulously wealthy. Philo himself was a patriotic Jew. He was also an eager student of Greek philosophy, especially that of Plato, the Stoics, and the Neo-Pythagoreans. His goal was to interpret the Old Testament in the light of Greek philosophy. He developed a system of hermeneutics based on an allegorical interpretation of the Scriptures, pressed to the point of absurdity. He was, nevertheless, one of the most influential Jews of his day. Apollos was an Alexandrian and would have found it difficult to escape the influence of Philo. Apollos, well versed in the Old Testament Scriptures, probably the Septuagint version, pointed to Christ, even though his understanding of the gospel was defective at first. It is very likely that Apollos favored Philo's allegorical hermeneutics. In any case, his style, so unlike Paul's, appealed to many.[13]

The writer of Acts gives the indication that Paul was aware of Apollos's faulty gospel that resulted in his baptizing converts with John's baptism. Paul's attempt in Ephesus to explain to Apollos's converts that John was pointing the people to Christ, and the fact that he was the one who baptized Apollos's converts in the name of Jesus, are instructive (Acts 19:1–7). All this happened because, while claiming to be preaching Christ as a powerful public speaker (Acts 18:28), Apollos was baptizing his converts with John's baptism (Acts 18:25).

The chiasm with which the roles of the layer of the foundation and the builder upon the foundation are presented is of interest:

A ὡς σοφὸς ἀρχιτέκτων θεμέλιον θηκα,
   B ἄλλος δὲ ἐποικοδομεῖ.
   B¹ ἕκαστος δὲ βλεπέτω πῶς ἐποικοδομεῖ.
A¹ θεμέλιον γὰρ ἄλλον οὐδεὶς δύναται θεῖναι παρὰ τὸν κείμενον, ὅς ἐστιν Ἰησοῦς Χριστός. (1 Cor 3:10–11)

While A focuses on the role of Paul as the wise (skillful) layer of the foundation, A¹ identifies the foundation with Jesus, and rules out the possibility of another foundation. Sandwiched between them are B and B¹. B indicates that another person (ἄλλος) is building on the foundation. B¹ cautions the one building on it to take care *how* (πῶς) he builds on the

---

13. Phillips, *Exploring 1 Corinthians*, 68.

foundation. The use of ἕκαστος (each) should be understood in light of the preceding ἄλλος (another) since they play the same role in referring to the builder upon the foundation. It is a matter of curious interest that the one who needs to exercise the caution is not the layer of the foundation, but the one building upon the foundation. This is because the layer of the foundation has done his work as a "wise" (σοφὸς) builder (1 Cor 3:10). He has no need for a call to be careful in how he does his work, but the builder upon the foundation has need of such a call. While Paul describes himself in his role as "wise" (σοφὸς), he fails to qualify Apollos with such a positive modifier in his role. This is deliberative.

In what follows (1 Cor 3:12), the focus is fixed on the role identified with Apollos. Paul continues with his use of distinctio in order to remove all ambiguity about whose role he has issues with. The introductory "Now if anyone builds on the foundation" (εἰ δέ τις ἐποικοδομεῖ ἐπὶ τὸν θεμέλιον) clarifies whose role he is talking about between himself and Apollos. Using a number of objects for *analogy*, he indicates how depending upon the *manner* (how), the quality of the builder's work could be gold (χρυσόν), silver (ἄργυρον), precious stones (λίθους τιμίους), wood (ξύλα), hay (χόρτον), or straw (καλάμην). In this verse (1 Cor 3:13), Paul uses "each" (ἑκάστου) as a metonymy for Apollos, who will be judged for his work as a builder upon the foundation of Christ. With the use of this metonymy Paul generalizes the subject of the verb "builds" (ἐποικοδομεῖ) in order to make it less offensive to Apollos.[14] The judgment, which lies in the future, will make manifest (φανερὸν) the work (ἔργον) of the builder on the foundation (τις ἐποικοδομεῖ ἐπὶ τὸν θεμέλιον), and reveal by fire what sort of work it is. Worthy of note is the use of many words to indicate that the purpose of the judgment is to reveal the nature of the builder's work. This is evident in the following chiasm:

A ἑκάστου τὸ ἔργον φανερὸν γενήσεται,
  B ἡ γὰρ ἡμέρα δηλώσει,
  B¹ ὅτι ἐν πυρὶ ἀποκαλύπτεται.
A¹ καὶ ἑκάστου τὸ ἔργον ὁποῖόν ἐστιν τὸ πῦρ [αὐτὸ] δοκιμάσει (1 Cor 3:13)

The *chiastic* structure presents "the day" (ἡ ἡμέρα, B) and "fire" (πυρὶ, B¹) as the means by which the work of the builder will be assessed. These

14. The interpretation of the indefinite personal pronoun ἕκαστος (each) in 1 Corinthians 3:10c, as applicable to other workers (as Naylor and others have done), ignores Paul's expressed intent of applying his argument to Apollos and himself.

(B and B¹) are sandwiched between A and A¹, both of which state the object of the judgment (the work of the builder). In all the four lines of ABB¹A¹, there are words and expressions that show that the purpose of the judgment is to reveal the nature of the builder's work: A ("will become visible" [φανερὸν γενήσεται]), B ("will bring to light" [δηλώσει]), B¹ ("will be revealed" [ἀποκαλύπτεται]), and A¹ ("will test what sort of work," [ἔρον ὁποῖόν... δοκιμάσει]). The cumulative effect of these words and expressions establishes the certainty both of the judgment and the revelation of the sort of work in question. The fact that this judgment lies in the future indicates that the Corinthians' assessment of the builder is not final.[15]

Paul concludes the discourse on the judgment of the builder with two statements: εἴ τινος τὸ ἔργον μενεῖ ὃ ἐποικοδόμησεν, μισθὸν λήμψεται.

εἴ τινος τὸ ἔργον κατακαήσεται, ζημιωθήσεται, αὐτὸς δὲ σωθήσεται, οὕτως δὲ ὡς διὰ πυρός (1 Cor 3:14–15). The two concluding statements employ anaphora, which repeats εἴ τινος τὸ ἔργον at the initial position for emphatic effect. The two are antithetical statements in parallel structures. They describe two likely scenarios for the judgment of the one who builds on the foundation. After the testing on the Day by fire, his work will either stand or get burnt. If it stands, he will receive a reward (μισθὸν λήμψεται), but if it gets burnt, he will suffer loss (ζημιωθήσεται); and though he will be saved, it will be as through fire (αὐτὸς δὲ σωθήσεται, οὕτως δὲ ὡς διὰ πυρός). This judgment has no general application to the Corinthians as it deals specifically with the builder on the foundation and what he has built on the foundation (ἐποικοδόμησεν, 1 Cor 3:14). Paul is not talking about the eschatological judgment of all believers here. Its general application to all Christians and the resulting question of whether one can suffer loss and be saved are uncalled for, as such a question fails to appreciate the particular direction of Paul's argument.[16] Fee is one of those who give a general application of the judgment to the Corinthians:

> Paul is not so much making a soteriological statement as he is warning his Corinthian friends. He obviously, as elsewhere (e.g., 6:11), sees them as within the context of the faith; salvation after

15. Other future expressions are "he will receive a reward," (μισθὸν λήμψεται—1 Cor 3:14), "the work will be consumed," (τὸ ἔργον κατακαήσεται), "it will be lost," (ζημιωθήσεται), and "but he will be saved, but as through fire," (αὐτὸς δὲ σωθήσεται, οὕτως δὲ ὡς διὰ πυρός—1 Cor 3:15).

16. Fee tends to see the object of this judgment as the *psychikoi* in the Corinthian church, but strictly speaking, that is not the case. (Fee, *First Epistle to the Corinthians*, 128).

> all is by grace, not by one's own works. But also as elsewhere he expects the warnings to be taken seriously. Here the word of warning and the word of hope are one. He wants them to desist from their current worldly wisdom; he wants them, with him, to be saved and to experience reward. But their current behavior is so seriously aberrant that he must warn them yet once more (3 vv. 16–17), this time in the strongest terms yet: those who persist in these activities and attitudes are in fact in eternal danger.[17]

Fee's general application of the judgment of the builder to the Corinthians fails to recognize the fact that Paul does not depict the readers as builders, but as God's building. Conzelmann holds that the judgment applies to Paul also. He maintains, "By drawing attention to the judgment to which his own work will be exposed, Paul sets himself on the same footing as the other workers and party heads."[18] Much as Conzelmann's view is theologically sound and consistent with Paul's theology of the eschatological judgment, this is not what Paul states here. He deliberately leaves the wise layer of the foundation out of the judgment in order to focus on the one who builds on the foundation.

With two rhetorical questions in a single sentence, Paul now turns the attention away from Apollos the builder to the readers: Οὐκ οἴδατε ὅτι ναὸς θεοῦ ἐστε καὶ τὸ πνεῦμα τοῦ θεοῦ οἰκεῖ ἐν ὑμῖν (1 Cor 3:16); Paul establishes in these two rhetorical questions the fact that, together, the readers constitute the temple of God (ναὸς θεοῦ ἐστε) and that God's Spirit dwells in them (τὸ πνεῦμα τοῦ θεοῦ οἰκεῖ ἐν ὑμῖν). Keener lists ancient sources that indicate the view that God's people constituted his temple.[19] The introductory οὐκ οἴδατε ὅτι calls attention to their failure to appreciate these facts in their attitude of division. These two rhetorical questions become the basis for one of Paul's most serious pronouncements of judgment on the Corinthians. It should be noted that, rhetorically, "God's temple" (ναὸς θεοῦ) is a metonymy for "God's building" (θεοῦ οἰκοδομή [1 Cor 3:9]), as they refer to the same people.

In the following verse (1 Cor 3:17), Paul makes use of anadiplosis. The final word ("destroy" [φθείρει]) of the first clause is repeated at the beginning of the second clause: εἴ τις τὸν ναὸν τοῦ θεοῦ φθείρει, φθερεῖ τοῦτον ὁ θεός.

---

17. Fee, *First Epistle to the Corinthians*, 144–45.

18. Conzelmann, *Commentary on the First Epistle*, 75–76.

19. 1QS 8.5–9; 9:6; CD 3.19A; 2.10, 13B; 4Q511 frg. 35.2–3. See Keener, *1–2 Corinthians*, 43.

This anadiplosis is Paul's way of calling loud attention to God's destruction (φθερεῖ) of those who destroy (φθερεῖ) God's temple (ναὸς τοῦ θεοῦ)—which the Corinthians collectively constitute (οἵτινές ἐστε ὑμεῖς). The rhetorical device allows for the verb φθερεῖ (destroy) to be heard successively for the intended impact.

It is because God's temple is holy that those who destroy it will be destroyed (1 Cor 3:16–17). In his use of the sanctuary (τὸν ναὸν), Paul is drawing on the building metaphor used in (1 Cor 3:9) so that the layer of the foundation is Paul, the builder upon the foundation is Apollos, and the foundation on which the building stands is Christ. The believers together constitute the building and the sanctuary of God. If the believers together constitute the temple/building of God, then their division constitutes the breaking up of that building. Earlier, Paul had spoken of the division as implying dividing Christ when he asked, "is Christ divided?" (μεμέρισται ὁ Χριστός; [1 Cor 1:13a]).

For Paul therefore, the division in the church is not harmless; it has a disastrous effect on the body of Christ and the temple of God as it results in the dividing of Christ and the destruction of the temple of God. Fee recognizes that Christ, used as metonymy for the church (1 Cor 12:12), could mean the Corinthians were dividing Christ himself "by their divisions." His abandonment of this view is due to his taking the fourth slogan about Christ too seriously rather than as hypothetical. His difficulty is how such a question ("is Christ divided?") could have logically followed the fourth slogan ("I belong to Christ"). Accordingly, he maintains that the response of the Christ party to Paul's question would be "Of course Christ is not divided, we are following him."[20]

Barton finds this appeal to the temple metaphor as "a specific corrective to claims by the self-styled 'spiritual ones' (*hoi pneumatikoi*) in the fellowship that they alone possess the Spirit."[21] While the metaphor can be

---

20. Fee, *First Epistle to the Corinthians*, 60.

21. Barton calls attention to the shift from the architectural metaphor of a building that enables Paul to address the leadership styles in the Corinthian church, to another architectural metaphor of the temple of God with which he addresses the nature of the believing community itself. He identifies in the background "Gentiles worshipping in temples dedicated variously to a pantheon of gods and Jews worshipping . . . in the temple in Jerusalem or constituting themselves as an 'alternative temple' at Qumran" (Barton, "1 Corinthians," 1321). Both metaphors, however, enable Paul to point out the destructive effect of their division on who they are as God's building and God's temple, which cannot stand when divided (1 Cor 3:17). It is in this sense that their division is presented as amounting to the destruction of God's temple, an effect which can also be

stretched generally as a corrective to such an exclusivist view of spirituality, it is not intended for such a purpose in Paul's argument here. In both architectural metaphors of God's building and temple, Paul's focus is on the disintegration and profaning of the holy community by the Corinthians' division.

In this rhetorical division, Paul employs simile to describe himself in his role as a wise layer of the foundation, which is Christ. He further uses commoratio with indirect references to restate the role of Apollos, who is a worker with Paul both in God's field and God's building. With the use of distinctio by means of chiasm, Paul once again clarifies his role and that of Apollos in order to remove any ambiguity about his role as the layer of the foundation that is made up of Christ alone. The judgment of the builder upon the foundation is presented with the aid of parallelism that describes the two possible scenarios of its outcome. With a rhetorical question, he confronts the readers with who they are as the temple of God, using the temple of God as a metonymy for the readers. The use of anadiplosis enables him to put the needed emphasis on the verb that calls attention to God's destruction of those who destroy his temple.

EXHORTATION TO BECOME FOOLS IN ORDER TO BE WISE: AGAINST THE FOOLISHNESS OF BOASTING IN HUMAN LEADERS

1 Corinthians 3:18–23

> 18 Μηδεὶς ἑαυτὸν ἐξαπατάτω. εἴ τις δοκεῖ σοφὸς εἶναι ἐν ὑμῖν ἐν τῷ αἰῶνι τούτῳ, μωρὸς γενέσθω, ἵνα γένηται σοφός. 19 ἡ γὰρ σοφία τοῦ κόσμου τούτου μωρία παρὰ τῷ θεῷ ἐστιν. γέγραπται γάρ. ὁ δρασσόμενος τοὺς σοφοὺς ἐν τῇ πανουργίᾳ αὐτῶν. 20 καὶ πάλιν. κύριος γινώσκει τοὺς διαλογισμοὺς τῶν σοφῶν ὅτι εἰσὶν μάταιοι. 21 ὥστε μηδεὶς καυχάσθω ἐν ἀνθρώποις. πάντα γὰρ ὑμῶν ἐστιν, 22 εἴτε Παῦλος εἴτε Ἀπολλῶς εἴτε Κηφᾶς, εἴτε κόσμος εἴτε ζωὴ εἴτε θάνατος, εἴτε ἐνεστῶτα εἴτε μέλλοντα. πάντα ὑμῶν, 23 ὑμεῖς δὲ Χριστοῦ, Χριστὸς δὲ θεοῦ.

> 18 No one should deceive himself. If anyone among you thinks he is wise in this age, he must become foolish so that he can become wise. 19 For the wisdom of this world is foolishness with God,

---

appreciated from the perspective of dividing Christ (1 Cor 1:13).

since it is written: He catches the wise in their craftiness; 20 and again, The Lord knows that the reasonings of the wise are meaningless. 21 So no one should boast in human leaders, for everything is yours—22 whether Paul or Apollos or Cephas or the world or life or death or things present or things to come—everything is yours, 23 and you belong to Christ, and Christ belongs to God.

From 1 Corinthians 3:18, Paul begins to apply all he has said to the readers. He employs two antithetical adjectival nouns to call his readers to order in what can be described as irony: Μηδεὶς ἑαυτὸν ἐξαπατάτω. εἴ τις δοκεῖ σοφὸς εἶναι ἐν ὑμῖν ἐν τῷ αἰῶνι τούτῳ, μωρὸς γενέσθω, ἵνα γένηται σοφός. The introductory imperative, μηδεὶς ἑαυτὸν ἐξαπατάτω, expresses Paul's conviction that his readers have been deceived into relying on the wisdom of this age. "If someone thinks he is wise among you in this age" (εἴ τις δοκεῖ σοφὸς εἶναι ἐν ὑμῖν ἐν τῷ αἰῶνι τούτῳ) represents the self-perception of those being addressed. His solution for them is expressed in the irony of becoming fools (μωρὸς γενέσθω) so that they would become wise (ἵνα γένηται σοφός). "Becoming a fool" (1 Cor 3:18) recalls Paul's earlier assertion that the message of the cross is foolishness to those who are perishing (1 Cor 1:18). It should also bring to mind an earlier statement to the effect that the foolishness of God is wiser than men (1 Cor 1:25). He calls on the readers as wise people of this age to become fools so that they will become wise in Christ. In other words, when they have become what seems to them as fools, that is when they will become truly wise in Christ. The language here is forensic as it implies the Corinthians are actually fools who need to become wise by yielding to his appeal.

The reasons for this prescribed course of action are presented by way of enumeratio, which gives amplification to the prescribed course of action. The first of the reasons is: "for the wisdom of this world is foolishness with God (ἡ γὰρ σοφία τοῦ κόσμου τούτου μωρία παρὰ τῷ θεῷ ἐστιν). The comparative effect of the dative τῷ θεῷ, coming after παρὰ, is as though the wisdom of this world were placed beside God's wisdom against which the wisdom of this world appears as foolishness. Two quotations follow in the enumeratio as further reasons in support of the prescribed course of action. The first, a quotation from Job 5:13,[22] insists that God catches the wise in their craftiness (ὁ δρασσόμενος τοὺς σοφοὺς ἐν τῇ πανουργίᾳ αὐτῶν [1 Cor 3:19]). The second, introduced by καὶ πάλιν (and again), has a copula-

---

22. "He catches the wise in their own craftiness, and the schemes of the wily are brought to a quick end."

Wisdom, Knowledge, and Spirituality in Self-defense

tive effect in reinforcing the import of the first quotation. It states, "the Lord knows that the thoughts of the wise are futile" (κύριος γινώσκει τοὺς διαλογισμοὺς τῶν σοφῶν ὅτι εἰσὶν μάταιοι, 1 Cor 3:20).

Paul gives another prescribed course of action for the Corinthians (1 Cor 3:21). With ὥστε (so that), he indicates the purpose for his argument. This course of action stands in one simple, complete sense: "let no one boast in men" (μηδεὶς καυχάσθω ἐν ἀνθρώποις). The *dehortatio*, "let no one boast in men" (μηδεὶς καυχάσθω ἐν ἀνθρώποις), is an imperative that tells them how not to act. It indicates that the situation Paul was dealing with had to do with "boasting in men." To dissuade them from boasting in men, he offers a reason, which is, "all things are yours" (πάντα . . . ὑμῶν ἐστιν).[23] He resorts to distinctio by means of enumeratio with the provision of a list that should leave them in no doubt about what things are theirs. The list is presented with such impressive anaphora in which εἴτε occurs eight times:

εἴτε Παῦλος
εἴτε Ἀπολλῶς
εἴτε Κηφᾶς,
εἴτε κόσμος
εἴτε ζωὴ
εἴτε θάνατος,
εἴτε ἐνεστῶτα
εἴτε μέλλοντα.
πάντα ὑμῶν, (1 Cor 3:22).

In the first three, Paul, Apollos, and Cephas are listed, each preceded by εἴτε (whether). The first comma in this amplification separates the list of these three leaders from the second list of three which has the world, life, and death. Another comma separates this second list of three from the third list of two: the present and the future. To precede the list with the statement, "All things are yours" (πάντα ὑμῶν), and end with the same statement, makes Paul's intent loud. πάντα ὑμῶν at the end of the list in 1 Corinthians 3:22 therefore forms an inclusio with πάντα γὰρ ὑμῶν ἐστιν (1 Cor 3:21b), with the two enclosing clauses giving meaning to the tall list given between them. If Paul should subsequently refer to anything they have, it should be

---

23. Conzelmann observes that there is an appeal to a Stoic maxim here ("All things are yours"). The Stoic understanding of the maxim holds that the wise man is master of all that comes to him from without. Paul employs this to the effect that boasting about any of the things that belong to them makes no sense. This use of the maxim by Paul is closer in meaning to the Stoic teaching that one must not allow anything external to change one's mood or emotions. Conzelmann, *Commentary on the First Epistle*, 80.

understood in light of the list here. In other words, what they have (what is also referred to in "all things are yours," [1 Cor 3:21b; 3:22, cf. 1 Cor 4:7b]) are spelled out in the list as: Paul, Apollos, Cephas, the world, life, death, the present, and the future (things to come).

With two more clauses, Paul brings to an end the amplification of the reasons given for why they should not boast. The two shift the focus from what belongs to the readers to whom the Corinthians belong to, Christ, and who Christ belongs to: God. Thus, ὑμεῖς δὲ Χριστοῦ, Χριστὸς δὲ θεοῦ (1 Cor 3:23). In these two concluding clauses we have a *climatic order* that begins from the list of the things that belong to the Corinthians. This can be summarized in the following:

πάντα ὑμῶν (all things are yours)
ὑμεῖς δὲ Χριστοῦ (you are Christ's)
Χριστὸς δὲ θεοῦ (Christ is God's)

In their boasting in human leaders, the Corinthians elevated the workers to a higher status than they had. Instead, the leaders were part of the "possession" of the Corinthians. The Corinthians do not belong to the leaders, the leaders (Paul and Apollos), rather, belong to them. The only one the Corinthians belong to is Christ. This recalls the essence of Paul's statements in 1 Corinthians 1:13: "Was it Paul who was crucified for you? Or were you baptized in Paul's name?" That is, the one who was crucified for them, and into whose name they were baptized is the one to whom they belong. At least two important notes should be carried from this discussion as we proceed to 1 Corinthians 4: (1) Paul and Apollos are among the things that belong to the Corinthians, and (2) the Corinthians are boasting in human leaders.

In this rhetorical division, Paul employs irony in calling on the readers to become fools so that they will become wise. He uses a forensic expression that implies that the readers are fools in their ways. Enumeratio, as a figure of amplification, is an important device for providing reasons why the readers should become wise by becoming fools. It is also used with inclusio for the purpose of distinctio, which clarifies in detail what Paul meant by "all things are yours." By means of dehortatio he dissuades them from boasting in men. His use of climatic order enables him to demonstrate whom the Corinthians and their leaders belong to. On the whole, he employs a number of reasons to build *logos* as the mode of appeal for this rhetorical division.

Chapter 5

Correction of Wrong Perception and Further Judgment

CORRECTION OF THE CORINTHIAN PERCEPTION RESPONSIBLE FOR THE DIVISION AND THEIR UNFAVORABLE RATING OF PAUL

1 Corinthians 4:1–7

> 1 Οὕτως ἡμᾶς λογιζέσθω ἄνθρωπος ὡς ὑπηρέτας Χριστοῦ καὶ οἰκονόμους μυστηρίων θεοῦ. 2 ὧδε λοιπὸν ζητεῖται ἐν τοῖς οἰκονόμοις, ἵνα πιστός τις εὑρεθῇ. 3 ἐμοὶ δὲ εἰς ἐλάχιστόν ἐστιν, ἵνα ὑφ' ὑμῶν ἀνακριθῶ ἢ ὑπὸ ἀνθρωπίνης ἡμέρας. ἀλλ' οὐδὲ ἐμαυτὸν ἀνακρίνω. 4 οὐδὲν γὰρ ἐμαυτῷ σύνοιδα, ἀλλ' οὐκ ἐν τούτῳ δεδικαίωμαι, ὁ δὲ ἀνακρίνων με κύριός ἐστιν. 5 ὥστε μὴ πρὸ καιροῦ τι κρίνετε ἕως ἂν ἔλθῃ ὁ κύριος, ὃς καὶ φωτίσει τὰ κρυπτὰ τοῦ σκότους καὶ φανερώσει τὰς βουλὰς τῶν καρδιῶν. καὶ τότε ὁ ἔπαινος γενήσεται ἑκάστῳ ἀπὸ τοῦ θεοῦ. 6 Ταῦτα δέ, ἀδελφοί, μετεσχημάτισα εἰς ἐμαυτὸν καὶ Ἀπολλῶν δι' ὑμᾶς, ἵνα ἐν ἡμῖν μάθητε τὸ μὴ ὑπὲρ ἃ γέγραπται, ἵνα μὴ εἷς ὑπὲρ τοῦ ἑνὸς φυσιοῦσθε κατὰ τοῦ ἑτέρου. 7 τίς γάρ σε διακρίνει; τί δὲ ἔχεις ὃ οὐκ ἔλαβες; εἰ δὲ καὶ ἔλαβες, τί καυχᾶσαι ὡς μὴ λαβών;

> This is how one should regard us, as servants of Christ and stewards of the mysteries of God. 2 Moreover, it is required of stewards that they be found faithful. 3 But with me it is a very small thing that I should be judged by you or by any human court. In fact, I

do not even judge myself. 4 For I am not aware of anything against myself, but I am not thereby acquitted. It is the Lord who judges me. 5 Therefore do not pronounce judgment before the time, before the Lord comes, who will bring to light the things now hidden in darkness and will disclose the purposes of the heart. Then each one will receive his commendation from God. 6 I have applied all these things to myself and Apollos for your benefit, brothers, that you may learn by us not to go beyond what is written, that none of you may be puffed up in favor of one against another. 7 For who sees anything different in you? What do you have that you did not receive? If then you received it, why do you boast as if you did not receive it?

In 1 Corinthians 4:1, Paul reiterates how Apollos and himself should be regarded—something he had done clearly enough.[1] Such repetitive emphasis has been noted over and over again. It is clear from the outset that Paul was dealing with a problem of perception. The statement, "In this way let a man reckon us" (οὕτως ἡμᾶς λογιζέσθω ἄνθρωπος) is indicative of Paul's recognition that the readers' problem had to do with misconception about who Paul and Apollos were. οὕτως (In this way [1 Cor 4:1]) is intended to make the readers identify the place of Apollos and Paul in the climatic order above—all things are yours, you are Christ's, and Christ is God's (1 Cor 3:22–23). In this climatic order, Apollos and Paul are servants of Christ and part of all the things that belong to the Corinthians. The Lord has freely given Paul and Apollos as servants to the Corinthians. They are gifts of servants to the Corinthians given by the Lord. Though Paul identifies himself and Apollos as servants (ὑπηρέτας) and stewards (οἰκονόμους) of the mysteries of God (μυστηρίων θεοῦ), it is all for the benefit of the Corinthians.

The one thing that is sought (ζητεῖται) in them as stewards (ἐν τοῖς οἰκονόμοις) is "faithfulness" (πιστός). Being found faithful (πιστός τις εὑρεθῇ) is "all that remains here" (ὧδε λοιπὸν) for them. In this way Paul draws attention to what for him is the most important virtue of a steward—to be found faithful (1 Cor 4:2).

Following from this, his assertion that it is the least thing (ἐλάχιστόν) for him (ἐμοὶ) to be judged by the readers (ὑφ' ὑμῶν ἀνακριθῶ) or by any human court (ἢ ὑπὸ ἀνθρωπίνης ἡμέρας [1 Cor 4:3]) points to Paul's conviction

---

1. This point has been made earlier in 1 Corinthians 3: Τί οὖν ἐστιν Ἀπολλῶς; τί δέ ἐστιν Παῦλος; διάκονοι δι' ὧν ἐπιστεύσατε, καὶ ἑκάστῳ ὡς ὁ κύριος ἔδωκεν (Who is Apollos? And Who is Paul? Servants through whom you believed, just as the Lord assigned to each—1 Cor 3:5).

Wisdom, Knowledge, and Spirituality in Self-defense

that he is blameless in the test of faithfulness expected of a servant. This finds further expression in "for I do not know anything against myself" (οὐδὲν γὰρ ἐμαυτῷ σύνοιδα). With this, he gives amplification by way of commoratio to his conviction that he stands as a faithful steward. By means of the following *metanoia,* he qualifies his earlier statement that he knows nothing against himself: "but in this I'm not justified, but it is the Lord who judges me" (ἀλλ' οὐκ ἐν τούτῳ δεδικαίωμαι, ὁ δὲ ἀνακρίνων με κύριός ἐστιν [1 Cor 4:4]). The comment of Anthony Thiselton is helpful. He maintains that Paul is liberated from concern about human judgments, which, though faulty, can be so distracting as well as his own evaluation of himself.[2] It will be an unfair comment to say that Paul lived an unexamined life because he said, "For I am not aware of anything against myself." He had intimated that he judges all things as one who has the mind of Christ (1 Cor 2:15–16). It is in his quality of judging all things that he sees faithfulness as what matters in stewardship. It is also because of this virtue that no other person's judgment can affect him. "It is the Lord who judges me" (1 Cor 4:4) depicts Paul's view of himself as one who has the mind of Christ. Christ judges him as he evaluates things with the mind of Christ.

First Corinthians 4:5 is Paul's direct reaction to the Corinthians' judgment of him. "For this reason" (ὥστε) indicates that what follows logically flows from "it is the Lord who judges me." He intends this to remind the readers that judgment belongs to the Lord. Therefore, they should not pronounce judgment before the Lord comes (μὴ πρὸ καιροῦ τι κρίνετε ἕως ἂν ἔλθῃ ὁ κύριος). What follows is enumeratio, specifying qualities about the Lord who judges. Firstly, he will bring the hidden things of darkness to light (ὃς καὶ φωτίσει τὰ κρυπτὰ τοῦ σκότους). Secondly, he will disclose the purpose of the heart (φανερώσει τὰς βουλὰς τῶν καρδιῶν). Thirdly, he will give each one his commendation from God (ὁ ἔπαινος γενήσεται ἑκάστῳ ἀπὸ τοῦ θεοῦ). By these details, Paul provides qualities that make the Lord the only one who qualified to judge. In light of these qualities, the Corinthians, and indeed all humans, lack the qualification to judge. This is why they should not pronounce judgment before the Lord comes.

First Corinthians 4:6 marks an important turning point in Paul's argument. His use of "brothers" (ἀδελφοί) to introduce a new phase of his discourse is well noted. He now moves into application by indicating that all the arguments he has made so far (ταῦτα) are applicable to himself and Apollos for the readers' sake (μετεσχημάτισα εἰς ἐμαυτὸν καὶ Ἀπολλῶν δι'

---

2. Thiselton, *1 Corinthians,* 72.

ὑμᾶς). How? For what purpose? The answer is, so that they may learn in Paul and Apollos two lessons (ἵνα ἐν ἡμῖν μάθητε). These two lessons lay in two imperatives in the form of dehortatio, by which they are exhorted on what not to do: (1) not to go beyond what is written (τὸ μὴ ὑπὲρ ἃ γέγραπται), and (2) not to be puffed up in favor of one (ἵνα μὴ εἷς ὑπὲρ τοῦ ἑνὸς φυσιοῦσθε) against the other (κατὰ τοῦ ἑτέρου). In other words, Paul is saying, "Look, this is what you are doing; you are boasting in favor of one of us (Paul and Apollos) against the other. Learn from the argument I have applied to myself and Apollos and stop this."

"What is written" appears to be a principle which is appealed to in this argument. But what is it? Craig Blomberg notes that it is written nowhere in Scripture that we should not go beyond what is written. He suggests among other things that Paul might be appealing to a popular saying of the day with which he calls on them to put an end to rivalries.[3] Sampley, for his part, understands Paul to be saying "'Be like me, your father in the faith, not like babies who cannot write between the lines (4:6).'"[4] By this understanding, Sampley takes the expression to mean a call to maturity. It should be argued, however, that Paul's own rhetoric holds the answer to what he means. He has just told them that they should not pronounce judgment before the Lord, who knows the intention of the heart, comes. He has also indicated the roles assigned to each one of them according to Scripture. The Lord's role is judgment; theirs is not to judge. Similarly, the role assigned to Paul and Apollos is that of servants, a role that erases any basis for the readers' boasting. These roles are, of course, scriptural. "Nothing beyond

---

3. Blomberg suggests that by the phrase "do not go beyond what is written," Paul is advocating for conduct that is consistent with scriptural principles which eschew being proud in favor of one against the other. He further suggests that the saying is a well-known proverb referring to either rules of arbitration between factions in conflict or children who have to trace letters as they learn to write. He is convinced that Paul might mean, "observe proper behaviour and put an end to rivalries" (Blomberg, *NIV Application Commentary*, 89.). One should agree with Blomberg's first suggestion that Paul was referring more generally to the need to remain within biblical standards. Specifically, he had appealed to the roles assigned to the readers and the leaders according to Scripture. He had indicated that he and Apollos were mere servants. He planted and Apollos watered (1 Cor 3:6). He laid the foundation, which is Christ, and Apollos built on it (1 Cor 3:10). As for the readers, they should not pronounce judgment as they had done because they did not qualify to do that. Neither the time nor the one who qualifies to judge had come. It is the Lord who judges and he would judge when he returned for that purpose (1 Cor 4:5). To ignore all these scriptural roles and act as judges would certainly amount to going beyond what is written.

4. Sampley, "1 Corinthians," 803.

Wisdom, Knowledge, and Spirituality in Self-defense

what is written" would then mean sticking to their roles as spelled out in Scripture, which certainly does not include judging others—the conduct that accounts for the problem of division and boasting in men. It is by going beyond what is written in judging their teachers that they do what is unacceptable—boasting on behalf of one against another. What is written, understood properly within the context of Paul's argument, refers to the roles of each of the players in the discourse as spelled out in Scripture.[5] The end of Paul's argument in this division is what Sampley has suggested: "Paul openly declares that, in what has preceded 4:6 ('all this'), he has used a common contemporary rhetorical device, 'indirect' or 'figured speech,' by which he has made a point with reference to himself and Apollos as a roundabout or oblique way of critiquing the Corinthians' predilection for contentions and divisions."[6]

Comments

Paul's explicit application of all this to himself and Apollos provides the direction and the interpretative framework for his argument. In this light, it is clear that the boasting (being puffed up) was the kind that set either Paul or Apollos against the other. To fail to recognize this is to ignore the purpose of his entire argument. Paul's concern about their boasting in favor of one against the other (that resulted in strife and division among them) is not about Cephas or Christ; it is all about Paul and Apollos. While one was honored in the addressees' eyes, the other was dishonored. The one was not just being honored, but his honor was being pressed to the shame of the other. This makes sense in light of the concept of limited good of the Mediterranean society, where one's honor meant the dishonor of all others. In this particular case, however, it appears there were conscious efforts to press one teacher's honor deliberately in order to shame the other. As this happens, the party of the one against whom the boasting is done feels the pinch, resulting in strife and envy, which Paul mentioned earlier in 1 Corinthians 3:3. It is particularly in the expression "in favor of one" (ὑπὲρ τοῦ

---

5. For Conzelmann, all attempts to explain the phrase "nothing beyond what is written" have produced guesswork. He thinks one should simply ignore it (*Commentary on the First Epistle*, 86). But as has just been pointed out, the readers were expected to refrain from behaving as judges of Paul as they were doing, when that is not the role Scripture assigns to them.

6. Sampley, "1 Corinthians," 803.

ἑνός) "against the other" (κατὰ τοῦ ἑτέρου) that the rivalry in the division and their boasting is felt most. The Corinthians, in this light, were behaving as they did toward *sophists*. It was a normal practice for students to evaluate their teachers and actively defend their favorites among them.

The implication of Paul's application of his argument to himself and Apollos can be outlined as follows:

1. That the real division had to do with Paul and Apollos. The inclusion of Cephas and Christ must be hypothetical and should be considered as a means of making a loud statement of the problem.[7]

2. It should mean that the contrast between the two styles of preaching—with wisdom of words and without wisdom of words—applies directly to the approaches adopted by Apollos and Paul. Now when Paul clearly spells out his style, as without the wisdom of words, the implication is that Apollos's style involved the wisdom of words.

3. It implies that Paul found fault with Apollos's work. When it comes to the judgment, the layer of the foundation has done an excellent work. As a wise builder, he laid the foundation of Christ and him crucified and nothing else (1 Cor 3:10–11). But the one who builds on the foundation needs to be careful how he builds on the foundation. It is his work that will be subjected to judgment and not that of the layer of the foundation (1 Cor 3:10d). This is not a general theological proposition; it is rather the case of Paul's argument here, and it is the more reason why it reflects Paul's perspective on Apollos. Though Paul believes that he will be judged too (1 Cor 4:4), his deliberate isolation of the one who builds on the foundation as the object of the judgment (1 Cor 3:12) is instructive.

4. It implies that Paul's emphasis on "motive" (1 Cor 4:5) as the important factor in God's judgment of the builder on the foundation, suggests that Apollos's motive for his work was questionable in Paul's view. It

---

7. Cephas is not known to have worked in Corinth, and neither did Jesus. It is a plausible assumption that their views or teaching could have earned them some admirers in Corinth in a remote sense, and groups of such admirers could have been formed. However, Paul's application of the argument to himself and Apollos implies the situation being addressed has to do specifically with those to whom it has been applied. Boring and Craddock's observation is right. They hold that the boasting in favor of one against the other is "probably not a generalization, but referring specifically to Apollos and Paul, whom the Corinthians consider to be rivals and alternatives" (Boring and Craddock, *People's New Testament Commentary*, 516).

suggests that Apollos may have acted like the *sophists* who sought to impress their audience in order to win their admiration and support. The tendency for one to be carried away by the wave of rhetoric at that time was high. Thiselton notes that, though the audience determined the fame granted to the rhetorician, the view of the audience was, however, "manipulated and shaped by sophistic rhetoricians in ancient Corinth" who adopted strategies that were deductive.[8] It is noted that emotional attachment to the teacher was necessary for the moral and intellectual development of students of philosophers.[9] Epicurus is said to have encouraged such emotional attachment as an important way of influencing his students "beyond abstract reasoning."[10] This has affinity with his view that philosophy is not studying merely what is written in books, but is what results from "examining a narrative of one's own life."[11] In this respect, the impression one has of a teacher's life could account for how the teacher's teaching is rated. Paul is likely to have found Apollos behaving similarly as a typical philosopher in Corinth. This tendency, for Paul, accounted for the teaching that was other than Christ (1 Cor 3:11), which Apollos taught. This is especially so when the teacher in view taught John's baptism and the wisdom of words.

The construction in 1 Corinthians 4:6 does not necessarily mean that Paul wants the Corinthians to learn from the example of peaceful coexistence and cooperation between Apollos and himself, as some suggest. This is more so since Paul and Apollos are not known to have worked together in Corinth during the same period. Moreover, the identification of the two as coworkers (1 Cor 3:9) does not necessarily imply working together peacefully. Coworkers are workers engaged in the same cause whether or not they agree or live in harmony. "So that you may learn by us" (ἵνα ἐν ἡμῖν μάθητε) is about the application of the argument to Paul and Apollos (those at the center of the division), rather than to their example of peaceful coexistence and cooperation.

Paul employs three rhetorical questions in order to address the Corinthians' self-image: τίς γάρ σε διακρίνει; τί δὲ ἔχεις ὃ οὐκ ἔλαβες; εἰ δὲ καὶ

---

8. Thiselton, *1 Corinthians*, 16.
9. Keener, *IVP Bible Background Commentary*, 455.
10. Ghaemi, *Concept of Psychiatry*, 118.
11. Ghaemi, *Concept of Psychiatry*, 118.

ἔλαβες, τί καυχᾶσαι ὡς μὴ λαβών; (1 Cor 4:7) In the first question, Paul demands to know who assesses (rates) the Corinthians? That is, who gives them the self-image they have? The rendering of the question by HCSB as "for who makes you so superior?" speaks to their self-image. The second asks: What do they have that they did not receive? The third rhetorical question is introduced by an if clause after which the question comes as a tag. The introductory statement establishes that they *received* all they *have*. That is Paul's way of answering the preceding question for his infant audience. The question tag that follows the statement, "Why do you boast as if you did not receive it?" gives the indication that their boasting was based on what they *have* which they also *received*. The point in these three rhetorical questions is that there is no ground for boasting about things received.

It is important to find the meanings of the words *have* and *received* within Paul's own argument for the sake of coherence. Paul had earlier spoken of the things God had freely given the Corinthians (1 Cor 2:12). To remove any ambiguity from the things they have received from God (*what they have*), he gives the following list and insists that they are all *theirs*: Paul, Apollos, Cephas, the world, life, death, the present, and the future (1 Cor 3:22). The priority given to Paul and Apollos in the list is intentional. We should recall that Paul had applied all the argument to himself and Apollos (1 Cor 4:6). This implies that the rest of the items in the list are merely for the rhetorical effect of *accumulation* in the particular case being addressed. Now Paul and Apollos, who are *theirs* (what the Corinthians *have*), are also what they have received freely from God. For this reason, they have no need to boast of any of them as if they did not receive him. The only thing in this rhetorical subunit the Corinthians are said to boast of is either Paul or Apollos (1 Cor 1–4) of whom they are urged not to boast (1 Cor 3:21–22). The combination of the words *have* and *receive* in 1 Corinthians 4:7 is meant to be understood in terms of what is "freely given us by God" (1 Cor 2:12) and what is theirs (what they *have*, 1 Cor 3:21–22). This consideration makes what they *have* another expression of what they have *received* and the very thing they are boasting of—Paul or Apollos. It was to this end that Paul deliberately changes the object of what the Spirit enables the believer to understand from "the wisdom of God proclaimed in hidden mysteries" (1 Cor 2:7–10) to "the things freely given us by God" (1 Cor 2:12). This was a deliberate shift from the message of the cross to the identity of Paul and Apollos as freely given gifts of servants to the Corinthians, the things the

Wisdom, Knowledge, and Spirituality in Self-defense

Corinthians *have*, the things they have *received* on account of which they should not boast.

Now the problem of the Corinthians is that they do not understand who Paul and Apollos are. This lack of understanding is responsible for why they are boasting in favor of one against the other. This explains why as part of his argument, Paul clarifies repeatedly in no uncertain words the identity of Apollos and himself (1 Cor 3:5–9; 4:1, 6). The fact that Paul tells the readers not to boast in favor of one against the other (1 Cor 4:6), and in the succeeding verse (4:7) asks "Why do you boast as if you did not receive it?" means that Paul and Apollos are the key items among the things the Corinthians have in this argument. It is the two leaders that Paul explicitly describes as things they have (1 Cor 3:22) and boast of (1 Cor 4:6). It is rhetorically significant that boasting in men in 1 Corinthians 3:21 forms an inclusio with boasting "as if you did not receive it" in 1 Corinthians 4:7c. Between the two enclosing clauses of the inclusio is a discussion that begins with Paul and Apollos as things the Corinthians have (1 Cor 3:22) to the call that none of them should boast in favor of one against the other (1 Cor 4:6). The inclusio implies that Paul and Apollos are the things the readers have. It implies that it is one of the same people in favor of whom the boasting is being done, while the other is the one against whom they boast. To recap and illustrate the point, the first and last of the following quotations are the enclosing clauses of the inclusio: 1 Cor 3:21 and 1 Cor 4:7c, while lying in-between (1 Cor 3:22—4:7b) are the discussions that deal with Paul and Apollos as the things the readers have received, and their boasting of one of them as if they did not receive him. Together, the entire inclusio is 1 Corinthians 3:21—4:7 (3:21, 3:22—4:7b, 4:7c).

This division of Paul's argument combines both forensic language in Paul's defense of himself against the readers' judgment, and deliberative expressions that seek to persuade them from their attitude of judgment. He gives amplification by way of commoratio to his conviction that he stands guiltless as a faithful servant and that he knows nothing against himself. When he used *metanoia*, it was to qualify the statement that he knows nothing against himself. His use of enumeratio enables him to present qualities that make the Lord the only one who qualifies to judge. He employs dehortatio to dissuade the readers from engaging in two courses of action. He uses hypothetical items in a list to create the effect of accumulation in order to increase the impact of the statement of the problem. He employs inclusio to present Paul and Apollos as the men of whom they boast. The mode of appeal remains mainly *logos,* as it offers reasons against their perception of their leaders and their assessment of him.

SARCASTIC DEPICTION OF THE SELF-IMAGE OF THE CORINTHIANS

Paul devotes this rhetorical division to a description of the readers that plays back their bloated self-image to them. It marks a departure from Paul's discourse on the Corinthians' wrong perceptions and attitudes toward their teachers.

1 Corinthians 4:8–13

> 8 ἤδη κεκορεσμένοι ἐστέ, ἤδη ἐπλουτήσατε, χωρὶς ἡμῶν ἐβασιλεύσατε. καὶ ὄφελόν γε ἐβασιλεύσατε, ἵνα καὶ ἡμεῖς ὑμῖν συμβασιλεύσωμεν. 9 δοκῶ γάρ, ὁ θεὸς ἡμᾶς τοὺς ἀποστόλους ἐσχάτους ἀπέδειξεν ὡς ἐπιθανατίους, ὅτι θέατρον ἐγενήθημεν τῷ κόσμῳ καὶ ἀγγέλοις καὶ ἀνθρώποις. 10 ἡμεῖς μωροὶ διὰ Χριστόν, ὑμεῖς δὲ φρόνιμοι ἐν Χριστῷ. ἡμεῖς ἀσθενεῖς, ὑμεῖς δὲ ἰσχυροί. ὑμεῖς ἔνδοξοι, ἡμεῖς δὲ ἄτιμοι. 11 ἄχρι τῆς ἄρτι ὥρας καὶ πεινῶμεν καὶ διψῶμεν καὶ γυμνιτεύομεν καὶ κολαφιζόμεθα καὶ ἀστατοῦμεν 12 καὶ κοπιῶμεν ἐργαζόμενοι ταῖς ἰδίαις χερσίν. λοιδορούμενοι εὐλογοῦμεν, διωκόμενοι ἀνεχόμεθα, 13 δυσφημούμενοι παρακαλοῦμεν. ὡς περικαθάρματα τοῦ κόσμου ἐγενήθημεν, πάντων περίψημα ἕως ἄρτι.

> 8 Already you have all you want! Already you have become rich! Without us you have become kings! And would that you did reign, so that we might share the rule with you! 9 For I think that God has exhibited us apostles as last of all, like men sentenced to death, because we have become a spectacle to the world, to angels, and to men. 10 We are fools for Christ's sake, but you are wise in Christ. We are weak, but you are strong. You are held in honor, but we in disrepute. 11 To the present hour we hunger and thirst, we are poorly dressed and buffeted and homeless, 12 and we labor, working with our own hands. When reviled, we bless; when persecuted, we endure; 13 when slandered, we entreat. We have become, and are still, like the scum of the world, the refuse of all things.

In the next few statements, Paul gives a description of the Corinthians that reflects their attitude toward him. The description also reflects their bloated self-image which he had just alluded to in 1 Corinthians 4:7a: "For who makes you so superior?" The depiction of their self-image in 1

Wisdom, Knowledge, and Spirituality in Self-defense

Corinthians 4:8 is loud, especially with the combination of several rhetorical devices used to express it. First is the use of commoratio. Three different expressions are used to describe the bloated self-image of the readers: "you have become full" (κεκορεσμένοι ἐστέ), "you have become rich" (ἐπλουτήσατε), and "you have become kings" (ἐβασιλεύσατε) all speak to the same self-perception as observed in their attitude. Secondly, the repetition of various forms of the verb βασιλεύω at the end of three successive clauses presents us with *epistrophe* (epiphora or *antistrophe*). At the same time, the repetition of ἤδη in the initial position of the first two clauses gives us anaphora:

> ἤδη κεκορεσμένοι ἐστέ,
> ἤδη ἐπλουτήσατε,
> χωρὶς ἡμῶν ἐβασιλεύσατε.
> καὶ ὄφελόν γε ἐβασιλεύσατε,
> ἵνα καὶ ἡμεῖς ὑμῖν συμβασιλεύσωμεν. (1 Cor 4:8)

Even in the English some of the rhetorical features can be discerned:

> "*Already* you have all you want!"
> "*Already* you have become rich!"
> "Without us you have become *kings*!"
> "And would that you did *reign*,"
> "so that we might share the *rule with you*!"

While "already" is repeated at the beginning of the first two clauses, "kings," "reign," and "rule" are placed at the end of the last three clauses. The different expressions (kings, reign, and rule) in the English, however, weakens the effect of the words in the Greek, where all three have forms of βασιλεύω.

With these rhetorical devices, Paul resorts to such sarcasm that falls a little short of insult. In this ridiculing depiction, he describes the readers with some honorable expressions, which are obviously untrue. Both Paul and the readers know the recipients are not kings. They know they are not reigning. Yet Paul finds them in their bloated self-image behaving as reigning kings. He felt the Corinthians had placed themselves so high as though they were far above him. This is the feeling expressed in "Who rates you so? Or what gives you such rating" (τίς γάρ σε διακρίνει; 1 Cor 4:7a)? The phrase "without us," in the third statement, says it all—their attitude presents them not as people brought to faith and nurtured by Paul. The first two statements describe their sense of self-sufficiency, while the phrase "without us" drives forcefully home their ingratitude and brushing-off attitude toward Paul. In what follows, he engages in a description primarily of himself in which the first-person plural is once again used as a metonymy for him. He describes himself *vis-à-vis* the Corinthians.

In the first sentence, Paul appeals to the imagery of the procession of a victor returning from war. With this he depicts how he feels as a result of the Corinthians' attitude toward him (1 Cor 4:9). The introductory "For it seems to me" (δοκῶ γάρ), makes the sentence Paul's personal assessment. Though the place he gives to himself as an apostle in this imagery is that of the king, his lot does not reflect the honor of a king. His emphasis is on the reproach and agony of the one who occupies the last position in the procession (ἐσχάτους ἀπέδειξεν). His agony is of one condemned to die (ἐπιθανάτιος). It is in such an agony that he has become (ἐγενήθημεν) a spectacle as one on display in a theater (θέατρον) to the world (τῷ κόσμῳ), to angels (ἀγγέλοις), and to men (ἀνθρώποις).

As noted before, he uses the first-person plural to speak of his lot as an apostle. This will become clear as the rest of his argument unfolds. The negative image of himself here is not a self-wish, but one that plays back to the Corinthians their perception of him and how they have subsequently treated him and made him to feel. The polysyndeton employed in the repeated καὶ (and) in τῷ κόσμῳ καὶ ἀγγέλοις καὶ ἀνθρώποις is Paul's way of highlighting the totality of his feeling of reproach. It calls attention to the angels and men, in addition to the world, as the spectators of his display. In other words, there is no escape from his shame with all these spectators.

To give further amplification to his feeling about his image in the eyes of the Corinthians, Paul resorts to the alternative use of "you" (ὑμεῖς) and "we" (ἡμεῖς), the regular pattern of which changes toward the end. With such alternation he contrasts his feeling as felt in their treatment of him and that of the readers:

> ἡμεῖς μωροὶ διὰ Χριστόν,
> ὑμεῖς δὲ φρόνιμοι ἐν Χριστῷ.
> ἡμεῖς ἀσθενεῖς,
> ὑμεῖς δὲ ἰσχυροί.
> ὑμεῖς ἔνδοξοι,
> ἡμεῖς δὲ ἄτιμοι. (1 Cor 4:10)

The alternation between ἡμεῖς (we) and ὑμεῖς (you) is regularly repeated in the first two pairs of clauses. The antithetical δὲ in the second line of each pair establishes a *sarcastic* contrast. In the series, all the positive

Wisdom, Knowledge, and Spirituality in Self-defense

attributes are given to the Corinthian believers represented by "you" (ὑμεῖς), while all the negative and unpleasant attributes are given to Paul (ἡμεῖς). Paul is a fool because of Christ (μωροὶ διὰ Χριστόν), but the Corinthians are wise in Christ (φρόνιμοι ἐν Χριστῷ); Paul is weak (ἀσθενεῖς), but the Corinthians are strong (ἰσχυροί). In the third pair, the Corinthians are honored (ἔνδοξοι), but Paul is without honor (ἄτιμοι). The interruption of the pattern—ἡμεῖς... ὑμεῖς—in the last pair enables Paul to attribute two powerful qualities (strength and honor) in succession to the Corinthians in the last two pairs. This disruption creates a chiasm in the last two pairs as follows:

A ἡμεῖς ἀσθενεῖς,
B ὑμεῖς δὲ ἰσχυροί.
B ὑμεῖς ἔνδοξοι,
A ἡμεῖς δὲ ἄτιμοι.

This *we-you-you-we* chiasm affords Paul the chance to end these sarcastic contrasts on the note of his unfavorable image as the dishonored (ἄτιμος). To end on such a dishonorable note of the Corinthians' perception of him after two successive powerful and honorable imageries for the readers (strong and honored) is a deliberate contrast meant to highlight the lowly image they have of Paul. This is beside his being seen as a fool (which for him is because of Christ) while the Corinthians are seen as wise (which for him is of the pattern of this world). The priority given to the fool-wise contrast emphasizes the key perception undergirding their judgment of Paul (1 Cor 4:3, 10). It is from their judgment of him as one without the wisdom they have that results in the low image and perception they have of him. Paul has failed to impress them as a teacher of wisdom as Apollos has done. Having believed, imbibed, and worked with the teaching of Apollos, they know that they are wiser than Paul, who never teaches with such wisdom associated with what they know. Their judgment is therefore not a simple matter of Paul not being wise; rather, he goes down in their judgment together with the message he preaches. In this light, anytime Paul raises questions and doubts about their knowledge and wisdom, he is judging the Corinthians with the very judgment with which they have judged him. In other words, he judges the readers on the same bases on which they have judged him. His call on them to become fools in order to become wise (1 Cor 3:18) is meant to be a pronouncement on their failure to attain true wisdom in Christ. At the same time, his insistence on preaching nothing but Christ and him crucified (1 Cor 2:2), a message of foolishness and a stumbling block (1 Cor 1:23), is Paul's way of confronting them with what he gets right—the foolishness of God which is wiser than that of humans, and the weakness of God which is stronger than that of humans (1 Cor 1:25). He knows that Christ is the power of God and the wisdom of God (1 Cor 1:24), his wisdom from God, his righteousness, and his sanctification and redemption (1 Cor 1:30), so he resolves never to preach him with the wisdom of word which the Corinthians have come to rely on (1 Cor 1:17; 2:1).

If inspired men were the teachers of wisdom, it also meant for the Corinthians that the one who fails the test of a teacher of wisdom lacks the spirituality that goes with the vocation. This explains the pride and arrogance of those who considered themselves to be spiritual and prophets. Paul speaks of such people as having the tendency to reject his teaching (1 Cor 14:37-38). But for Paul they were mistaken; such members could not appreciate that their sexually immoral act called for mourning rather than pride (1 Cor 5:2). He was never pleased with the arrogance of such members (1 Cor 4:18-19) on whom he turns back their judgment of him when he declares that he could not address them as spiritual, but as fleshly and babes capable of taking in only milk (1 Cor 3:1-2). In this light, his claim that it takes those who possess the Spirit of God to understand the message he preaches (1 Cor 2:13) is instructive on how Paul rates the readers as people who have failed to understand the mysteries of God which he preached (1 Cor 3:2). In other words, if they were spiritual, they would have understood the message he as a spiritual person had preached by means of the Spirit (1 Cor 2:13).

The foregoing chiasm provides a logical link to six clauses in the next sentence which describe what has happened to Paul up to the present (ἄχρι τῆς ἄρτι ὥρας). Sliding away from the contrast of himself with the Corinthians, Paul now gives further amplification that focuses solely on his *sarcastic* depiction of himself. The polysyndeton in his abundant use of the preposition καὶ in the initial position creates the effect of anaphora:

καὶ πεινῶμεν
καὶ διψῶμεν
καὶ γυμνιτεύομεν
καὶ κολαφιζόμεθα
καὶ ἀστατοῦμεν
καὶ κοπιῶμεν ἐργαζόμενοι ταῖς ἰδίαις χερσίν (1 Cor 4:11-12a)

While the anaphora provides the sound effect that calls attention to his argument, the enumeratio (the six clauses that provide details of Paul's state) gives the cumulative effect of emphasizing the unfavorable lot of Paul. With the foregoing, Paul describes his condition as one suffering hunger and thirst, as being poorly clothed, brutally treated, homeless, and working with his own hands.

After focusing solely on his lot with the enumeratio above, Paul returns to another series of contrasts. In this series, he contrasts his attitude with that of the Corinthians. These contrasts depart from the *sarcastic* tone of the preceding contrasts and focuses on the attitudes of the Corinthians and on his. By ending this series with ἕως ἄρτι ("until now," 1 Cor 4:13), Paul provides the indication that this last series of contrasts form an inclusio with "until now" (ἄχρι τῆς ἄρτι) in 1 Corinthians 4:11. As such, Paul intends everything he has said in between these two phrases to be understood in the light of the bracketing phrases. This implies that all that is presented between the phrases forming the inclusio represent Paul's image and the Corinthians' treatment of him until now—an enduring unfortunate lot of an apostle:

> λοιδορούμενοι εὐλογοῦμεν,
> διωκόμενοι ἀνεχόμεθα,
> δυσφημούμενοι παρακαλοῦμεν.
> ὡς περικαθάρματα τοῦ κόσμου ἐγενήθημεν,
> πάντων περίψημα ἕως ἄρτι. (1 Cor 4:12:b–13)

The first part of each contrast deals with how Paul is treated by the Corinthians (employing the passive voice to avoid direct reference to the readers). The second part then indicates how he responds to them. Once again, he uses the first-person plural to speak about himself in the second part of the contrasts. Thus, when he is reviled (λοιδορούμενοι), he blesses (εὐλογοῦμεν); when he is persecuted (διωκόμενοι), he puts up with it (ἀνεχόμεθα); when slandered (δυσφημούμενοι), he entreats (παρακαλοῦμεν). By placing the verb ἐγενήθημεν last, Paul gives priority and emphasis to the scum of the world he has become (ὡς περικαθάρματα τοῦ κόσμου). The scam receives further amplification by way of commoratio in the next phrase "refuse of all things" (πάντων περίψημα). The *rhyme* and assonance in the words ending with νοι and μεν (both of which occur not less than three times) have their significance in the attention they call to the contrasts.

Though it appears negative, the unfavorable self-description Paul gives himself is meant to go to his advantage. It is an ironic presentation of himself as a more spiritual person who bears the reproach similar to that of Christ. Barton points to Paul's advantage here: "The irony is built around the well-known rhetorical practice of comparison *(synkrisis)* in which, in the competition between factions, one *sophos* is compared with another to establish who is superior."[12] He explains,

> In Paul's admonition, the spiritual exaltation of the Corinthians is compared and contrasted with the material and physical humiliation of their apostle. To assist in his argument, Paul uses a particular rhetorical trope: the catalogue of sufferings *(peristaseis)* cited to demonstrate the integrity and honor of the wise man and the truth of his teaching.[13]

Similarly, Keener observes, "Like a philosopher, Paul proved his character and provided a model by a hardship list (1 Cor 4:11–13)."[14]

Comment

We have in Paul's first description of himself the imagery of a king captured in war and displayed at the end of the procession. The lot of such a king is ridicule in an agonizing expectation of a shameful and painful death at the hands of his captor. The second part of the description points to the negative attention, comments, and assessments he attracts from the "spectators" (in this case, the Corinthians). If the expressed purpose of his argument is for the Corinthians not to boast in favor of one against the other, then the expression of how he feels as one of the two is important. His feelings do not present him as the one in favor of whom the boasting was done. The view that the boasting was not in favor of Paul, but against him, is shared by Fee.[15] In a similar vein, Tim MacBride recognizes that the divisions in the Corinthian church "involved setting Apollos over against Paul.[16] The following table shows how Paul is preoccupied with his unfavorable image in the treatment of the Corinthians (1 Cor 4:10–13):

---

12. Barton, "1 Corinthians," 1322.
13. Barton, "1 Corinthians," 1322.
14. Keener, *1–2 Corinthians*, 9.
15. He maintains, "Given the express statement in 4:18 that some are 'puffed up' against Paul, and the indication in 4:6 that some are 'puffed up' *for* one (apparently Apollos in this case), *against* the other (probably Paul), it seems altogether likely that the quarreling over their leaders is not just *for* Apollos or Cephas, but is decidedly *over against* Paul at the same time" (Fee, *First Epistle to the Corinthians*, 49).
16. MacBride, *Preaching the New Testament*, 90.

Wisdom, Knowledge, and Spirituality in Self-defense

Paul	The Corinthians
1) We are fools for Christ's sake	But you are wise in Christ
2) We are weak	But you are strong
3) We are in disrepute	You are held in honor
4) To the present hour we hunger and thirst, we are poorly dressed and buffeted and homeless, and we labor, working with our own hands	[But you do not share such struggles]
5) When reviled, we bless	[You revile us]
6) When persecuted, we endure it	[You persecute us]
7) When slandered, we entreat	[You slander us]
8) We have become, and are still, like the scum of the world, the refuse of all things	[You are honored]

The consistency of Paul's argument is amazing. He is able to sustain the coherence of his argument through the various stages. Firstly, "We are fools for Christ" finds expression in Paul's resolution to stick to the message of the cross preached without human wisdom. Since this message is foolishness to the world, the carrier must consequently appear foolish.

"We are weak" is also meaningful in light of Paul's observation that the message of the cross as the weakness of God is stronger than that of men (1 Cor 1:25). So the carrier of the weakness of God must appear weak to the Corinthians. This explains why when he resolved to know nothing except Christ and him crucified, he appeared in weakness and in fear and much trembling (1 Cor 2:3). To state here that "we are weak" is very consistent and logical to those preceding statements. The third contrast in the table is logical to the first two: wise and strong (powerful) people are honored.

Everything Paul says from 1 Corinthians 4:8–13 speaks about him, spelling out how he feels about the estimation and attitude of the Corinthians. First Corinthians 4:11–13 describes his economic and social hardships and hostilities. He is hungry and thirsty, poorly clothed, roughly treated and homeless, laboring and working with own hands in contradistinction to Apollos and the readers. He suffers insults, persecution, and slander, all of which leave him as scum and refuse of all things.

First Corinthians 4:12 shows how Paul behaves as a fool for Christ's sake. He blesses in response to being reviled. Certainly he does feel reviled by the Corinthians, but reviled as he feels, he still refrains from reviling back and, instead, speaks kindly of them. Even when he sounds sarcastic, he insists it is meant for their good and not to put them down. Similarly, when persecuted, he endures it. When slandered, he responds graciously. In failing to pay back evil for evil, Paul behaves in accordance with the teaching of Christ as opposed to the envy and strife among the Corinthians. "We have become, and are still, like the scum of the world, the refuse of all things" (1 Cor 4:13) sums up how Paul sees himself in the attitudes expressed by his own church members—the dirt of all manner of things that no one would tolerate even on their footwear.

In depicting the bloated self-image of the readers in this rhetorical division, Paul's use of commoratio enables him to use different expressions to describe the same self-image of the readers. Epistrophe and anaphora make important aspects of the argument catchy. With sarcasm that mocks their bloated self-image, Paul employs ironic contrasts to confront his readers with their false self-image. It further uses irony by way of contrasts that depict Paul and the readers in images contrary to who they really are. Paul uses polysyndeton to increase the cumulative impact of two lists that describe his unfavorable lot. The contrast between Paul and the readers is given a *chiastic* structure, while enumeratio provides the needed details of Paul's condition in support of his image among the Corinthians. The sarcastic tone of Paul's depiction of the Corinthians and himself in images that are contrary to who they really are, reverses the Corinthians' judgment of Paul back to them.

FINAL EXHORTATION FOR CHANGE IN ATTITUDE AND WARNING TO THE ARROGANT

1 Corinthians 4:14–21

> 14 Οὐκ ἐντρέπων ὑμᾶς γράφω ταῦτα ἀλλ' ὡς τέκνα μου ἀγαπητὰ νουθετῶ[ν]. 15 ἐὰν γὰρ μυρίους παιδαγωγοὺς ἔχητε ἐν Χριστῷ ἀλλ' οὐ πολλοὺς πατέρας. ἐν γὰρ Χριστῷ Ἰησοῦ διὰ τοῦ εὐαγγελίου ἐγὼ ὑμᾶς ἐγέννησα. 16 Παρακαλῶ οὖν ὑμᾶς, μιμηταί μου γίνεσθε. 17 Διὰ τοῦτο ἔπεμψα ὑμῖν Τιμόθεον, ὅς ἐστίν μου τέκνον ἀγαπητὸν καὶ πιστὸν ἐν κυρίῳ, ὃς ὑμᾶς ἀναμνήσει τὰς ὁδούς μου τὰς ἐν Χριστῷ [Ἰησοῦ], καθὼς πανταχοῦ ἐν πάσῃ ἐκκλησίᾳ διδάσκω. 18 Ὡς μὴ ἐρχομένου δέ μου πρὸς ὑμᾶς ἐφυσιώθησάν τινες. 19 ἐλεύσομαι δὲ ταχέως πρὸς ὑμᾶς ἐὰν ὁ κύριος θελήσῃ, καὶ γνώσομαι οὐ τὸν λόγον τῶν πεφυσιωμένων ἀλλὰ τὴν δύναμιν. 20 οὐ γὰρ ἐν λόγῳ ἡ βασιλεία τοῦ θεοῦ ἀλλ' ἐν δυνάμει. 21 τί θέλετε; ἐν ῥάβδῳ ἔλθω πρὸς ὑμᾶς ἢ ἐν ἀγάπῃ πνεύματί τε πραΰτητος;

> 14 I do not write these things to make you ashamed, but to admonish you as my beloved children. 15 For though you have countless guides in Christ, you do not have many fathers. For I became your father in Christ Jesus through the gospel. 16 I urge you, then, be imitators of me. 17 That is why I sent you Timothy, my beloved and faithful child in the Lord, to remind you of my ways in Christ, as I teach them everywhere in every church. 18 Some are arrogant, as though I were not coming to you. 19 But I will come to you soon, if the Lord wills, and I will find out not the talk of these arrogant people but their power. 20 For the kingdom of God does not consist in talk but in power. 21 What do you wish? Shall I come to you with a rod, or with love in a spirit of gentleness?

The priority given to "not to shame you" (οὐκ ἐντρέπων ὑμᾶς [1 Cor 4:14]) in this division sets the tone for the succeeding discourse. Paul employs *apophasis* by denying that his reason for writing these things is to shame the readers. He insists that he is admonishing (νουθετῶ[ν]) them as beloved children. While this indirect appeal to shame builds *pathos*, it is incorporated into an argument, which largely employs an *ethos* mode of appeal in which Paul dwells on his status as the father of the believers. He argues that even if they have many guardians in Christ (ἐὰν γὰρ μυρίους παιδαγωγοὺς ἔχητε ἐν Χριστῷ), they do not have many fathers because he gave birth to them (ὑμᾶς ἐγέννησα) in Christ through the gospel (1 Cor 4:15).

In pursuit of his admonishing, Paul resorts to entreating the Corinthians (παρακαλῶ οὖν ὑμᾶς). The use of "therefore" (οὖν) makes the inference from the preceding claim obvious (1 Cor 4:16). His appeal for the readers to become (γίνεσθε) his imitators (μιμηταί μου) is in line with the Mediterranean social script governing relationship and interaction within the family. This social script expects children to behave like the one who gave birth to them. Once their being children of Paul in Christ has been established, there is ground for expecting and demanding the parent's way of life from them. Sampley's comments are apt:

> The *pater familias* ("head of the household") was responsible for all who lived there; in particular the children's comportment and wellbeing were in the father's hand. The children learned modeling after their father, learned whatever trade the household was involved with, but much more fundamentally, learned appropriate

conduct. Accordingly, as their father, Paul has written in warning or admonition (4:14) and enjoins them to model after him.[17]

Paul further appeals to his past effort—he sent Timothy to them (1 Cor 4:17). The reason for sending Timothy was to remind them of Paul's ways (τὰς ὁδούς μου) in the Lord as he taught them everywhere in every church (καθὼς πανταχοῦ ἐν πάσῃ ἐκκλησίᾳ διδάσκω.). That is to say, he is not demanding that they learn from him only because of the current situation. This is what he has always expected from them, which is the reason for which he sent Timothy.

Employing the genitive absolute ἐρχομένου . . . μου, together with ὡς μὴ, Paul discloses his knowledge of those (τινες) who were behaving as though he were not coming to them (πρὸς ὑμᾶς). Because of their assumption that Paul was not coming to them, they had become arrogant (ἐφυσιώθησάν, 1 Cor 4:18). Paul now dares them: "I will come to you soon" (ἐλεύσομαι δὲ ταχέως πρὸς ὑμᾶς) "if the Lord wills" (ἐὰν ὁ κύριος θελήσῃ). His warning that he would find out (γνώσομαι) not the talk of the proud (πεφυσιωμένων) but their power (δύναμιν, 1 Cor 4:19) is instructive. The power here is not the demonstration of the Spirit in mighty acts of miracles as some may suggest. Paul has already clarified what the power of God means in the discourse of 1 Corinthians 1:10—4:21. This power is the message of the cross which, though it is foolishness and weakness, represents God's wisdom and power for those who are called. It is God's weakness that is stronger than man's, God's foolishness that is wiser than man's. It is this same power of God that Paul demonstrated in his preaching of the cross, which also yielded the fruit of the conversion of the Corinthians who are now in Christ.

The Corinthians know that Paul is unparalleled in demonstrating this power of God (2 Cor 10:10). Paul testifies of his use of this power to destroy strongholds of arguments, thoughts, and everything that exalts itself against the knowledge of God (2 Cor 10:4). The reason why Paul would find out their power is introduced by the inferential γὰρ (therefore). The priority given to "not in talk" (οὐ . . . ἐν λόγῳ) in relation to "the kingdom of God" (ἡ βασιλεία τοῦ θεοῦ, 1 Cor 4:20) is meant to stress the futility of considering talk as that in which the kingdom of God consists. Once the futility of talk has been established, the contrast, "but in power" (ἀλλ' ἐν δυνάμει) becomes the constitutive essence of the kingdom of God. Paul therefore establishes power as the most important thing in the kingdom of God as far as his argument is concerned. But this power is not what the Corinthians

---

17. Sampley, "1 Corinthians," 803.

count on for their evaluation of the teachers as they judge them in terms of words of wisdom and persuasion, rather than the power of God in the folly of the message of the cross, the criterion on which the Corinthians cannot match Paul.

The subunit of 1 Corinthians 1:10—4:21 ends with a rhetorical question which comes in two parts. The readers are asked to indicate what they want (τί θέλετε;). The choice is about how Paul should come to them in his next visit. They are to choose between coming to them with a rod (ἐν ῥάβδῳ ἔλθω πρὸς ὑμᾶς) or in a spirit of love and gentleness (ἐν ἀγάπῃ πνεύματί τε πραΰτητος; 1 Cor 4:21). In this question, Paul resorts to *argumentum ad baculum*, threatening to come to the readers, if need be, with a rod to settle the matter of their arrogance. The rhetorical question requires the audience to make a choice. The Corinthians would have to effect the needed change of humility and submission to Paul's authority, which then implies opting for a spirit of love and gentleness. The question could also express *aporia*, in which Paul is trying to settle a dilemma on how to go to the Corinthians in his next visit. However it is considered, the rhetorical question points to the rod-deserving attitude of the Corinthians, as well as Paul's hesitance in applying the rod. In this light, the rhetorical question should be considered as a means to dissuade the readers from their pride so that Paul could come to them in a gentle spirit.

COMMENT

In 2 Corinthians 10:1, Paul was responding to a similar attitude of arrogance toward him from the same congregation. They claimed he was humble when face-to-face with them, but only bold when he was away. He faced the same temptation of coming to them to show boldness to those who thought he was walking according to the flesh (2 Cor 10:2). It is a similar situation we find in 1 Corinthians where he threatens to come with a rod to find out the power of those who are arrogant toward him. The accusation that he walks in the flesh leads him to say he does not wage war according to the flesh, though he walks in the flesh (2 Cor 10:3). He does not only indicate that the weapons of his warfare have divine power to destroy strongholds (2 Cor 10:4), but also goes ahead to show what strongholds they destroy. These strongholds are arguments and every lofty opinion raised against the knowledge of God. They include every thought which he takes captive in order to obey Christ (2 Cor 10:5). This is exactly the power and effect of Paul's letters admitted by the Corinthians: "For they say, 'his letters are weighty and strong, but his bodily presence is weak, and his speech of no account'" (2 Cor 10:10). Now, here in 2 Corinthians, as well as what we are dealing with in 1 Corinthians, the temptation was for Paul to come and show that same power which is felt in his letters. Paul admits this in saying "let such a person understand that what we say by letter when absent, we do when present" (2 Cor 10:11). If Paul has power to demonstrate to the readers in his next visit, it should be nothing apart from what is found in his letters, namely, the power of his word.

We should now go back to 1 Corinthians 4:19–21, where he challenges the arrogant members, stating that he would come and find out their power and not their talk. He had indicated that "the kingdom of God does not consist in talk but in power" (1 Cor 4:20). All his talk about the Spirit in this rhetorical unit has centered on the role of the Spirit in aiding understanding and communication of the message of the cross. He challenges the readers that the power of his message of the cross can also be felt when face-to-face with them. It is not merely their talk, but the power of God at work in that talk that Paul seeks to find out. That is the crux of the matter, and where Paul has the upper hand.

This rhetorical division reveals the use of apophasis as Paul denies that his reason for writing is to shame the readers. He builds *ethos* as he appeals to himself as the only father of the readers who also brought them to faith, and whose character they should emulate. Moreover, his indirect appeal to shame builds *pathos*. He resorts to *argumentum ad baculum* in appealing to the rod. But with a rhetorical question, he expresses his dilemma (*aporia*) while at the same time giving the readers the option to choose between the rod and a spirit of gentleness.

SUMMARY OF 1 CORINTHIANS 1:10-4:21

In a nutshell, this is what Paul is trying to tell the Corinthian believers: "My brothers and sisters, the division among you has disastrous effects. With your factions you are dividing Christ and destroying the temple (building) of God, which you all constitute. You have come to this state of affairs because you have relied on the wisdom of this world by accepting the preaching of the good news with persuasive words. Because of this you cannot understand spiritual things as meant for spiritual and mature believers. For instance, you cannot understand that Apollos and I are among the things

Wisdom, Knowledge, and Spirituality in Self-defense

God has freely given you, and that you should not boast in us—we are mere workers through whom you came to believe in Christ. Instead, you have treated us as though we were the ones who were crucified for you. See how you have developed envy and strife among you by giving your allegiance to mere servants who are part of your possession?

"I knew that when the gospel is preached with the wisdom of words it would make you rely on human wisdom rather than on the power of God. That is why I decided to stick to the message of the cross though it appears to you foolish and weak. If I appeared among you as one who is in weakness and in fear and much trembling, it is precisely because I came to you with the message which is neither wise nor powerful in your sight.

"I want you to know that your assessment of me does not mean anything to me because as a spiritual person and one having the mind of Christ, I have already assessed everything so well, and I know that your rating of me is wrong. You present yourselves as rich, reigning kings. You behave as if I'm not the one who brought you to faith in Christ.

"As I have always tried to teach you, learn from me as your only father. The example I have given you of my life eschews arrogance. Even when I was at the receiving end of ill treatment I refrained from paying back with evil. Heed my word so that I can return to you in a gentle spirit.

SUMMARY OF SOME RECOGNIZABLE RHETORICAL DEVICES IN 1 CORINTHIANS 1-4

It has come to light that 1 Corinthians 1:10—4:21 employs language typical of all three forms of rhetoric: forensic, deliberative, and epideictic. It combines all three modes of appeal—*ethos*, *logos*, and *pathos* at various points. In this rhetorical subunit, Paul uses a number of rhetorical devices for his rhetorical strategies in order to achieve persuasion. These rhetorical devices, occurring in different frequencies, include: chiasm, rhetorical questions, commoratio, enumeratio, amplification, contrast, and irony. Mention can also be made of exemplum, parallelism, sententia, antithesis, bending syllogism, and hypophora. The others are contrast, nonfallacious ad hominem, distinctio, metonymy, accumulation, climatic order, dehortatio, and sarcasm. The rhetorical figures in sound that enhance the empathic effect of the various arguments include: anaphora, conduplicatio, anadiplosis, epiphora, alliteration, assonance, polysyndeton, and epistrophe. Paul's use of parallelism, amplification commoratio, enumeratio, and distinctio in particular, enabled him to treat his readers in accordance with his view of them as infants and fleshly people.

A KEY TEXT IN PAUL'S ARGUMENT

It can be argued that 1 Corinthians 2:14–16 holds the key to Paul's evaluation of the Corinthians and himself. Everything he says about the Corinthians and himself in this rhetorical subunit can be explained in terms of these three verses:

1 Corinthians 2:14–16

> 14 ψυχικὸς δὲ ἄνθρωπος οὐ δέχεται τὰ τοῦ πνεύματος τοῦ θεοῦ μωρία γὰρ αὐτῷ ἐστιν καὶ οὐ δύναται γνῶναι, ὅτι πνευματικῶς ἀνακρίνεται. 15 ὁ δὲ πνευματικὸς ἀνακρίνει [τὰ] πάντα, αὐτὸς δὲ ὑπ' οὐδενὸς ἀνακρίνεται. 16 τίς γὰρ ἔγνω νοῦν κυρίου, ὃς συμβιβάσει αὐτόν; ἡμεῖς δὲ νοῦν Χριστοῦ ἔχομεν.

> 14 The natural person does not accept the things of the Spirit of God, for they are folly to him, and he is not able to understand them because they are spiritually discerned. 15 The spiritual person judges all things, but is himself to be judged by no one. 16 "For who has understood the mind of the Lord so as to instruct him?" But we have the mind of Christ.

In these three verses are clauses that define the unspiritual and the spiritual person. The discussion of these clauses will focus first on the unspiritual person.

The Unspiritual Person

The defining clauses of the unspiritual person come in two pairs. The first clause of each pair expresses an attitude the reason for which is given in the second clause. Thus,

> *1st Pair:*
>
> The unspiritual person
>
> A Does not accept the things of the Spirit of God (effect—action/attitude)
>
> > B Because they are folly to him or her (cause—reason for action/attitude)

Wisdom, Knowledge, and Spirituality in Self-defense

2nd Pair:

A¹ He is not able to understand them (effect—action/attitude)

B¹ Because they [the spiritual things] are spiritually discerned (cause—reason for action/attitude).

The second pair, taken as a whole, is the reason that accounts for the first pair. Thus, because the fleshly person cannot discern the things of the spirit of God (B¹), he or she is not able to understand them (A¹). The two (B¹ and A¹) account for why the things of God's Spirit are folly to him or her (B) and why he or she does not accept them (A). To appreciate the relevance of these statements about the unspiritual person in Paul's argument, we should reverse Paul's order by moving from the cause (B¹ and A¹) to the effect (B and A). Because the things of the Spirit of God are spiritually discerned, the unspiritual person cannot understand them (B¹ and A¹). Because of this, they are folly to him or her, and he or she does not accept them (B and A).

Application to the Corinthians

How do these verses find expression in Paul's argument? Certain statements in Paul's argument point to the Corinthians' lack of spiritual understanding. This lack of understanding is the reason for what Paul considers to be the unacceptable conduct and attitudes of his readers.

First, he states that the Corinthians are unspiritual, citing two reasons in support of this: (1) their inability to understand his teaching (βρῶμα, solid food) for which reason he resorts to feeding them with milk (γάλα); and (2) their division as demonstrated in their claims of allegiance to human leaders (1 Cor 3:1–4). Paul therefore demonstrates that the Corinthians are unspiritual in their lack of understanding of two things—his message and the identity of Paul and Apollos. These two deserve some explanation.

The Corinthians' Misunderstanding of Paul's Message as Evidence of Their Unspiritual State

Paul argues that it takes the Holy Spirit for one to understand his message of the cross (1 Cor 2:14; cf. 3:1–3). Understood by the aid of the Spirit, the message of the cross is God's power unto salvation (1 Cor 1:18), the wisdom of God, and the power of God (1 Cor 1:24). It is the foolishness of

God, which is wiser than men, and the weakness of God, which is stronger than men (1 Cor 1:25). But because the Corinthians cannot understand this message, it seems to be foolishness to them as wise people of the age. It is this lack of understanding of Paul's message that leads them to see Paul as one in weakness and in much fear and trembling, the image of one who carries a message they consider to be folly and weak. Paul wants them to understand things by the Spirit so they might become fools (to the world) and thereby become wise in Christ (1 Cor 3:18). If it takes the Spirit to understand the message proclaimed in hidden mysteries (1 Cor 2:7, 13), then the fact that the Corinthians do no understand it means that they are not spiritual. In a nutshell, their inability to understand things spiritually led to their misconceptions about themselves and about Paul and Apollos.

The Corinthians' Misconception of Paul's and Apollos's Identities as Indications of Their Being Unspiritual

Paul's conviction that the Corinthians' division stems from their misconception about the leaders is evident in the two rhetorical questions that immediately follow the statement of the problem (1 Cor 3:4–5). He inquires, "Who then is Apollos?" (Τί οὖν ἐστιν Ἀπολλῶς;) followed by "And who is Paul" (τί δέ ἐστιν Παῦλος; 1 Cor 3:5)? To correct their misconception, Paul indicates who the leaders are: they are servants (according to God's appointment) through whom the Corinthians believed (διάκονοι δι' ὧν ἐπιστεύσατε, καὶ ἑκάστῳ ὡς ὁ κύριος ἔδωκεν). The Corinthians' apparent lack of understanding here implies that they perceived Paul and Apollos differently. It is instructive that earlier, following the first statement of the division, two rhetorical questions (1 Cor 1:12–13) spoke to the Corinthians' misconception, which overrates the leaders as worthy of the Corinthians' allegiance. The implications of these rhetorical questions are obvious: "Was Paul crucified for you? Or were you baptized in the name of Paul" (1 Cor 1:13)?

This should explain why Paul explains over and over again who he and Apollos are. He maintains he and Apollos are coworkers. He plants, Apollos waters (1 Cor 3:6–9). He lays the foundation, Apollos builds on it (1 Cor 3:10). He restates the same point: "This is how one should regard us, as servants of Christ and stewards of the mysteries of God" (1 Cor 4:1). The lengthy enumeratio of the one who builds on the foundation (Apollos) is meant to correct the same misconception about the leaders (particularly that of Apollos, 1 Cor 3:11–15). Paul leaves no stone unturned just to make his point clear: "So neither he who plants nor he who waters is anything, but only God who gives the growth" (1 Cor 3:7). This is a direct response to their overestimation of Paul and Apollos—Paul says he and Apollos are nothing in their roles as compared to that of God.

The foregoing establishes one thing—that the Corinthians are not spiritual. This shows in two main ways—their failure to understand the message of God's saving power in the cross, and their failure to appreciate who Paul and Apollos are. This also gives meaning to why they do not receive the things of the Spirit of God. Because they cannot understand the two objects of God's giving—the message of the cross on the one hand, and Paul and Apollos on the other hand, they do not receive them. While they rely rather on the wisdom of this world, they take Paul and Apollos not as free gifts of God but as objects of their allegiance. So though they receive Paul and Apollos, they do not do so as to things freely given to them by the Spirit (1 Cor 2:12) for they do not understand them as such. They rather understand them as objects of their allegiance. This is why they boast in them as though they did not receive them (1 Cor 4:7; cf. 3:21–23). It is in this sense that the listing of Paul and Apollos in the things the Corinthians have (things that are theirs) makes sense. This gives meaning to the question: "What do you have that you did not receive? If then you received it, why do you boast as if you did not receive it?" (1 Cor 4:7). Of course, the Corinthians were boasting of their leaders (who were part of the things they have, 1 Cor 4:6c) as though did not receive them, when indeed there is nothing they have which they did not receive (1 Cor 4:7). When they failed to receive Paul and Apollos as things freely given, they were demonstrating that they could not regard the two leaders as such. If only they could understand them this way, they would have accepted them so. For Paul, this demonstrates their condition as unspiritual people.

The Spiritual Person

Two very instructive statements define the spiritual person in the three verses under consideration. The first statement has two clauses: (a) the spiritual person judges all things, and (b) he is himself to be judged by no one (1 Cor 2:15).

The first clause states what the spiritual person does; the second states what the spiritual person does not need one to do to him. Whereas the spiritual person judges (evaluates, ἀνακρίνει) all things (a), he or she needs no one to judges him or her (b). The reason why nobody judges him or her (b) is that he or she judges all things (a). Having judged everything so well as a spiritual person, the judgment of others about what he or she has judged does not matter to the spiritual person.

Two other important statements follow by way of enumeratio, offering reasons why the spiritual person judges all things while he or she is not judged. The first establishes the impossibility of one knowing the Lord's mind to the point where one could instruct the Lord in the things of the Lord. Thus, "For who has understood the mind of the Lord so as to instruct him?" (1 Cor 2:16a). The answer to this is obviously, "NO one!" In essence, this rhetorical question amplifies by way of commoratio the preceding clause, "but is himself to be judged by no one" (1 Cor 2:15). In this way, Paul establishes the freedom of the spiritual person from the judgment of all others. In other words, a spiritual person is free from the opinion and evaluation of other people.

By saying "But we have the mind of Christ (1 Cor 2:14–16), Paul is claiming that no one can judge him in the things of God as one who has the mind of Christ. If it is impossible to know the mind of the Lord so as to instruct him, then no one can judge him as one who has (not who knows) the mind of the Lord. No one can *know* more of the things of the Lord than him who *has* the mind of Christ. We noted earlier two things: (1) Paul's use of "the Lord" as a metonymy for himself in 1 Cor 3:16, and (2) the fact that Paul places himself higher in spiritual understanding—that is, as one having the mind of Christ—over those who might claim to know the mind of the Lord. The one who has the mind of Christ is logically, Christ the Lord. Having the mind of Christ therefore makes Paul Christ the Lord insofar as his rhetorical strategy is concerned. The implied superior understanding of spiritual things exhibited in the ability of the spiritual person to judge things appropriately explains why the judgments of others do not matter to him or her. How does Paul demonstrate that this is applicable to him in his argument?

When he declared, "But with me it is a very small thing that I should be judged by you or by any human court," he was confronting the readers with his virtue as a spiritual person whom no one judges (one to whom the judgment of others does not matter). It is this practice of judging all things that resulted in his claim that he does not even know anything against himself (1 Cor 4:4). When he declares, "In fact, I do not even judge myself," it is to be understood in the light of his having the mind of Christ, so that his judgment of all things is actually the judgment of Christ. "It is the Lord who judges me" (1 Cor 4:4), therefore expresses his judgment of himself with the mind of Christ. When he judges himself with the mind of Christ, then the Lord judges him.

The fact that Paul sees himself as a spiritual person who judges all things with the mind of Christ explains a number of things in his argument. It explains why he decides to stick to the message of Christ and him crucified (1 Cor 2:1–2) though that made him appear as one in weakness and in fear and in much trembling (1 Cor 2:3). It explains why he saw the message of the cross as the power of God unto salvation (1 Cor 1:18) when it appeared as foolishness and a stumbling block to others (1 Cor 1:23). It explains why he is content with his image as a fool for Christ, weak, held in disrepute (1 Cor 4:10), and as the scum of the world, the refuse of all things (1 Cor 4:13). It explains why Paul would not treat the Corinthians the way they treated him: so when he is reviled, he blesses; when persecuted, he endures; when slandered, he entreats (1 Cor 4:12). Indeed, by acting this way, Paul presents himself as the spiritual person who judges all things, and is himself not judged.

CHAPTER 6

Sexual Immorality as Evidence of Lack of Sound Knowledge and Spirituality

FIRST CORINTHIANS 5–6 CONSTITUTE the second rhetorical subunit of the letter. The judgmental language of the argument of 1 Corinthians 5 makes it forensic. It deals with the first of two conducts of the Corinthians over which Paul expresses great surprise and perplexity. The second receives attention in the succeeding chapter.

RHETORICAL DIVISION, INTRODUCTION, AND PAUL'S ARGUMENT ON THE SIN OF INCEST

First Corinthians 5:1–2 is the introductory and summary presentation of the entire argument. The rest of the chapter gives amplification to it. Acting like a prosecutor and a judge, Paul presents a case for the guilt of the immoral man and the church's failure to take the appropriate action. He then pronounces severe punishment on the immoral man.

1 Corinthians 5:1–3

> 1 Ὅλως ἀκούεται ἐν ὑμῖν πορνεία, καὶ τοιαύτη πορνεία ἥτις οὐδὲ ἐν τοῖς ἔθνεσιν, ὥστε γυναῖκά τινα τοῦ πατρὸς ἔχειν. 2 καὶ ὑμεῖς πεφυσιωμένοι ἐστὲ καὶ οὐχὶ μᾶλλον ἐπενθήσατε, ἵνα ἀρθῇ ἐκ μέσου ὑμῶν ὁ τὸ ἔργον τοῦτο πράξας; 3 ἐγὼ μὲν γάρ, ἀπὼν τῷ σώματι παρὼν δὲ τῷ πνεύματι, ἤδη κέκρικα ὡς παρὼν τὸν οὕτως τοῦτο κατεργασάμενον.

> 1 It is actually reported that there is sexual immorality among you, and of a kind that is not tolerated even among pagans, for a man has his father's wife. 2 And you are arrogant! Ought you not rather to mourn? Let him who has done this be removed from among you. 3 For though absent in body, I am present in spirit; and as if present, I have already pronounced judgment on the one who did such a thing.

The importance of the first two verses lies in their rhetorical significance. They appear in Greek as follows:

> *Announcement of the problem:* Ὅλως ἀκούεται ἐν ὑμῖν πορνεία
>
> *The nature of the problem:* καὶ τοιαύτη πορνεία ἥτις οὐδὲ ἐν τοῖς ἔθνεσιν
>
> *The specific sin:* γυναῖκά τινα τοῦ πατρὸς ἔχειν
>
> *Paul's disappointment with their reaction:* ὑμεῖς πεφυσιωμένοι ἐστὲ
>
> *Their expected reaction:* οὐχὶ μᾶλλον ἐπενθήσατε
>
> *Paul's verdict:* ἵνα ἀρθῇ ἐκ μέσου ὑμῶν ὁ τὸ ἔργον τοῦτο πράξας (1 Cor 5:1–2)

In English we have:

> *Announcement of the problem:* It is reported that there is sexual immorality among you
>
> *The nature of the problem:* The kind of sexual immorality not found even among the gentiles
>
> *The specific sin:* A man has his father's wife
>
> *Paul's disappointment with their reaction:* You are proud (in spite of this)
>
> *Their expected reaction:* Ought you not rather to mourn?
>
> *Paul's verdict:* The one who has done this act should be removed from among you

ὅλως, as translated by many English versions, expresses the veracity of the report of the scandal. But taken as the adverbial form of ὅλος, ὅλως may indicate how widespread the news of the incest had been. This is the sense found in the HCSB.[1] The problem itself is sexual immorality among them (ἐν ὑμῖν πορνεία). The following clause provides the description of the problem. The repetition of πορνεία (sexual immorality) instead of its

---

1. The HCSB translates ὅλως ἀκούεται "It is widely reported."

relative pronoun in the defining clause is emphatic in effect (1 Cor 5:1). Preceding πορνεία with the conjunction καὶ (and) and the correlative adjective τοιαύτη (such) calls curious attention to the nature of the problem. Two details are given in enumeratio in the description of the sexual act: (1) it is one that is not found even among the gentiles ("Ἥτις οὐδὲ ἐν τοῖς ἔθνεσιν), and (2) it is about a man having his father's wife (ὥστε γυναῖκά τινα τοῦ πατρὸς ἔχειν). The two details provide both the nature of the problem and what it specifically involves. ὥστε (so that) functions as γάρ (for), implying that the clause indicates the reason why the act would hardly be found even among gentiles, who were generally perceived to have a loose moral life. The present infinitive ἔχειν (to have) is indicative of the fact that the man was still living in the sinful act.

In spite of the amplification, given the problem, some details remain unclear. One of such details is the relationship between the man and woman involved in the incestuous act. Conzelmann rules out marriage with the man's own mother as well as an adulterous relationship with his stepmother. He suggests marriage or concubinate with his stepmother after the father's death, or after his father had secured divorce.[2]

The disposition of the Corinthians in the face of the incestuous act was a major factor for Paul's disappointment. Paul is surprised that they are proud (ὑμεῖς πεφυσιωμένοι ἐστέ). The succeeding rhetorical question indicates what should have been their appropriate disposition—to mourn (οὐχὶ μᾶλλον ἐπενθήσατε, 1 Cor 5:2). Their failure to assume the right disposition of remorse in the face of the sin elicits Paul's condemnation and judgment—the man who did such a thing must be removed from among them (ἵνα ἀρθῇ ἐκ μέσου ὑμῶν ὁ τὸ ἔργον τοῦτο πράξας). The foregoing finds its full expression in the form of amplification in the rest of 1 Corinthians 5.

In 1 Corinthians 5:3, Paul gives clear instructions on how his judgment of the immoral man should be carried out. He maintains that though absent in body (ἀπὼν τῷ σώματι), he is present in spirit (παρὼν δὲ τῷ πνεύματι), and has already pronounced judgment (κέκρικα), as though present (ὡς παρὼν), on the one who had done such a thing (1 Cor 5:3). The indication that he has already pronounced judgment is superfluous because that is clear from the previous verse (1 Cor 5:2). This repetition is, however, for a deliberate emphatic effect, and as has been observed over and over again, an appropriate way for addressing a fleshly and infant audiece.

2. Conzelmann, *Commentary on the First Epistle*, 96.

Wisdom, Knowledge, and Spirituality in Self-defense

MOCKERY OF THE CORINTHIANS' WISDOM AND THEIR FAILURE TO APPRECIATE THE DANGERS OF SEXUAL IMMORALITY

1 Corinthians 5:4–13

4 ἐν τῷ ὀνόματι τοῦ κυρίου [ἡμῶν] Ἰησοῦ συναχθέντων ὑμῶν καὶ τοῦ ἐμοῦ πνεύματος σὺν τῇ δυνάμει τοῦ κυρίου ἡμῶν Ἰησοῦ, 5 παραδοῦναι τὸν τοιοῦτον τῷ σατανᾷ εἰς ὄλεθρον τῆς σαρκός, ἵνα τὸ πνεῦμα σωθῇ ἐν τῇ ἡμέρᾳ τοῦ κυρίου. 6 Οὐ καλὸν τὸ καύχημα ὑμῶν. οὐκ οἴδατε ὅτι μικρὰ ζύμη ὅλον τὸ φύραμα ⌜ζυμοῖ; 7 ἐκκαθάρατε ⊤ τὴν παλαιὰν ζύμην, ἵνα ἦτε νέον φύραμα, καθώς ἐστε ἄζυμοι. καὶ γὰρ τὸ πάσχα ἡμῶν ⊤ ἐτύθη Χριστός. 8 ὥστε ἑορτάζωμεν μὴ ἐν ζύμῃ παλαιᾷ ⌜μηδὲ ἐν ζύμῃ κακίας καὶ ⌜πονηρίας ἀλλ' ἐν ἀζύμοις εἰλικρινείας καὶ ἀληθείας. 9 Ἔγραψα ὑμῖν ἐν τῇ ἐπιστολῇ μὴ ⌜συναναμίγνυσθαι πόρνοις, 10 ⊤οὐ πάντως τοῖς πόρνοις τοῦ κόσμου τούτου ἢ τοῖς πλεονέκταις ⌜καὶ ἅρπαξιν ἢ εἰδωλολάτραις, ἐπεὶ ⌜ὠφείλετε ἄρα ἐκ τοῦ κόσμου ἐξελθεῖν. 11 ⌜νῦν δὲ ἔγραψα ὑμῖν μὴ συναναμίγνυσθαι ἐάν τις ἀδελφὸς ὀνομαζόμενος ⌜ἢ πόρνος ἢ πλεονέκτης ἢ εἰδωλολάτρης ἢ λοίδορος ἢ μέθυσος ἢ ἅρπαξ, τῷ τοιούτῳ μηδὲ συνεσθίειν. 12 τί γάρ μοι ⊤ τοὺς ἔξω κρίνειν; ⌜οὐχὶ τοὺς ἔσω ὑμεῖς κρίνετε⌝; 13 τοὺς δὲ ἔξω ὁ θεὸς ⌜κρινεῖ. ⌜ἐξάρατε τὸν πονηρὸν ἐξ ὑμῶν αὐτῶν.

4 When you are assembled in the name of the Lord Jesus and my spirit is present, with the power of our Lord Jesus, 5 you are to deliver this man to Satan for the destruction of the flesh, so that his spirit may be saved in the day of the Lord. 6 Your boasting is not good. Do you not know that a little leaven leavens the whole lump? 7 Cleanse out the old leaven that you may be a new lump, as you really are unleavened. For Christ, our Passover lamb, has been sacrificed. 8 Let us therefore celebrate the festival, not with the old leaven, the leaven of malice and evil, but with the unleavened bread of sincerity and truth. 9 I wrote to you in my letter not to associate with sexually immoral people—10 not at all meaning the sexually immoral of this world, or the greedy and swindlers, or idolaters, since then you would need to go out of the world. 11 But now I am writing to you not to associate with anyone who bears the name of brother if he is guilty of sexual immorality or greed, or is an idolater, reviler, drunkard, or swindler—not even to eat with such a one. 12 For what have I to do with judging outsiders? Is it not those inside the church whom you are to judge? 13 God judges those outside. "Purge the evil person from among you."

The additional information in 1 Corinthians 5:4 is the amplification that provides the procedure to be followed for executing Paul's judgment. Thus, they should meet (συναχθέντων ὑμῶν) in the name of the Lord (ἐν τῷ ὀνόματι τοῦ κυρίου), and recognize the presence of Paul's spirit (ἐμοῦ πνεύματος) and the power of our Lord Jesus (σὺν τῇ δυνάμει τοῦ κυρίου ἡμῶν Ἰησοῦ, 1 Cor 5:4). It is in this setting that they should deliver the judgment. Though what follows, 1 Corinthians 5:5, appears to be a restatement of the verdict to "remove the man from among them" (commoratio, 1 Cor 5:2), that is not the case. What follows in 1 Corinthians 5:5 begins the portrayal of the folly of the wisdom with which the Corinthians were acting in the matter of sexual immorality. It represents their underlying views with a mocking imagery that should leave them confounded. They are to deliver (παραδοῦναι) this kind of person (τὸν τοιοῦτον) to Satan (τῷ σατανᾷ). The purpose for handing him over to Satan is one—that his spirit would be saved in the day of the Lord (ἵνα τὸ πνεῦμα σωθῇ ἐν τῇ ἡμέρᾳ τοῦ κυρίου). The use of ἵνα (so that) is significant in pointing to the purpose (1 Cor 5:5). This purpose should be achieved by the destruction of the man's flesh for which he is to be handed over to Satan (εἰς ὄλεθρον τῆς σαρκός). Satan now becomes the agent who acts for the salvation of the man's soul. It is the folly of such a view found in the action of the immoral man and the church's attitude that is thrown back to the readers in this imagery. They have acted as though, by giving one's body to sexual immorality, one's spirit could still be saved because what happens to one's body has no effect on one's spirit. It is no wonder that just after this, Paul tells them, "Your boasting is not good" (Οὐ καλὸν τὸ καύχημα ὑμῶν), and begins to paint the right picture of the incestuous act. The impracticable literal execution of this injunction of the judgment is meant to force the readers to come to terms with the folly of their action as represented in the contradictory, ridiculing sarcasm,[3] which itself is a judgment on their knowledge and wisdom, not to mention their spiritual state. This impracticability is not necessarily about handing the man over to Satan, but about the destruction of his body as an act meant for his salvation.

The process for carrying out the verdict is simple but spiritually intense. The presence of the spirit of Paul and the power of the Lord Jesus

---

3. The use of "ridiculing" and "sarcasm" is deliberate and intended to create a cumulative effect. How would they hand him over to Satan? Some have sought to explain that removing him from among them (excommunication) means casting the man into the domain of Satan where he lacks the protection of God. However, taking the injunction as a whole in context, this falls short of a satisfactory explanation.

Wisdom, Knowledge, and Spirituality in Self-defense

makes the jury very powerful. While this spiritually intense atmosphere is meant to make the members of the jury bold enough to carry out Paul's verdict of removing the man from among them, it is also meant to make the verdict unquestionable. In terms of Paul's theology, the puzzle of this judgment lies mainly with what appears to be his separation of the flesh and the Spirit of the immoral man. By failing to see it as a sarcastic representation of their underlying views, this puzzle has become a matter of curious interest to scholars. Fee, for instance, argues, "It is simply foreign to Paul's usage for the 'flesh/spirit' contrast to refer to the body as doomed to destruction but the 'spirit' (inner, real person?) as destined for salvation. Such a view stands in contradiction to Paul's express doctrine of the resurrection of the body and in fact would fit nicely into the Corinthians' own view (see on 6:12–14)."[4] He maintains, "it is out of character with Paul's theology as we meet it elsewhere that one who sins within the Christian community should be so punished in the present age that he lies beyond the redemptive, restorative love of that community."[5] He cites Paul's counsel to the Corinthians concerning a brother who needed correction (2 Cor 2:5–11) as opposed to his attitude here.[6] Fee cautions against making the text the basis for a "canon law" because of the "*ad hoc*" nature of the "church discipline" here.[7]

Subsequent to the instruction on how the immoral man should be dealt with, and Paul's sarcastic depiction of their views and action, he now evaluates their attitude of pride (τὸ καύχημα ὑμῶν), which is not good (οὐ καλὸν, 1 Cor 5:6), according to Paul. This verdict on their pride points to their lack of understanding as unspiritual people. To explain this inappropriate boasting, the folly of their views and action in the immoral sexual act, Paul resorts to the imagery of the Passover with which the immoral man is presented as unfit for their assembly. He begins with a rhetorical question which confronts them with their inability to discern the danger in the current situation: "Do you not know that a little leaven leavens the whole lump" (οὐκ οἴδατε ὅτι μικρὰ ζύμη ὅλον τὸ φύραμα ζυμοῖ;)? With "Do you not know?" Paul touches on an important motif found at various points in the second rhetorical subunit. On Paul's use of the rhetorical device "Do you not know that…?" it has been argued that "the fact that he will use this

---

4. Fee, *First Epistle to the Corinthians*, 211.
5. Fee, *First Epistle to the Corinthians*, 212.
6. Fee, *First Epistle to the Corinthians*, 212.
7. Fee, *First Epistle to the Corinthians*, 213.

Sexual Immorality as Evidence of Lack of Sound Knowledge and Spirituality

device ten times in this letter, chiefly in contexts where he is exercised, and that it occurs only one other time in his letters (Rom 6:16), probably says much about his feelings toward the Corinthians and their behavior."[8] Not only could they not discern the wisdom and power of the message of the cross, nor recognize the apostles as servants of Christ through whom they believed, but also, they could not recognize the danger of the sin of incest they were entertaining—that it is a little yeast that will leaven the whole lump (μικρὰ ζύμη ὅλον τὸ φύραμα ζυμοῖ, 1 Cor 5:6).

While using the Passover imagery to establish the inappropriateness of the incestuous act and their boasting, the imagery also enables Paul to restate his verdict and make it urgent. His logic is simple; people who cannot recognize the danger in a situation can hardly take the right step to remedy the situation. He must therefore help them recognize the damaging implications of their actions and tell them what to do about it. The imperative "cleanse out" (ἐκκαθάρατε) is not an appeal but an unambiguous command. The accusative τὴν παλαιὰν ζύμην makes "the old leaven" unmistakably the object of the action. With ἵνα he points to the expected result of this cleansing: "to be a new batch of dough" (ἵνα ἦτε νέον φύραμα). The two subsequent clauses provide the indicative for the preceding imperative: "Cleanse out the old leaven." The two indicatives answer the question: "Why should we cleanse out the old leaven?" They are: (1) "You are unleavened" (καθώς ἐστε ἄζυμοι), and (2) "Christ, our Passover lamb has been sacrificed" (καὶ γὰρ τὸ πάσχα ἡμῶν ἐτύθη Χριστός). While the first one indicates who they are (unleavened), the second indicates the reason for what they are—the divine initiative (Christ our Passover lamp has been sacrificed). The truth of the first indicative is presented as given with καθώς (even as) standing first in the clause. The conjunction γὰρ (for) makes the second indicative that from which the first indicative derives. The two indicatives also lead to another imperative. ὥστε, at the beginning of this imperative, has two functions; while it makes the preceding indicative the reason for the imperative, it also presents the imperative as the intended result of the indicative (1 Cor 5:8). The second-person subjunctive "Let us celebrate the festival" (ἑορτάζωμεν) is *cohortatory* as it calls on the readers to join in a celebration with Paul. The focus of this imperative, however, is the manner in which the celebration is to be done. The appropriateness of the dough (ζύμη) used determines the worthiness of one's celebration. The first three adjectives speak of the

---

8. Fee, *First Epistle to the Corinthians*, 146.

Wisdom, Knowledge, and Spirituality in Self-defense

inappropriateness of old leaven (ζύμῃ παλαιᾷ), leaven of evil (ζύμῃ κακίας), and of wickedness (πονηρίας):

μὴ ἐν ζύμῃ παλαιᾷ …
μηδὲ ἐν ζύμῃ κακίας
καὶ πονηρίας
ἀλλ' ἐν ἀζύμοις εἰλικρινείας καὶ ἀληθείας (1 Cor 5:8).

The καὶ in the third line above has the effect of negating πονηρίας (of evil) just like the negative particle μὴ and the conjunction μηδὲ in the two preceding lines. The fourth line provides the kind of dough that is acceptable for the celebration. The contrast between "the unleavened bread of sincerity (ἀζύμοις εἰλικρινείας) and of truth (καὶ ἀληθείας) on the one hand, and the leaven of malice and evil on the other, is made explicit by the preceding ἀλλ' (but) of the last line.

The metaphor of the Passover is intended to provide a framework in which Paul's verdict on the immoral man finds support and urgency—the need to remove the immoral man as old leaven. During the entire period of the Passover feast, nothing leaven must be eaten. For this reason, the preparation of the Passover involves the removal of all things leaven in the house in order to celebrate the festival in a worthy manner. Paul goes straightway to the essence of the metaphor: he recalls his earlier instruction to the readers not to associate with (συναναμίγνυσθαι) the sexually immoral (πόρνοις). He follows this up with the explanation that he certainly was not referring to the sexually immoral of this world (οὐ πάντως τοῖς πόρνοις τοῦ κόσμου τούτου). He was neither referring to the greedy (τοῖς πλεονέκταις), nor the swindler (ἅρπαξιν), nor the idolater (εἰδωλολάτραις) of this world (1 Cor 5:10). If it were so, then they would have to (ἐπεὶ ὠφείλετε) leave the world (ἐκ τοῦ κόσμου ἐξελθεῖν). So what did he mean? He explains this with a long sentence containing five noun phrases and an adjectival phrase which acts like the preceding noun phrases. In the function of enumeratio, these phrases provide details of the people Paul considers inappropriate for believers to associate with:

νῦν δὲ ἔγραψα ὑμῖν μὴ συναναμίγνυσθαι ἐάν τις ἀδελφὸς ὀνομαζόμενος
ἢ πόρνος
ἢ πλεονέκτης
ἢ εἰδωλολάτρης
ἢ λοίδορος
ἢ μέθυσος
ἢ ἅρπαξ,

τῷ τοιούτῳ μηδὲ συνεσθίειν (1 Cor 5:11)

"And now" (νῦν δὲ) marks the turning point in the discourse where Paul makes clear the kind of immoral persons he asked them not to associate with. The "or" (ἢ) in each noun phrase has the effect of the initial third-person singular subjunctive "being" ᾖ (in ᾖ πόρνος). By listing the kind of members to be avoided, Paul leaves no stone unturned to ensure that his babes in Christ understand what he means. They are not to associate with members who are sexually immoral (πόρνος), or greedy (πλεονέκτης), or idolaters (εἰδωλολάτρης), or slanderers (λοίδορος), or drunkards (μέθυσος), or swindlers (ἅρπαξ). This is another instance of dehortatio in which the readers are told what not to do. The polysyndeton in the abundant use of the conjunction ἢ, together with the anaphora of the repetition of the same conjunction in the initial position of each phrase, highlight the attention the list deserves. The concluding clause, "not even to eat with such a one" (τῷ τοιούτῳ μηδὲ συνεσθίειν, 1 Cor 5:11) following the list forms an inclusio with "not to associate with the sexually immoral" (1 Cor 5:9), bracketing 1 Corinthians 5:9–11 as addressing what associations they must avoid. Once that has been established, he justifies his injunction with two rhetorical questions: τί γάρ μοι τοὺς ἔξω κρίνειν and οὐχὶ τοὺς ἔσω ὑμεῖς κρίνετε.

The switch from the first-person singular (μοι, in the first question) to the second-person plural (ὑμεῖς, in the second question) is instructive. While the first question indicates that Paul has nothing to do with judging those outside (τοὺς ἔξω), the second question draws attention to what the Corinthians do—they judge those inside (the in-group of the believers). At the very least they have judged Paul (1 Cor 9:3; cf. 4:3), a member of their in-group. οὐχὶ demands the answer "Yes" to the question, "Do you not judge insiders" (οὐχὶ τοὺς ἔσω ὑμεῖς κρίνετε)? In the next two sentences, he establishes whose duty it is to judge the outsiders and calls on the readers to do what they should do as judges of insiders. For those outside, it is God who judges them (τοὺς δὲ ἔξω ὁ θεὸς κρινεῖ). But since the readers judge those inside, they should now expel the evil man from among them (ἐξάρατε τὸν πονηρὸν ἐξ ὑμῶν αὐτῶν). The rendering of the indicative κρίνετε in the ESV, NIV, and ISV as "Is it not those inside the church whom you are to judge?" (1 Cor 5:12) weakens the effect of the verb as indicating what the Corinthians do. The ASV, HSCB, KJV, and NKJV are to be preferred here. They have "Don't you judge those who are inside?" To put it bluntly, Paul was saying, "If you judge insiders (me), judge this man who has done this." Their judgment of him becomes a rhetorical tool by which he highlights their failure to judge the immoral man. The concluding imperative acts as the *peroratio* that sums up the action they are required to take on the immoral man.

Paul's appeal to the readers in the imagery of the Passover feast can be represented in the following parallelism:

> A ἐκκαθάρατε τὴν παλαιὰν ζύμην
> > B ἵνα ἦτε νέον φύραμα (καθώς ἐστε ἄζυμοι) καὶ γὰρ τὸ πάσχα ἡμῶν ἐτύθη Χριστός
>
> A¹ ὥστε ἑορτάζωμεν μὴ ἐν ζύμῃ παλαιᾷ μηδὲ ἐν ζύμῃ κακίας καὶ πονηρίας
> > B¹ ἀλλ' ἐν ἀζύμοις εἰλικρινείας καὶ ἀληθείας

The *parallelism* can be appreciated in English as well:

> A Clean out the old leaven
> > B In order that you might be a new batch of dough (just as you are unleavened). For also Christ our Passover lamb has been sacrificed
>
> A¹ Therefore let us celebrate the feast not with the old leaven, neither with the leaven of evil nor of wickedness,
> > B¹ But with the unleavened bread of sincerity and truth.

Both statements in A and A¹ deal with what must be cleaned out while those of B and B¹ refer to what they are (the indicative) which they must maintain by removing the old leaven. That is to say, they should become what they already are: they are unleavened, so they should clean out the old leaven and become the unleavened they are. The peroratio therefore represents how Paul wants the believers to live in the imagery of the Passover feast. If they remove the sexually immoral man from among them, they would be celebrating the feast with the unleavened bread. The metaphor of the Passover serves to make the removal of the immoral man an urgent act, and to reinforce that imperative. Once the Passover lamb (Christ) has been sacrificed, the only bread that is suitable for the celebration is the unleavened bread. The aorist passive, ἐτύθη is therefore meant to have a present effect as in the perfect tense. The translation of the aorist passive as "has been sacrificed" in the HCSB is therefore appropriate for the intended rhetorical effect. The present effect of the sacrifice demands that they remain unleavened.

Comment

One may be critical of Paul for pronouncing judgment even before meeting on the case as well as of his failure to give the immoral man a hearing, a violation of common law. Fee, for instance, finds Paul's judgment *ad hoc*.[9] However, Paul must have found the case conclusive enough, and must have thought that, with its heinous nature, he was right in what he did. But this does not end the discussion.

If Paul knew that lack of spiritual understanding was responsible for such conduct as he indicates in the following chapter (1 Cor 6), why did he not seek to correct them in a gentle spirit as he advocates in Galatians 6:1? But before one jumps on Paul with criticism, one should put oneself in the shoes of Paul as a pastor. It should be pointed out that the problem in 1 Corinthians 5 was particularly embarrassing for him. The seriousness of the issue was due particularly to the failure of the man to repent and the public affront of this to the church. The church's compromising stance was another bother. Once this public affront of the act to the church is appreciated, the indignation of Paul as a pastor with passion for the right image of his church may appear understandable. But there were other sentiments. The Corinthians' arrogance and judgmental attitude toward Paul may have played a role in the path Paul took to address the problem (see 1 Cor 4:3,18–19; 5:2; 9:3; 14:37–38; cf. 13:4).

What exactly was the church expected to do about this matter and how? It is not clear if the church had a duly constituted body of leadership overseeing it in the absence of Paul. Paul's expectation that they should have removed the culprit suggests that they had the authority to do so. His unilateral pronouncement of judgment, and the fact that he did not instruct a group within the church to meet on the issue (but the whole church) point to one thing: the absence of a body of leadership with authority to deal with such issues within the church. This observation, however, cannot conclusively settle the question of why the church failed to deal with the issue. Other important observations should be made.

The verdict on the immoral man was quite clear—he should be removed from among them—excommunicated. As has already been pointed out, what is problematic, however, is his instruction to "deliver this man to Satan for the destruction of the flesh, so that his spirit may be saved in the day of the Lord." Though this has received what might be considered

---

9. Fee, *First Epistle to the Corinthians*, 213.

Wisdom, Knowledge, and Spirituality in Self-defense

enough attention, its nature as a long-standing puzzle demands some further discussion. What does Paul really mean? The person should be handed over to Satan? How? Does excommunication mean being handed over to Satan?[10] How is his flesh to be destroyed by Satan, and how can this destruction of his flesh result in the salvation of his soul? How can Satan's work in a man produce the man's salvation? Conzelmann is of the view that "The destruction of the flesh can hardly mean anything else but death."[11] But that does not settle the question. How can death merely result in the salvation of one's soul?

Paul's concern for the salvation of the man's spirit in isolation appears to support the Corinthians' view, which Paul himself opposes. This will be made clear in 1 Corinthians 6. The use of the rhetorical device of question-and-answer (hypophora) will help in analyzing Paul's instruction for the man to be handed over to Satan and the difficulties involved:

> Whose weapon is the flesh?[12]—Satan.
> Whose interest is it to destroy the flesh?—God, not Satan. If Satan destroys the flesh as Paul urges, Satan is fighting against his own kingdom.
> Who is interested in saving the man's spirit?—God.
> What does Satan do to the soul?—Destroy it. For Paul to urge that Satan should destroy the flesh (Satan's own weapon) for the soul to be saved (against Satan's purpose) appears contradictory. Satan will not fight against himself.

In light of the foregoing, Paul appears to be using irony to shame the readers for their failure to recognize the folly of the view underlying the sexually immoral act. The irony points out the folly of the Corinthians' belief that one could give one's body to sexual immorality without any adverse effect on one's spirit. Indeed, the man had given his body to Satan for destruction in the incestuous act, trusting that the salvation of his soul was

---

10. Many commentators argue that excommunication meant handing over the man to Satan since he would then be in the sphere of Satan.

11. Conzelmann, *Commentary on the First Epistle*, 97.

12. The analysis by Achtemeier, Green, and Thompson of Paul's use of the terms "flesh" and "body" reveal that Paul uses the two terms in both positive and negative senses. They argue therefore that the context of each use of these terms should be examined to ascertain the sense in which it is used (Achtemeier et al., *Introducing the New Testament*, 318). Here, the use of "flesh" is a sarcastic depiction of the Corinthians' view that one could engage in sexual immorality and still have the salvation of one's soul unaffected because the act affects only the body and not the soul.

still intact. This is what Paul is making a mockery of. The expression "Hand him over to Satan" is therefore not another way of expressing the verdict of excommunication, but a sarcastic depiction of the perception responsible for the unacceptable act. The verdict was for the man to be excommunicated. Nothing more, nothing less! The difficulty in the interpretation of this expression in most commentaries stems from attempts to interpret it literally as an instruction to hand over the man to Satan.

In this rhetorical division, one encounters a language that is mainly forensic due to its judgmental tone. The overall mode of appeal is *logos* as it advances reasons for which the Corinthians are misguided and guilty in their actions. There is extensive use of enumeratio as a tool of amplification to provide the needed detail to help the readers understand what is meant. Paul employs several rhetorical questions to raise important points they have ignored or shown ignorance of in their actions. His use of cohortatory injunctions is meant to invite the readers to join in what is right for their current situation. There is also the use of dehortatio in which the readers are told what not to do. The peroratio gives the conclusion on the subject in which his intent is clarified. Parallelism is used to state important points that deserve attention with the use of similar patterns. He employs irony to shame the Corinthians for their lack of sound judgment. Hypophora is an important way by which Paul treats his readers as children unworthy of solid food in providing them with even obvious answers to his questions. Finally, anaphora and polysyndeton are two rhetorical figures in sound that drew attention to important parts of his argument.

CHAPTER 7

Lawsuits among the Corinthians —A Sign of Spiritual Degeneracy

LAWSUITS AS INAPPROPRIATE FOR SANCTIFIED PEOPLE

1 Corinthians 6:1-11

1 Τολμᾷ τις ᵀ ὑμῶν πρᾶγμα ἔχων πρὸς τὸν ἕτερον κρίνεσθαι ἐπὶ τῶν ἀδίκων καὶ οὐχὶ ἐπὶ τῶν ἁγίων; 2 ἢ οὐκ οἴδατε ὅτι οἱ ἅγιοι τὸν κόσμον ⌜κρινοῦσιν; καὶ εἰ ἐν ὑμῖν κρίνεται ὁ κόσμος, ἀνάξιοί ἐστε κριτηρίων ἐλαχίστων; 3 οὐκ οἴδατε ὅτι ἀγγέλους κρινοῦμεν, μήτι γε βιωτικά; 4 βιωτικὰ μὲν οὖν κριτήρια ἐὰν ἔχητε, τοὺς ἐξουθενημένους ἐν τῇ ἐκκλησίᾳ, τούτους καθίζετε; 5 πρὸς ἐντροπὴν ὑμῖν ⌜λέγω. οὕτως οὐκ ⌜ᶠἔνι ἐν ὑμῖν ⌜οὐδεὶς σοφός⌝, ὃς δυνήσεται διακρῖναι ἀνὰ μέσον τοῦ ἀδελφοῦ αὐτοῦ; 6 ἀλλ' ἀδελφὸς μετὰ ἀδελφοῦ κρίνεται καὶ τοῦτο ἐπὶ ἀπίστων; 7 Ἤδη μὲν [οὖν] ὅλως ἥττημα ὑμῖν ἐστιν ὅτι ⌜κρίματα ἔχετε μεθ' ἑαυτῶν. διὰ τί οὐχὶ μᾶλλον ἀδικεῖσθε; διὰ τί οὐχὶ μᾶλλον ἀποστερεῖσθε; 8 ἀλλ' ὑμεῖς ἀδικεῖτε καὶ ἀποστερεῖτε, καὶ ⌜τοῦτο ἀδελφούς. 9 Ἢ οὐκ οἴδατε ὅτι ἄδικοι θεοῦ βασιλείαν οὐ κληρονομήσουσιν; μὴ πλανᾶσθε. οὔτε πόρνοι οὔτε εἰδωλολάτραι οὔτε μοιχοὶ οὔτε μαλακοὶ οὔτε ἀρσενοκοῖται 10 οὔτε κλέπται οὔτε πλεονέκται, ⌜οὐ μέθυσοι, οὐ λοίδοροι, οὐχ ἅρπαγες βασιλείαν θεοῦ ᵀ κληρονομήσουσιν. 11 καὶ ταῦτά τινες ἦτε. ἀλλ' ἀπελούσασθε, ἀλλ' ἡγιάσθητε, ἀλλ' ἐδικαιώθητε ἐν τῷ ὀνόματι τοῦ κυρίου ⌜Ἰησοῦ Χριστοῦ⌝ καὶ ἐν τῷ πνεύματι τοῦ θεοῦ ἡμῶν.

Lawsuits among the Corinthians—A Sign of Spiritual Degeneracy

1 When one of you has a grievance against another, does he dare go to law before the unrighteous instead of the saints? 2 Or do you not know that the saints will judge the world? And if the world is to be judged by you, are you incompetent to try trivial cases? 3 Do you not know that we are to judge angels? How much more, then, matters pertaining to this life! 4 So if you have such cases, why do you lay them before those who have no standing in the church? 5 I say this to your shame. Can it be that there is no one among you wise enough to settle a dispute between the brothers, 6 but brother goes to law against brother, and that before unbelievers? 7 To have lawsuits at all with one another is already a defeat for you. Why not rather suffer wrong? Why not rather be defrauded? 8 But you yourselves wrong and defraud—even your own brothers!
9 Or do you not know that the unrighteous will not inherit the kingdom of God? Do not be deceived: neither the sexually immoral, nor idolaters, nor adulterers, nor men who practice homosexuality, 10 nor thieves, nor the greedy, nor drunkards, nor revilers, nor swindlers will inherit the kingdom of God. 11 And such were some of you. But you were washed, you were sanctified, you were justified in the name of the Lord Jesus Christ and by the Spirit of our God.

This chapter belongs to the same rhetorical unit with the previous one (1 Cor 5). It opens with the expression of surprise in disappointment over another practice of some of the Corinthians. The excessive use of rhetorical questions in this division is indicative of Paul's astonishment and perplexity. Beginning a new discourse with the following ten successive rhetorical questions directed against the readers is indicative of the number of issues at stake:

(1) Τολμᾷ τις ὑμῶν πρᾶγμα ἔχων πρὸς τὸν ἕτερον κρίνεσθαι ἐπὶ τῶν ἀδίκων καὶ οὐχὶ ἐπὶ τῶν ἁγίων;

(2) ἢ οὐκ οἴδατε ὅτι οἱ ἅγιοι τὸν κόσμον κρινοῦσιν;

(3) καὶ εἰ ἐν ὑμῖν κρίνεται ὁ κόσμος, ἀνάξιοί ἐστε κριτηρίων ἐλαχίστων;

(4) οὐκ οἴδατε ὅτι ἀγγέλους κρινοῦμεν, μήτι γε βιωτικά;

(5) βιωτικὰ μὲν οὖν κριτήρια ἐὰν ἔχητε, τοὺς ἐξουθενημένους ἐν τῇ ἐκκλησίᾳ, τούτους καθίζετε;

(6) πρὸς ἐντροπὴν ὑμῖν λέγω. οὕτως οὐκ ἔνι ἐν ὑμῖν οὐδεὶς σοφός, ὃς δυνήσεται διακρῖναι ἀνὰ μέσον τοῦ ἀδελφοῦ αὐτοῦ;

(7) ἀλλὰ ἀδελφὸς μετὰ ἀδελφοῦ κρίνεται καὶ τοῦτο ἐπὶ ἀπίστων;

(8) Ἤδη μὲν [οὖν] ὅλως ἥττημα ὑμῖν ἐστιν ὅτι κρίματα ἔχετε μεθ' ἑαυτῶν. διὰ τί οὐχὶ μᾶλλον ἀδικεῖσθε;

(9) διὰ τί οὐχὶ μᾶλλον ἀποστερεῖσθε;

(10) ἀλλ' ὑμεῖς ἀδικεῖτε καὶ ἀποστερεῖτε, καὶ τοῦτο ἀδελφούς. Ἢ οὐκ οἴδατε ὅτι ἄδικοι θεοῦ βασιλείαν οὐ κληρονομήσουσιν; (1 Cor 6:1–9)

By placing τολμᾷ τις . . . (does one dare. . . ?) first in the sentence, Paul highlights the surprising boldness of the Corinthians in taking their internal cases before unbelievers for settlement (1 Cor 6:1). The first of the ten rhetorical questions plays a dual role since it introduces the problem and establishes the inappropriateness of believers taking one another to unbelievers to have their cases settled. The main concern is expressed in "before the unrighteous and not the righteous" (ἐπὶ τῶν ἀδίκων καὶ οὐχὶ ἐπὶ τῶν ἁγίων;)? The second rhetorical question suggests their ignorance accounts for the conduct in question. If they knew that they would judge the world (οὐκ οἴδατε ὅτι οἱ ἅγιοι τὸν κόσμον κρινοῦσιν [1 Cor 6:2]), they would not take their matters to unbelievers for settlement. Paul's designation of the unbelievers before whom the Corinthians brought their cases as "the unrighteous" (τῶν ἀδίκων) shows the folly of the readers' action as righteous people. The irony is meant to heighten the folly of their action. What follows is a series of arguments to prove that the readers have acted out of folly and ignorance on the matter. The effect of Paul's repeated use of "Do you not know . . . ?" is significant in this light.

In the third rhetorical question, ἐν ὑμῖν should be considered a dative expressing agency. The dative is also meant to signify the sphere of the authority where the judgment of the world is to take place, that is, among the saints. The nominative ὁ κόσμος makes the world the subject upon which κρίνεται (is to be judged) acts as a passive verb. The third rhetorical question has two parts (1 Cor 6:2)—an if clause and a question tag. The if clause establishes the fact that the saints will judge the world (a restatement of the preceding rhetorical question). The question tag presents the task of judging the world in the if clause as a greater task for which judging issues among the saints becomes the least of cases (κριτηρίων ἐλαχίστων). The argument is *a fortiori* and argues from the greater to the lesser (*a maiore ad minus*). That is, "If you are going to judge major cases such as of the world, are you unworthy (ἀνάξιοί ἐστε) to judge minor cases among you?"

The fourth rhetorical question is parallel and an amplification of the third. It comes in two parts—one main question and its implication by extension. It wonders if the Corinthians do not know that they would judge angels (οὐκ οἴδατε ἀγγέλους κρινοῦμεν [1 Cor 6:3]). This is followed by the implication, an extension of the question—"not to mention ordinary matters" (μήτι γε βιωτικά;)? The extension of the *question* establishes the readers' utter failure in being capable of dealing with ordinary matters. Like the preceding (third) rhetorical question, the first part provides the basis for Paul to present the cases among the saints as lesser issues of this life (βιωτικά) compared with the angels they would judge. Here is another *a maiore ad minus* type of *a fortiori* argument. On the saints judging the world, Datiri provides passages that suggest that the saints will sit in judgment with Christ in the last day (Dan 7:22; Matt 19:28; Luke 22:30; Rev 3:21; 20:4).[1] Keener gives some ancient sources that touch on the subject of believers judging the world.[2] On judging angels, however, Keener finds it rare at the time and holds that it could be Paul's extrapolation.[3] Fee suggests that believers judging angels reflects an "apocalyptic motif" about the "judgment of fallen angels."[4] Rhetorically, Paul needs such statements that hold up the greater roles believers are able to play in judgment in order to heighten the readers' failure to judge little matters among them.

The fifth question comes as an amplification of their failure as mentioned in the fourth question. Given the greater cases they will judge, should they present the lesser cases of life among them (βιωτικὰ μὲν οὖν κριτήρια ἐὰν ἔχητε; 1 Cor 6:4) before those who have no standing in the church [unbelievers] for settlement (τοὺς ἐξουθενημένους ἐν τῇ ἐκκλησίᾳ, τούτους καθίζετε)? That is to say, while emphasizing the insignificance of the cases they have among them, the fifth question also stresses the inappropriateness of their action in terms of the people before whom they lay their cases for settlement. This recalls Paul's earlier sentiment in 1 Corinthians 6:1 ("before the unrighteous," ἐπὶ τῶν ἀδίκων). It comes as repeated emphasis (the fourth instance of him making similar statements) on the incongruous act of going before unbelievers with little cases. Such an emphasis expresses Paul's perplexity and shock as well as his felt need to treat his readers as infants who must have all solid foods turned into liquid for their consumption. Barton indicates that the practice of settling disputes within by members of a group was widespread. He mentions that Deuteronomy

1. Datiri, "1 Corinthians," 1383.
2. *1 En.* 95:3; 1QpHab 5.4; 4Q418 69 II, 7–8; *Sipre Deut.* 47.2.8
3. Keener, *1–2 Corinthians*, 53.
4. Fee, *First Epistle to the Corinthians*, 234.

Wisdom, Knowledge, and Spirituality in Self-defense

1:9–18 and 16:18–20 urged that judges be appointed from among the people to settle disputes. He also mentions the Qumran community, the Jews in the diaspora, cult groups, and voluntary associations in the Roman Empire as some of those who followed similar practices.[5] Keener makes a similar observation by stating that some resident alien communities and philosophical groups resented taking matters to the law court and preferred settling matters within their group at the time.[6]

Datiri holds that Paul's advice to the Corinthian believers is to the effect that they should rather appoint as judges even men of little account in the church (6:4). He argues that the word translated as "men of little account" (ἐξουθενημένους) is similar to the word translated as "despised" in 1 Corinthians 1:28. He maintains that, "No matter how insignificant these people may be in the church, Paul thinks it is better to take disputes to them than to unbelievers."[7] Contrary to Datiri's view, Paul was not referring to any insignificant members of the church. His concern was that the unbelievers before whom the Corinthians had presented their cases for settlement have no standing in the church, the very reason why the Corinthians should have refrained from what they did. "The people with no standing in the church" are therefore not "despised people" within the church, but the very unbelievers before whom the Corinthians had laid their cases for judgment. Paul's aversion to views that suggest that some are insignificant members of the church further makes Datiri's view unlikely (see 1 Cor 12:13–27).

In the sixth rhetorical question, two things should be noted concerning the statement preceding the question tag (1 Cor 6:5): while πρὸς is used to introduce the purpose for the rhetorical question, the accusative ἐντροπὴν makes "shame" its expressed object. The succeeding question is then what is said to their shame. Paul asks, "Can it be that there is not one wise person among you who is able to arbitrate between his brothers" (οὕτως οὐκ ἔνι ἐν ὑμῖν οὐδεὶς σοφός, ὃς δυνήσεται διακρῖναι ἀνὰ μέσον τοῦ ἀδελφοῦ αὐτοῦ)? While this particular question is what is said to their shame, the entire set of ten questions should also be seen as such (what is said to their shame). The shame in their failure to identify a wise person to settle disputes among them is intensified by its repeated depiction throughout the ten rhetorical questions. Their failure in the test of little cases is also magnified against

---

5. Barton, "1 Corinthians," 1326.
6. Keener, *1–2 Corinthians*, 53.
7. Datiri, "1 Corinthians," 1383.

the background of the major cases they are to judge, which involve angels and the world. Wise as the Corinthians saw themselves to be, their failure to identify one wise person capable of settling disputes among them (ὃς δυνήσεται διακρῖναι ἀνὰ μέσον) is an indictment on them. Pointing this out is certainly to their shame. By this, Paul calls to question the wisdom on which the readers had relied; that wisdom had not made them wise after all. In this sense, Paul incorporates *pathos* into his argument with an appeal to shame.

The introductory ἀλλὰ (but) of the seventh question expresses contrast between what is expected of the readers—finding a wise person among them to settle their disputes, and what they actually do—that is, instead, "a brother takes another to be judged before unbelievers" (ἀδελφὸς μετὰ ἀδελφοῦ κρίνεται καὶ τοῦτο ἐπὶ ἀπίστων, 1 Cor 6:6). The demonstrative τοῦτο (this) points back to the act of bringing one another before unbelievers, an act which καὶ (and) and τοῦτο (this) draw emphatic attention to.

A statement that establishes the presence of lawsuits among the Corinthians as defeat for them (κρίματα ἔχετε μεθ' ἑαυτῶν ἥττημα ὑμῖν ἐστιν) precedes the eighth rhetorical question (1 Cor 6:7). With this defeat in the background, Paul asks the readers, "Why not rather be wronged" (μᾶλλον ἀδικεῖσθε)? This is followed by the ninth question which comes as commoratio to the preceding question, asking the same question in another way—that is, "Why not rather be defrauded" (μᾶλλον ἀποστερεῖσθε)? If being wronged or defrauded is better than having lawsuits against one another, then having lawsuits against one another must be very evil (1 Cor 6:7).

In other words, Paul presents lawsuits against one another as more evil than being wronged or cheated. The readers' choice of the greater evil is therefore indicative of the poverty of their sense of judgment as infants in Christ. Paul Marsh observes that, "'Why not rather be wronged . . . be cheated?' reflects the law of Christ; (see Mt 5:39–41)."[8] The point in Paul's concern about the lawsuits was that the church was taking unpleasant internal affairs to the public. This amounted to shaming both the individuals concerned and the church.[9]

With ἀλλὰ, again, Paul introduces another contrast which precedes the tenth rhetorical question. Instead of accepting being defrauded or cheated, the readers rather cheat and defraud (ἀλλὰ ὑμεῖς ἀδικεῖτε καὶ ἀποστερεῖτε), and do this to their own brothers (καὶ τοῦτο ἀδελφούς, 1 Cor 6:8). Socrates

---

8. Marsh, "1 Corinthians," 1356.
9. Fee, *First Epistle to the Corinthians*, 237, 239.

Wisdom, Knowledge, and Spirituality in Self-defense

is said to have stated that it is better to suffer wrong than to do it. On the basis of this, Barton suggests (in agreement with Hays[10]) that the believers "are shown once again to be not as 'wise' as they think they are."[11] Barton further indicates that "the challenge of the 'hidden wisdom' of Paul's own practice" lay in the background when he challenged the readers to accept being wronged or defrauded instead of taking one another to the law court. Paul had indicated, "when reviled, we bless; when persecuted, we endure; when slandered, we speak kindly" (1 Cor 4:12–13).[12] Barton concludes that the conduct of the Corinthians falls short of "the best of pagan wisdom" as well as "the example of Paul in imitation of Christ."[13]

The tone of the tenth rhetorical question, "Or do you not know that the unrighteous will not inherit the kingdom of God?" (Ἢ οὐκ οἴδατε ὅτι ἄδικοι θεοῦ βασιλείαν οὐ κληρονομήσουσιν; μὴ πλανᾶσθε. [1 Cor 6:9]) has two effects: while casting doubt on their knowledge, it also implies that the readers are unrighteous by their involvement in the act in question. Once again, Paul does not leave anything to chance. He wants to ensure that his unspiritual and infant audience understands what he means. For this purpose, the succeeding enumeratio comes in handy as a list of specific people who are the unrighteous:

> μὴ πλανᾶσθε.
> οὔτε πόρνοι
> οὔτε εἰδωλολάτραι
> οὔτε μοιχοὶ
> οὔτε μαλακοὶ
> οὔτε ἀρσενοκοῖται
> οὔτε κλέπται
> οὔτε πλεονέκται,
> οὐ μέθυσοι,
> οὐ λοίδοροι,
> οὐχ ἅρπαγες
> βασιλείαν θεοῦ κληρονομήσουσιν (1 Cor 6:9b–10)

The introductory "Do not be deceived" (μὴ πλανᾶσθε) suggests that the subsequent list is meant to correct their misguided view of those worthy of the kingdom of God. The anaphora in the repetition of the conjunction

---

10. Hays, *First Corinthians*, 95–96.
11. Barton, "1 Corinthians," 1326.
12. Barton, "1 Corinthians," 1326.
13. Barton, "1 Corinthians," 1326.

οὔτε (neither) seven successive times in the initial position of each noun phrase is worth noting. The rhyme in the repetition of οι and αι in uneven alternation in the end of the phrases draws attention to the list with its literary beauty. The effect of the particle οὐ (not) repeated three times (with its form, οὐχ [not] in the third instance) has the same negative effect as οὔτε (neither). The implication is that none of those mentioned in the list will inherit the kingdom of God. The phrase "Will not inherit the kingdom of God" (οὐχ ... βασιλείαν θεοῦ κληρονομήσουσιν) in 1 Corinthians 6:10 forms an inclusio with "Will not inherit the kingdom of God" (θεοῦ βασιλείαν οὐ κληρονομήσουσιν) in 1 Corinthians 6:9. This inclusio answers the question, "Who are the unrighteous who will not inherit the kingdom of God?" Paul's answer lying between the two bracketing phrases of the inclusio is: "Neither the sexually immoral (πόρνοι), nor idolaters (εἰδωλολάτραι), nor adulterers (μοιχοί), nor men who practice homosexuality (μαλακοί, ἀρσενοκοῖται),[14] nor thieves (κλέπται), nor the greedy (πλεονέκται), nor drunkards (μέθυσοι), nor slanderers (λοίδοροι), nor swindlers (ἅρπαγες)."

On not inheriting the kingdom of God, Fee notes the difficulty of some scholars in conceiving that God's children can be disinherited. Such scholars consequently consider the warning hypothetical. Fee's disagreement with such scholars is premised on the view that the readers were involved in acts that belong to the realm of the condemned, acts which are inconsistent with them as people who do not belong to the realm of the condemned.[15]

A list of three divine acts is subsequently provided to establish why the readers' involvement in those unrighteous acts is inconsistent with who they are.

> ἀλλ' ἀπελούσασθε,
> ἀλλ' ἡγιάσθητε,
> ἀλλ' ἐδικαιώθητε
> ἐν τῷ ὀνόματι τοῦ κυρίου Ἰησοῦ Χριστοῦ καὶ ἐν τῷ πνεύματι τοῦ θεοῦ ἡμῶν. (1 Cor 6:11)

The polysyndeton of the repeated conjunction ἀλλ' (but) is intended to give the divine acts cumulative effect. At the same time, the anaphora of the repeated ἀλλ' (but) ensures the needed sound effect for the attention the enumeratio deserves. The list of the divine acts enables Paul to establish the

14. The ESV explains that the two Greek terms translated as "men who practice homosexuality" refer to the passive and active partners in consensual homosexual acts.

15. Fee, *First Epistle to the Corinthians*, 242.

contrast between the readers as people "washed" (ἀπελούσασθε), "sanctified" (ἡγιάσθητε), and "justified" (ἐδικαιώθητε) on the one hand, and the unrighteous people on the other. With instrumental dative, Paul identifies the name of the Lord Jesus Christ (ἐν τῷ ὀνόματι τοῦ κυρίου Ἰησοῦ Χριστοῦ) and the Spirit of our God (καὶ ἐν τῷ πνεύματι τοῦ θεοῦ ἡμῶν) as the means by which these divine acts were accomplished.

With this, Paul supplies the incentive and reason why the readers should not continue to walk in deception and unrighteousness—that is, they were washed, sanctified, and justified from these unrighteous lifestyles. This concluding part establishes four things: (1) it recalls what they were before coming into Christ, (2) it establishes what God did for them through the Christ event, (3) it calls attention to the result of the divine act through Christ, and (4) it establishes the indicative on the basis of which they should not walk in the deception of the unrighteous acts in question.

How does the list of unrighteous people relate to the issues addressed so far? Whereas the thieves, the greedy and the swindlers relate to actions that prompted the lawsuits,[16] the sexually immoral, the adulterers, and the homosexuals relate to the incident of incest.[17] Idolaters and drunkards may not have immediate connection with any of the issues discussed so far. In these two particular instances, the apostle is perhaps looking ahead to some of the issues yet to be addressed, such as the case of food offered to idols and the abuse of the Lord's Supper.

The accusing and judgmental tone of this rhetorical division makes it forensic. While the overriding mode of appeal is *logos*, it incorporates *pathos* with appeal to shame. It also employs contrasts to establish the readers'

---

16. Paul's insistence that they should rather be cheated or defrauded than take one another to court indicates that the lawsuits involves these acts.

17. Barton thinks greed lies at the center of the sin of incest and the lawsuits. He maintains "The offender is not only immoral but greedy: he has married for financial gain and the security and social advantage that go with it. In passing, this would explain why, in the lists of vices in 5:10 and 11, 'sexual immorality' (i.e., marrying within the laws of prohibited degrees) is followed immediately by 'greed.' It is not at all impossible, then that the lawsuits referred to in 6:1–11 are related in some measure to conflicting property interests arising out of the case of incest and others like it" (Barton, "1 Corinthians," 1325–26). It should, however, be pointed out that, given the maxims Paul attacks as responsible for the incest, as discussed below, the financial gain and security as the reason for both the sexual offense and the lawsuits is remote. If there is a relationship between the lawsuits and the sexually immoral act, it must be found in something else since greed is hardly put forth as a cause in Paul's argument. My suggestion is that the nexus between the two acts should be found in what they share in common—their public affront to the church.

Lawsuits among the Corinthians—A Sign of Spiritual Degeneracy

failure in their actions as against their expected conduct. The extensive use of rhetorical questions in this rhetorical division reveals Paul's amazement and shock at the conduct of the Corinthians. His use of ten rhetorical questions in succession is meant to show the readers' utter failure in taking their internal cases before unbelievers. His employment of irony heightens the folly of their actions, while the use of *a maiore ad minus* enables him to portray the misery of their failure in the least of things. Parallel structures are employed in enumeratio to achieve amplification in some instances. Commoratio is also used to restate a rhetorical question that highlights lawsuits among the readers as worse than being wronged or defrauded. There is also the use of polysyndeton and anaphora for repetition and *emphasis* that establish the cumulative effect of the enumeratio, which lists the divine acts that contrast the readers with unrighteous people.

REFUTATION OF MAXIMS AND AFFIRMATION OF THE BODY AS THE LORD'S

1 Corinthians 6:12–19

> 12 Πάντα μοι ἔξεστιν ἀλλ' οὐ πάντα συμφέρει. πάντα μοι ἔξεστιν ἀλλ' οὐκ ἐγὼ ἐξουσιασθήσομαι ὑπό τινος. 13 τὰ βρώματα τῇ κοιλίᾳ καὶ ἡ κοιλία τοῖς βρώμασιν, ὁ δὲ θεὸς καὶ ταύτην καὶ ταῦτα καταργήσει. τὸ δὲ σῶμα οὐ τῇ πορνείᾳ ἀλλὰ τῷ κυρίῳ, καὶ ὁ κύριος τῷ σώματι. 14 ὁ δὲ θεὸς καὶ τὸν κύριον ἤγειρεν καὶ ἡμᾶς ἐξεγερεῖ διὰ τῆς δυνάμεως αὐτοῦ. 15 οὐκ οἴδατε ὅτι τὰ σώματα ὑμῶν μέλη Χριστοῦ ἐστιν; ἄρας οὖν τὰ μέλη τοῦ Χριστοῦ ποιήσω πόρνης μέλη; μὴ γένοιτο. 16 [ἢ] οὐκ οἴδατε ὅτι ὁ κολλώμενος τῇ πόρνῃ ἓν σῶμά ἐστιν; ἔσονται γάρ, φησίν, οἱ δύο εἰς σάρκα μίαν. 17 ὁ δὲ κολλώμενος τῷ κυρίῳ ἓν πνεῦμά ἐστιν.

> 12 "All things are lawful for me," but not all things are helpful. "All things are lawful for me," but I will not be dominated by anything. 13 "Food is meant for the stomach and the stomach for food"—and God will destroy both one and the other. The body is not meant for sexual immorality, but for the Lord, and the Lord for the body. 14 And God raised the Lord and will also raise us up by his power. 15 Do you not know that your bodies are members of Christ? Shall I then take the members of Christ and make them members of a prostitute? Never! 16 Or do you not know that he who is joined to a prostitute becomes one body with her? For, as it is written, "The two will become one flesh." 17 But he who is joined to the Lord becomes one spirit with him.

Wisdom, Knowledge, and Spirituality in Self-defense

This rhetorical division is the *refutatio* and is forensic. It finds serious fault with their use of the maxims underlying their conduct in sexual immorality and lawsuits. Paul's return to the subject of sexual immorality gives the indication that he treats the two issues—sexual immorality and lawsuits against fellow believers—as a single rhetorical unit. In a style typical of Paul, he takes up their maxims (supporting claims for their actions) and raises caveats against them. His caveats come in antithetical clauses usually introduced by "but" (ἀλλά) or its equivalent. Conzelmann rightly suggests that, going by the way the first maxim is introduced and its repetition in 1 Corinthians 10:23, "it [the maxim] was known and used in Corinth."[18] On this basis, he contends that sexual immorality in Corinth was not just a legacy of pagan way of life, but it had "an active/speculative justification on the ground of this basic principle" of the maxim.[19] Keener's observation corroborates Conzelmann's point. He notes that in spite of the general attitude that looked down on the practice of incest, "some philosophers regarded incest as unobjectionable."[20] These observations provide grounds for assuming that philosophical concepts such as this must have accounted for why the Corinthians were indifferent to the sin of incest.

On the two caveats that are raised against this maxim, each is preceded by the maxim. The repetition of the maxim must be significant since the two caveats could have come together against the first statement of the maxim. The deliberate repetition holds up the maxim for repeated treatment of caution and contempt. Paul finds parallelism a useful rhetorical device for presenting the maxim and the two caveats:

A Πάντα μοι ἔξεστιν ἀλλ' οὐ πάντα συμφέρει.
A¹ πάντα μοι ἔξεστιν ἀλλ' οὐκ ἐγὼ ἐξουσιασθήσομαι ὑπό τινος (1 Cor 6:12)

The first, "but not all things are beneficial" (ἀλλ' οὐ πάντα συμφέρει) confronts the readers with the weakness of their knowledge that leads them into acts that are not beneficial. The second, "but I will not be mastered by anything" (ἀλλ' οὐκ ἐγὼ ἐξουσιασθήσομαι ὑπό τινος) confronts them with the enslaving effect of their use of the maxim, and hence the weakness of their knowledge. Without doubt, the Corinthians had used this prominent

---

18. Conzelmann, *Commentary on the First Epistle*, 251.

19. Conzelmann, *Commentary on the First Epistle*, 108. Fee also considers the first maxim, "All things are lawful" (Πάντα μοι ἔξεστιν) as "almost certainly a Corinthian theological slogan" (Fee, *First Epistle to the Corinthians*, 251).

20. Keener, *1–2 Corinthians*, 49.

Lawsuits among the Corinthians—A Sign of Spiritual Degeneracy

maxim to claim lawfulness of their actions in the two despicable acts addressed in 1 Corinthians 5–6. Paul's polemic against the maxim as part of his response to the two despicable acts undoubtedly indicates the maxim's role in those acts. Moreover, the fact that the readers were proud in spite of these contemptible acts explains how they had considered their actions lawful, understandably, on the basis of this maxim.

The second maxim is "food for the stomach and the stomach for food" (τὰ βρώματα τῇ κοιλίᾳ καὶ ἡ κοιλία τοῖς βρώμασιν). The chiasm of both the maxim and Paul's caveat is a matter of interest:

A τὰ βρώματα
  B τῇ κοιλίᾳ καὶ
  B¹ ἡ κοιλία
A¹ τοῖς βρώμασιν (1 Cor 6:13a)

The ABB¹A¹ chiasm presents us with *food-stomach-stomach-food* structure in which the stomach is sandwiched by food. This structure stresses the mutual and reciprocal purpose of each for the other.

Following the chiasm of the maxim is Paul's caveat, also presented in another chiasm:

A ὁ δὲ θεὸς
  B καὶ ταύτην
  B¹ καὶ ταῦτα
A¹ καταργήσει (1 Cor 6:13b)

The structure presents food and stomach as the objects (B and B¹) of God's action, and these are sandwiched between God and God's action of destruction (A and A¹). The singular and plural demonstratives (ταύτην [this] and ταῦτα [these]) in the caveat are significant as they refer back to the singular "stomach" (κοιλίᾳ) and the plural "food" (βρώματα and βρώμασιν) in the maxim. Both food and stomach are therefore caught between God and the divine act of destruction in the chiasm of the caveat. The adversative particle δὲ functions like ἀλλ' in the maxim, making the divine action antithetical to the view represented in the maxim.

What exactly was this particular maxim used for? Paul's next statement suggests, and rightly so, that it was used as the basis for giving their bodies to sexual immorality. Holding that food was meant for the stomach and the stomach for food, the Corinthians extended the principle to imply that the body was meant of sexual immorality (and the things it craved for). Paul therefore picks the idea up for correction in the emphatic statement:

"but the body is not meant for sexual immorality but to the Lord" (τὸ δὲ σῶμα οὐ τῇ πορνείᾳ ἀλλὰ τῷ κυρίῳ). The presence of δὲ is significant, though the ESV, HCSB, and ISV do not translate it. Its antithetical relevance comes up in translations like ASV, BBE, and NIV as "however." The KJV's and NKJV's translation of it as "now" fails to carry the antithetical force of δὲ. NLT's rendering: "But you can't say that our bodies were made for sexual immorality" is explicit on the intended antithetical function of δὲ. The presentation of the *refutation* of the "stomach for food" maxim in another chiasm points to the importance of the rhetorical device for Paul in his response to the sexual misconduct. The chiasm is *the body-the Lord-the Lord-the body* structure:

A τὸ δὲ σῶμα οὐ τῇ πορνείᾳ
  B ἀλλὰ τῷ κυρίῳ,
  B¹ καὶ ὁ κύριος
A¹ τῷ σώματι (1 Cor 6:13c)

The emphasis of the chiasm is on whom the body is meant for (the Lord). Its essence is the *refutation* of the notion that the body is meant for sexual immorality (οὐ τῇ πορνείᾳ). On the "stomach and food" maxim, the following explanation by Datiri is helpful:

> The Greeks were inclined to despise the human body. One of their proverbs stated, 'The body is a tomb,' and the Stoic philosopher Epictetus said, 'I am a poor soul shackled to a corpse.' This attitude produced two different ways of treating the body. Some Greeks adopted a rigorous asceticism in an attempt to control the body and humiliate its desires and instincts. Others, however, argued that since the body was totally worthless and only the spirit was important, it did not matter what the body did. Clearly, the Corinthians were inclined to the latter view. They felt free to indulge their bodily desires, arguing from the analogy that food is intended for the stomach and the stomach is intended for food.[21]

On Paul's caveat to the maxim, Fee observes,

> The affirmation stands in bold contrast to the Corinthian view of spirituality, which looked for 'spiritual' salvation that would finally be divested of the body. Lying behind this form of spirituality is a Greek view of the world that placed little or no value on the material order. Out of such a view developed the idea of the 'immortality of the soul,' that is, that the spirit is somehow immortal, but

---

21. Datiri, "1 Corinthians," 1384.

the body, along with the rest of the material order, is destined for destruction.²²

Further to his argument, Paul points out two things about the body that makes its use in sexual immorality evil. Firstly, he maintains that just as God raised the Lord (ὁ δὲ θεὸς καὶ τὸν κύριον ἤγειρεν), he will also raise us through his power (καὶ ἡμᾶς ἐξεγερεῖ διὰ τῆς δυνάμεως αὐτοῦ). Though the body is not mentioned here, the reference to the Lord's resurrection suggests a similar resurrection that involves the body. Secondly, Paul establishes by means of a rhetorical question that the readers' bodies are members of Christ (οὐκ οἴδατε ὅτι τὰ σώματα ὑμῶν μέλη Χριστοῦ ἐστιν;) These two indicatives provide the background against which the horrible nature of sexual immorality is going to be highlighted in the following hypophora:

The question: ἄρας οὖν τὰ μέλη τοῦ Χριστοῦ ποιήσω πόρνης μέλη;
The answer: μὴ γένοιτο.

That is,

The question: "Shall I then take the members of Christ and make them the members of a prostitute?"
The answer: "May it never happen!" (1 Cor 6:16a)

His use of the first-person singular in the question of the *ypophora* has the rhetorical effect of inviting the readers to judge the impropriety of the sin in question as though they were not the culprits. This is another example of Paul's creative and rhetorical use of pronouns. He indicates what the Corinthians have done using a pronoun that appears to point to him. Though he had provided the background against which the inaptness of the act should be obvious, he nonetheless goes ahead to answer the question. This way of dealing with the readers is consistent with Paul's rating of the Corinthians as babes in Christ. Even the obvious answer should be pointed out to them.

The succeeding quotation acts as *enumeratio*, giving further explanation to the inappropriateness of sexual immorality:

A ἔσονται γάρ,
  B φησίν, οἱ δύο εἰς
A¹ σάρκα μίαν. (1 Cor 6:16b)

---

22. Fee, *First Epistle to the Corinthians*, 257.

Wisdom, Knowledge, and Spirituality in Self-defense

The ABA¹ *chiastic* structure places at both ends the result of joining oneself to a prostitute. At the beginning is the future middle ἔσονται (will become, A), and at the end, σάρκα μίαν (one flesh, A¹). The two (οἱ δύο) is sandwiched between the split result, so that becoming one flesh may be stressed at the end. Paul follows this up with a contrast in the case of one who is joined to the Lord (ὁ δὲ κολλώμενος τῷ κυρίῳ). The adversative "but" (δὲ) stresses the contrast between the act (joining oneself to the Lord [κολλώμενος τῷ κυρίῳ]) and its result (being one spirit [with the Lord], ἓν πνεῦμά ἐστιν) on the one hand, and the joining of oneself to a prostitute with its result on the other.

Together, the two contrasts—joining oneself to a prostitute and joining oneself to the Lord—with their results, form yet another chiasm. The chiasm assigns theological reasons against which the gravity of sexual immorality is highlighted. Thus,

A οὐκ οἴδατε ὅτι τὰ σώματα ὑμῶν μέλη Χριστοῦ ἐστιν;
   B ἄρας οὖν τὰ μέλη τοῦ Χριστοῦ ποιήσω πόρνης μέλη; μὴ γένοιτο.
   B¹ [ἢ] οὐκ οἴδατε ὅτι ὁ κολλώμενος τῇ πόρνῃ ἓν σῶμά ἐστιν; ...
A¹ ὁ δὲ κολλώμενος τῷ κυρίῳ ἓν πνεῦμά ἐστιν.

A and A¹ speak to one thing: What the Corinthians are by divine initiative. They are the members of Christ (A), and if they remain joined to him they are one spirit with him (A¹). Sandwiched between the two are the statements of their inappropriate act and its result. As they join themselves to prostitutes (B), they become one flesh with the prostitute (B¹). The appropriateness of members of Christ remaining joined to the Lord and becoming one spirit with him is given both the first and last attention in the *chiastic* structure. This places the emphasis on the appropriate act. The identification of the believers as members of Christ is instructive. It is this identity of believers which makes the sin of sexual immorality spiritually destructive.

This rhetorical division witnesses the use of repetition in parallelism for the purpose of modifying maxims in *refutation*. With rhetorical questions Paul calls attention to important points that establish the seriousness of the negative spiritual effect their involvement in sexual immorality has. Paul's use of a quotation in enumeratio enables him to present an imagery of union that helps him to depict the implication of sexual immorality for one's spiritual life. His creative use of the first-person singular enables him to depersonalize the sin of sexual immorality for the readers in order for them to assess its inappropriateness for believers as judges with no interest in the matter. Nonetheless, the readers are treated as people who cannot be trusted to make the right assessment. He therefore employs hypophora by which the right answer is given. The use of chiasm in this division is remarkable. It has instances in which smaller *chiastic* structures are built into a bigger chiasm. This is particularly used to emphasize the sinfulness of sexual immorality as sin against the body of Christ.

CONCLUSION AND PRACTICAL IMPLICATIONS OF THE ARGUMENT

1 Corinthians 6:18–20

> 18 Φεύγετε τὴν πορνείαν. πᾶν ἁμάρτημα ὃ ἐὰν ποιήσῃ ἄνθρωπος ἐκτὸς τοῦ σώματός ἐστιν. ὁ δὲ πορνεύων εἰς τὸ ἴδιον σῶμα ἁμαρτάνει. 19 ἢ οὐκ οἴδατε ὅτι τὸ σῶμα ὑμῶν ναὸς τοῦ ἐν ὑμῖν ἁγίου πνεύματός ἐστιν οὗ ἔχετε ἀπὸ θεοῦ, καὶ οὐκ ἐστὲ ἑαυτῶν; 20 ἠγοράσθητε γὰρ τιμῆς. δοξάσατε δὴ τὸν θεὸν ἐν τῷ σώματι ὑμῶν.

> 18 Flee from sexual immorality. Every other sin a person commits is outside the body, but the sexually immoral person sins against his own body. 19 Or do you not know that your body is a temple of the Holy Spirit within you, whom you have from God? You are not your own, 20 for you were bought with a price. So glorify God in your body.

Paul now concludes with a peroratio which brings out the essence of his argument in the second major rhetorical subunit. This comes in the form of two imperatives between which he provides a series of statements in amplification of the imperatives. The second-person plural "flee" (φεύγετε, 1 Cor 6:18) in the introductory imperative confronts the readers with what they should do with respect to sexual immorality (τὴν πορνείαν). Then the concluding imperative exhorts them to "glorify God" in their bodies (δοξάσατε δὴ τὸν θεὸν ἐν τῷ σώματι ὑμῶν, 1 Cor 6:20). Paul's use of the particle δή (therefore) shows the urgency of the imperative as a deduction from the preceding statements.

The intervening amplification between the two imperatives supplies the reason for the two imperatives. It comes in the form of *metanoia* in which sexual immorality is described as a sin against one's own body (ὁ δὲ πορνεύων εἰς τὸ ἴδιον σῶμα ἁμαρτάνει) only for the body to be described as not one's own (καὶ οὐκ ἐστὲ ἑαυτῶν, 1 Cor 6:19c) but the temple of the Holy

Wisdom, Knowledge, and Spirituality in Self-defense

Spirit (ναὸς τοῦ ἐν ὑμῖν ἁγίου πνεύματός ἐστιν, 1 Cor 6:19b). Two important questions emerge here—in what sense is sexual immorality a sin against ones body, and whose is the body? Following Hans Lietzmann, C. K. Barrett observes, "In fact, gluttony, drunkenness, self-mutilation and suicide also are crimes against one's own body."[23] Fee observes "the statement [. . . sins against his own body] has long exercised Christians, who see other sins as also 'against one's body.'"[24] A discussion of the suggested meaning to this expression is narrowed down to two of the most plausible sins out of twenty or thirty. The first considers the expression as a slogan of the Corinthians, which is qualified by Paul (1 Cor 6:12–13). It is paraphrased as "All sin, whatever it is that a man commits, is outside the body, you say (or, you say?) To the contrary, there is one sin in particular that is against one's own physical body, namely sexual immorality."[25] The second sees the statement as coming from Paul, which should be understood in terms of the theological implication of joining a member of Christ to a prostitute and becoming one with her.[26]

But why did Paul mention sin against one's own body here? He used it as an important rhetorical tool to highlight the seriousness of sexual immorality by presenting the body as more than one's own. The denial of the body as one's own after what appears to say it is one's own, amounts to the refutation of a concept of the body that led to its misuse in sexual immorality as though it had no effect on the spirit of the readers, which the readers believed belongs to the Lord. It meant that the body was not the Lord's, but one's own, and one could do as one pleased with it. Sin against one's body is therefore held up here only to be refuted by the claim that it is rather a sin against the body of Christ. Therefore, whether or not there are other sins that work against the body should not lessen the rhetorical effect of the statement in Paul's argument.

The two clauses in the succeeding question function in two ways: they question the knowledge of the readers and establish the fact that their bodies are individually the temples of the Holy Spirit they received from God. Thus, "Or do you not know that your body is a temple of the Holy Spirit in you which you have from God, and that you are not your own (ἢ οὐκ οἴδατε ὅτι τὸ σῶμα ὑμῶν ναὸς τοῦ ἐν ὑμῖν ἁγίου πνεύματός ἐστιν οὗ ἔχετε ἀπὸ θεοῦ,

---

23. See Barrett, *Commentary on the First Epistle*, 150.
24. Fee, *First Epistle to the Corinthians*, 261.
25. Fee, *First Epistle to the Corinthians*, 261–62.
26. Fee, *First Epistle to the Corinthians*, 261–62.

Lawsuits among the Corinthians—A Sign of Spiritual Degeneracy

καὶ οὐκ ἐστὲ ἑαυτῶν; 1 Cor 6:19)? The use of "Do you not know. . . ?" (οὐκ οἴδατε. . .) has been recurrent and it always impresses upon the readers the knowledge they ignored or are ignorant of. The preceding "or" (ἤ) suggests the knowledge is obvious and expected to have been appropriately applied in the conduct of the readers. Placing "in you" (ἐν ὑμῖν) between "temple of the" (ναὸς τοῦ) and "Holy Spirit" (ἁγίου πνεύματός) is a deliberate way of emphasising the divine presence in the bodies of the readers: ἤ οὐκ οἴδατε ὅτι τὸ σῶμα ὑμῶν ναὸς τοῦ ἐν ὑμῖν ἁγίου πνεύματός ἐστιν οὗ ἔχετε ἀπὸ θεοῦ.

The second clause of the rhetorical question "and that you are not your own?" (καὶ οὐκ ἐστὲ ἑαυτῶν) reinforces the metanoia that says the readers are not their own—a denial of the idea that the body is their own as suggested in the earlier phrase—"sins against *his own body*."[27] The readers' bodies are indeed not their own because they are the temple of the Holy Spirit. "You were bought with a price" (ἠγοράσθητε γὰρ τιμῆς) gives further amplification in commoratio to "you are not your own." One may decide to sin against one's body, but certainly, not against the temple of the Holy Spirit which is bought with a price. The imperative, "therefore glorify God in your body" (δοξάσατε δὴ τὸν θεὸν ἐν τῷ σώματι ὑμῶν) brings the peroratio to a head. First Corinthians 6:20 should therefore be seen as the sententia, which sums up the essence of Paul's polemic on sexual immorality—"For you were bought with a price; therefore glorify God in your body" (ἠγοράσθητε γὰρ τιμῆς. δοξάσατε δὴ τὸν θεὸν ἐν τῷ σώματι ὑμῶν).

The idea of glorifying God in one's body is radical in a world in which material things had very little spiritual significance. As C.K Barrett notes, glorifying God in one's body is opposed to the view of Seneca, for whom only the soul and spirit could glorify the gods, but not "the contemptible body, which always threatens the purity of the spirit."[28] That such a concept accounted for the pride of the Corinthians while they remained unrepentant of sexual immorality is not implausible.

This last rhetorical division presents the peroratio that concludes Paul's argument with the summary of its essence and its practical import for the readers. By employing *metanoia,* he clarifies what the sin of sexual immorality is against. This is reinforced by the use of commoratio that gives amplification to the idea that the believers are not their own. The fact that the body is the temple of the Holy Spirit, and the object bought with a price, makes the sin against the body a very serious sin. The peroratio comes with

27. Italics are mine.
28. See Barrett, *Commentary on the First Epistle,* 152.

a sententia which instructs the readers on how they ought to live as people who are bought with a price—the very essence of Paul's rhetoric on the sexually immoral act.

CHAPTER 8

Concluding Remarks on 1 Corinthians 1–6

THIS BOOK HAS SOUGHT to demonstrate how Paul's response to the Corinthians was shaped by the Corinthians' judgment of him, a fact which results in a tone that makes 1 Corinthians unique among all his letters. Of course he does not hide his emotions, or rather they give him away. He threatens to come to them with a rod (1 Cor 4:21). He dares those who have become arrogant that he will come and find out their power and not their talk (1 Cor 4:19). He is also clear on his disposition toward defending himself (1 Cor 9:3; cf. 4:3). He is in this mood because he is aware of their judgmental view of him, which he plays back to them with many rhetorical devices, including sarcasm. His gospel was one of foolishness and weakness, yet that was all he knew. As a result, they saw him as one in weakness, in fear, and in much trembling. So he is a fool, but the Corinthians are wise; he is weak, but they are strong; he is held in disrepute, but they in honor. Going hungry and thirsty, being poorly dressed, buffeted, and homeless, and laboring and working with his hands are all evidence for the Corinthians that Paul has failed in his career as a teacher of wisdom.

If it is the number of loyal students one has and the amount of sponsorship one wins that indicates the success of a teacher of wisdom, then Paul has failed in his career by having such a poor lifestyle. The interconnection between wisdom, knowledge, oratory, persuasion, and inspiration also means that Paul's failure to use persuasive words disqualifies him as an inspired speaker. Depicting all these in his own letter to the Corinthians meant that he was fully aware of the Corinthians' judgmental view of

Wisdom, Knowledge, and Spirituality in Self-defense

him. These parameters of the Corinthians' judgment of Paul are the lenses through which Paul presents his own assessment of them.

His rhetorical strategies involve many rhetorical devices that prove that the readers fail woefully in the very assessment they have subjected him to. He not only finds them to lack sound wisdom and knowledge, but they also lack the inspiration to understand spiritual things. To prove their lack of sound wisdom and knowledge, he resorts to three strategies: (1) the repetitive depiction of their wisdom and knowledge in a negative light, (2) the deliberate overelaboration and emphasis on issues, and (3) the provision of obvious answers to questions. A few details on how he used these strategies by way of recap will be helpful here:

(1) For the first strategy of the repetitive depiction of their wisdom in a negative light, Paul mainly employs rhetorical questions. The tone of such rhetorical questions shows his amazement and perplexity about their lack of wisdom and knowledge. Such rhetorical questions usually come with the formula "Do you not know. . . ?" These questions are framed against backgrounds that are meant to heighten the failure of the wisdom and knowledge the Corinthians have relied on, and to make them feel ashamed. On one occasion, he intimates that he says such things to their shame. On one other occasion, he employs apophasis by denying that his reason for writing was to shame them.

(2) On the deliberate overelaboration of issues, Paul finds a number or rhetorical devices to be useful. His use of commoratio enables him to restate the same point in different words. With enumeratio, he provides details to support even points that have already been clearly made. He also employs two rhetorical devices in order to clarify issues. When he employs *metanoia*, he states a point only to deny that that is what it is. This is done purposefully to refute wrong views of the readers, which are put forth and then refuted later. With distinctio, he clarifies a number of things he had said by stating what he means just to remove any ambiguity, and sometimes supporting it with details. In one instance, he does this by pointing to their mistaken view of what he had previously instructed them not to do, which resulted in their current unacceptable conduct.

(3) On the provision of obvious answers, the main rhetorical device was hypophora. Paul asks a question, and instead of expecting his readers to assume the right answer as in a rhetorical question, he provides the

answer. This is meant to ensure that the Corinthians do not assume the wrong answer even in instances where the answer is so obvious.

Paul combines all these rhetorical strategies to demonstrate that his readers are indeed infants and lack the spiritual substance with which one can understand spiritual things meant for the mature in Christ. While the foregoing touch more on the strategies used to indicate their lack of sound wisdom and knowledge, others are employed to show that they are not spiritual.

Paul employs *bending* syllogism in order to identify his gospel, himself, and Apollos as objects, the true understanding of which requires one's possession of the Spirit of God. The fact that the Corinthians do not appreciate these objects for what they are means that they do not have the Spirit of God. It is for this reason that they regard Paul's gospel as weakness instead of the power of God unto salvation, and as foolishness instead of the wisdom of God. They fail to see how the gospel as God's foolishness is wiser than human wisdom, and how as God's weakness, it is stronger than human strength. Similarly, being unspiritual makes them reckon Paul and Apollos wrongly. They cannot appreciate that Paul and Apollos are mere servants through whom they believed. They cannot appreciate that Paul, who planted, and Apollos, who watered, are nothing, and that the one who matters is God alone who grants the growth. For this lack of spiritual understanding, they align themselves to the two teachers as though the teachers were those who died for them, or as the ones into whose names they were baptized. Being unspiritual, they would not accept Paul and Apollos as things freely given to them, mere servants through whom they believed, and part of the things that are theirs, not objects of their allegiance.

Another rhetorical device Paul employs to demonstrate the Corinthians' condition as unspiritual is nonfallacious argumentum ad hominem by which he points to their character in support of his claim that they are not spiritual. He appeals to their jealousy and strife as attitudes which are inconsistent with spiritual people. The fact is, their failure to appoint a wise person among them to settle their cases, and their failure to recognize the spiritual risk involved in the immoral sexual act they were entertaining, corroborate Paul's claim that they are fleshly and behaving like ordinary people.

Paul's response to the readers in 1 Corinthians not only has the effect of judging the readers, but it also justifies him and proves him blameless in relation to the wisdom and power of his gospel and his spirituality. Apart

Wisdom, Knowledge, and Spirituality in Self-defense

from the justification of his gospel as the wisdom and power of God, Paul pitches himself against the hero of the Corinthians in order to clear his image since it is against their hero that the Corinthians' unfavorable assessment of Paul was done. Paul speaks of the excellence of his work and the blameworthy work of Apollos in Corinth. Pointing to his (Paul's) role as the sole layer of the foundation, he speaks of how he did his work as a wise person, and his foundation as made up of nothing but Christ. But he does not make any such excellent remarks of Apollos's work of building upon the foundation. Apollos is to be careful how he builds on the foundation Paul laid, and he should be aware that no other foundation can be laid apart from what Paul had laid, which is Christ. Paul singles out Apollos's work of building upon the foundation for judgment in a manner that makes him appear suspicious of Apollos.

It is clear from Paul's application of the entire argument to himself and Apollos, and from the role of building on the foundation, which is the focus of the judgment, that Apollos is the intended object of this judgment. If the entire argument is applicable to Paul and Apollos, and Paul's role is the layer of the foundation while Apollos's is that of the builder upon the foundation, then which of the two will be judged if it is the one who builds on the foundation who will be judged (1 Cor 3:14)? The fact that Paul speaks of judgment for the role of only one of the two leaders, something that is out of touch with his general view of the eschatological judgment, reveals Paul's deliberate intent here—pointing accusing fingers at Apollos. Paul's deviation from his norm in this particular case is the more reason why the isolation of one particular role (relating to one of them—Apollos) for judgment must be taken seriously. By this, Paul provides the rhetorical clue for his argument. In this judgment, Apollos's motive and the secrets of his heart will be made manifest. On the basis of this, if his work stands, he will be rewarded. But if it gets burned, then he will suffer loss, getting saved only as through fire.

In light of the foregoing, 1 Corinthians 1–6 can rightly be described as Paul's self-defense, a self-defense in which his foolishness becomes the foolishness of God, which is wiser than men; a self-defense in which his weakness becomes the weakness of God, that is stronger than men; a self-defense in which he has the mind of Christ, which makes all other judgments directed against him come to naught. It is precisely because his readers lack sound wisdom, knowledge, and spirituality that they have misjudged him.

Concluding Remarks on 1 Corinthians 1–6

To make this study relevant to today's church, it is important that we reflect on some important questions. Does the ability to speak persuasively like an orator necessarily indicate the presence of superior inspiration in a person? Can the ministry of the word of one who does not speak so persuasively still have the desired effect of regeneration and proper nurture? Are there some things from our traditional way of life (religion in particular) that shape the way we perceive leaders we consider to be spiritual and powerful? What different perceptions do members have of leaders who demonstrate charisma in speech and those who do not? How do these perceptions affect the attitude of members toward these two groups of leaders? Do leaders who have particular gifts consciously or unconsciously act in ways that promote unhealthy attitudes among members toward other leaders who do not have the same gifts? What are the implications of such attitudes on the general life and atmosphere of the church? Are there lessons that leaders and members have to learn in order to protect the church from the effects of members' unhealthy attitudes toward leaders based on the leaders' charisma? What specifically should leaders and members understand, be prepared for, and resolve to do in order not to allow tention, strife, division, rivalry, and unhealthy competition among leaders and members to destroy the life and ministry of the church as a family of God's people?

Glossary

Accumulation: A figure of speech in which similar items are piled up for emphasis.

Alliteration: One of the figures of sound which comes with the repetition of the same consonants in more than one word in a phrase, clause, or sentence or across a number of phrases, clauses, and sentences.

Amplification: A rhetorical device used to increase the impact of a statement by adding some further information to it.

Anadiplosis: A rhetorical device in which the same word ending one clause is repeated at the beginning of the subsequent clause.

Anaphora: A literary and rhetorical device in which the same word or words are repeated at the beginning of two or more clauses or sentences.

Antithesis: Juxtaposing two opposing ideas in order to highlight the contrast.

Apophasis: A rhetorical device by which a speaker brings up an idea by denying it.

Aporia: A rhetorical device which expresses the dilemma of a speaker who now wants the listeners to tell him or her what to do.

Argumentum a maiore ad minus: A kind of *a fortiori* argument in which it is argued that what is applicable to a greater situation is also applicable to a lesser situation.

Argumentum ad baculum: An appeal to threat or force in an argument.

Assonance: Repetition of same or similar vowels in words with different consonants.

Glossary

Bending syllogism: A form of deductive reasoning that comes from major and minor premises that are supposed to suggest an obvious conclusion. When a speaker, instead of the obvious conclusion provides another conclusion, we have a bending syllogism in which the twisted conclusion provides the direction of the speaker's argument.

Cacophony: Use of harsh and inharmonious sounds in a clause, sentence, or a passage. These sounds usually consist of hard consonants.

Chiasm: The presentation of two or more phrases, clauses, or sentences in a particular order and repetition of these in the reverse order, usually not with the same, but similar, wording. In some instances, it is the arrangement of ideas in such order.

Climatic order: Arrangement of words, phrases, or other items in an ascending order of importance.

Cohortatory: Part of an argument that urges the audience to join the author in a course of action.

Commoratio: Repeating the same point in different ways. It is a device of amplification.

Conduplicatio: Repetition of a word or words in successive clauses or sentences.

Contrast: A speaker uses contrast to establish the difference between two people or objects.

Cumulative: Use of many words, clauses, or sentences to describe something in order to increase its significance and effect.

Dehortatio: A rhetorical device employed by speakers to dissuade the audience from taking a particular cause of action. It comes with words like "Do not."

Deliberative rhetoric: One of the three major branches of rhetoric that seeks to persuade an audience to take or not to take some action.

Distinctio: A figure of speech employed to make a point explicit by clarifying it and removing all ambiguity from it.

Enumeratio: A figure of amplification that provides details of a point made in a step-by-step manner in order to enhance the force of the point.

Epideictic rhetoric: One of the three branches of rhetoric concerned with praise and blame of things or people.

Epiphora/epistrophe/antistrophe: The same word or phrase appearing at the end of successive phrases, clauses, or sentences.

Ethos: One of the three modes of persuasion. With this mode of persuasion, the speaker appeals to his or her credibility by way of position, experience, expertise, or any other way in an attempt to make the listeners accept what he or she says.

Exemplum: The use of an example to buttress a point.

Exordium: The introduction of a speech where the author tries to establish a rapport with the audience, and present himself or herself as worthy of the audience's attention. It also provides hints of the themes to be addressed in the speech.

Forensic/legal/judicial rhetoric: One of the branches of rhetoric which focuses on actions in the past. The speaker behaves as one defending his or her case while attacking the opponent in an attempt to establish one's guilt or blamelessness.

Hypophora: A figure of speech in which a speaker answers his own question.

Imperative: Part of a speech in which the speaker exhorts or commands the audience to take some particular course of action. The imperative is usually hortatory in nature, requiring the audience to act, or not to act, in a particular way.

Indicative: The part of speech which establishes who one is, what one is worthy of, capable of, or has the potential of doing. The indicative is presented as the basis from which the exhortation in the imperative is derived. The indicative establishes the necessity and urgency of the imperative.

Irony: A figure of speech in which words or expressions have different meanings from their actual meanings.

Logos: One of the three modes of persuasion. Presentation of facts and logical reasons is the means by which logos, as a mode of appeal, is built.

Metanoia: A rhetorical device used to modify a statement by expressing it in a better way.

Metonymy: Replacing the name of an object or an idea with a different related word or expression.

Narratio: The part of the argument where the speaker gives account of what happened and the nature of the case.

Nonfallacious ad hominem: An appeal to one's character in an argument. Unlike a typical *fallacious ad hominem* argument in which the character of the opponent does not support the speaker's argument, in *nonfallacious ad hominem,* the character of the opponent provides sound basis that supports the speaker's argument.

Parallelism: Ideas coming in successive phrases, clauses, and sentences that have similar syntactical structures.

Partitio: The part of the speech where the speaker sets out the main points and structure of his speech.

Pathos: One of the three modes of persuasion. It seeks to achieve persuasion by appealing to the emotion.

Peroratio: The final part of a speech that recapitulates the main points or essence of the argument in order to make the final appeal to the audience.

Polysyndeton: The deliberate use of many conjunctions in successive words, phrases, clauses, or sentences for stylistic or rhetorical effect.

Refutation: The part of the argument where the speaker tries to undermine or defeat the opponent's claims or arguments.

Repetition: Repeating words or expressions for the sake of emphasis.

Rhetoric: The effective use of language in speech or writing in order to achieve persuasion.

Rhetorical question: A question to which the speaker expects no answer, either because it has no answer or because the answer is obvious.

Sarcasm: The use of irony to make mockery of, or ridicule, someone or something.

Sententia: A quotation, maxim, aphorism, or any such thing that captures the essence of one's point in an argument.

Bibliography

Achtemeier, Paul J., et al. *Introducing the New Testament: Its Literature and Theology.* Grand Rapids: Eerdmans, 2001.
Anum, Eric. "Division and Reconciliation in Pauline Letters." Unpublished article, Microsoft Word file.
Barrett, C. K. *A Commentary on the First Epistle to the Corinthians.* 2nd ed. London: Adam and Charles Black, 1971.
Barton, Stephen C. "1 Corinthians." In *Eerdmans Commentary on the Bible,* edited by James D. G. Dunn and John W. Rogerson, 1314–52. Grand Rapids: Eerdmans, 2003.
Blomberg, Craig L. *The NIV Application Commentary: 1 Corinthians—From Biblical text . . . to Contemporary Life.* Grand Rapids: Zondervan, 1994.
Boring, M. Eugene and Fred B. Craddock. *The People's New Testament Commentary.* Louisville, Kentucky: Westminster John Knox, 2009.
Brookins, Timothy A. "The Wise Man among the Corinthians: Rethinking Their Wisdom in the Light of Ancient Stoicism and Studies on Ancient Economy." PhD diss., Baylor University, 2012.
Charles, Ronald. "The Report of 1 Corinthians 5 in Critical Dialogue with Foucalult," *JCRT* 11.1 (2010) 142–58.
Collins, Raymond F. *First Corinthians.* Edited by Daniel J. Harrington. Collegeville, MN: Liturgical, 1999.
Conzelmann, Hans. *A Commentary on the First Epistle to the Corinthians.* Philadelphia: Fortress, 1975.
Datiri, Dachollom. "1 Corinthians." In *Africa Bible Commentary,* edited by Tokunboh Adeyemo et al., 1377–98. Nairobi: WordAlive, 2006.
Drane, John. *Introducing the New Testament.* Rev. ed. Oxford: Lion Hudson, 1986.
Ellis, E. Earle. "'Wisdom' and 'Knowledge' in Corinthians." *Tyndale Bulletin* 25 (1974) 82–94.
Erickson, Richard J. *A Beginner's Guide to New Testament Exegesis.* Downers Grove, IL: InterVarsity, 2005.
Fee, Gordon D. *The First Epistle to the Corinthians.* The New International Commentary on the New Testament. Grand Rapids: Eerdmans, 1987.
Finney, Mark T. "Honor, Rhetoric and Factionalism in the Ancient World: 1 Corinthians 1–4 in its Social Context." *Biblical Theology Bulletin* 4.1 (2009) 1–10.
Ghaemi, S. Nassir. *The Concept of Psychiatry: A Pluralistic Approach to the Mind and Mental Illness.* Baltimore: Johns Hopkins University, 2003.

Bibliography

Grant, Robert M. *Paul in the Roman World: The Conflict at Corinth.* Louisville: Westminster John Knox, 1989.

Hardison, O. B., Jr. *Poetics and Praxis, Understanding and Imagination: The Collected Essays of O.B. Hardison.* Edited by Arthur F. Kinney. London: University of Georgia Press, 1997.

Harmening, William M. *Mystery at Corinth: Seeking a Jewish Answer to a Christian Mystery.* New York: iUniverse, 2006.

Hartin, Patrick J. *Apollos: Paul's Partner or Rival?* Collegeville, MN: Liturgical, 2009.

Hays, Richard. *First Corinthians.* Louisville: Westminster John Knox, 1997.

Heil, John Paul. *The Rhetorical Role of Scripture in 1 Corinthians—Society of Biblical Literature Studies in Biblical Literature.* Atlanta: Society of Biblical Literature, 2005.

Hogeterp, Albert Livinus Augustinus. *Paul and God's Temple: A Historical Interpretation of Cultic Imagery in the Corinthian Correspondence.* Leuven, Belgium: Peeters, 2006.

Holladay, Carl R. *A Critical Introduction to the New Testament: Interpreting the Message and Meanings of Jesus Christ.* Nashville: Abingdon, 2005.

House, H. Wayne. "Tongues and the Mystery Religions of Corinth." *Bibliotheca Sacra* 140 (April-June 1983) 131–51.

Howell, Don N., Jr. *Servants of the Servant: A Biblical Theology of Leadership.* Eugene, OR: Wipf & Stock, 2003.

Jaśelsner, Singh Mann. "Cultural Memory, Religious Practice, and the Invention of Tradition: Some Thoughts on Philostratus' Account of the Cult of Palaemon." In *Cultural Memories in the Roman Empire,* edited by Karl Galinsky and Kenneth Lapatin, 101–15. Los Angeles: Getty, 2015.

Johnson, Luke Timothy. *Hebrews: A Commentary.* Louisville: Westminster John Knox, 2006.

Keener, Craig S. *The IVP Bible Background Commentary.* Downers Grove, IL: InterVarsity, 1993.

———. *1–2 Corinthians.* The New Cambridge Bible Commentary. Cambridge: Cambridge University Press, 2005.

Kissi, Seth. *The Gifts and Spirituality: Understanding the Subject in the Context of First Corinthians—Addressing some Popular Misconceptions.* Accra, Ghana: African Christian, 2014.

Kwon, Oh-Young. *1 Corinthians 1–4: Reconstructing its Social and Rhetorical Situation and Re-reading it Cross-culturally for Korean-Confucian Christians Today.* Eugene, OR: Wipf & Stock, 2010.

MacArthur, John F. *1 Corinthians.* The MacArthur New Testament Commentary. Chicago: Moody, 1984.

MacBride, Tim. *Preaching the New Testament as Rhetoric: The Promise of Rhetorical Criticism for Expository Preaching.* Eugene, OR: Wipf & Stock, 2014.

Malcolm, Matthew R. *Paul and the Rhetoric of Reversal in 1 Corinthians: The Impact of Paul's Gospel on His Macro-Rhetoric.* Cambridge: Cambridge University Press, 2013.

Marsh, Paul W. "1 Corinthians." In *New International Bible Commentary Based on the NIV Translation,* edited by F. F. Bruce, 1347–88. Grand Rapids: Zondervan, 1979.

Matsen, Patricia P., et al., eds. *Readings from Classical Rhetoric.* Garbonadale, IL: Southern Illinois University Press, 1990.

Mihaila, Corin. *The Paul-Apollos Relationship and Paul's Stance towards Greco-Roman Rhetoric: An Exegetical and Socio-Historical Study of 1 Corinthians 1–4.* LNTS 402. London: T. & T. Clark, 2009.

Miller, Mark Heber. *The Nazarene Commentary with 21st Century Version of the Christian Scriptures: Pauline Teachings—Romans to Hebrews.* N.p.: Xlibris, 2010.

Naylor, Peter. *A Study Commentary on 1 Corinthians.* Darlington, UK: Evangelical, 2004.

Nguyen, V. Henry T. *Christian Identity in Corinth: A Comparative Study of 2 Corinthians, Epictetus and Valerius Maximus.* Tübingen: Mohr Siebeck, 2008.

Patterson, Stephen J. *The Lost Way: How Two Forgotten Gospels are Rewriting the Story of Christian Origins.* New York: Harper One, 2014.

Phillips, John. *Exploring 1 Corinthians: An Expository Commentary.* Grand Rapids: Kregel, 2002.

Powell, Mark Allan. *Introducing the New Testament: A Historical, Literary, and Theological Survey.* Grand Rapids: Baker, 2009.

Sampley, Paul. "1 Corinthians." In *The New Interpreter's Bible Commentary*, vol. 10, edited by Leander E. Keck et al., 773–1003. Nashville: Abingdon, 2002.

Simutowe, Alice Nyirenda. "A Rhetorical Exegetical Study of the Warning Passage in Hebrews Chapter 6 in the Light of its Old Testament Background." Masters Thesis, South African Theological Seminary, 2013.

Snyman, Andries. H. "1 Corinthians 1:18–31 from a Rhetorical Perspective." *Acta Theologica* 1 (2009) 130–44.

Thiselton, Anthony C. *1 Corinthians: A Shorter Exegetical and Pastoral Commentary.* Grand Rapids: Eerdmans, 2006.

Tomlison, F. Alan. "1 Corinthians." In *Holman Illustrated Bible Commentary*, edited by E. Ray Clendenen and Jeremy Royal Howard, 1229–50. Nashville: B & H, 2015.

Witherington, Ben, and Darlene Hyatt. *Paul's Letter to the Romans: A Socio-Rhetorical Commentary.* Grand Rapids: Eerdmans, 2004.

Index

a fortiori argument, 134
a maiore ad minus type, of *a fortiori* argument, 135
ABA1 chiastic structure, 145–46
ABB1A1 chiastic structure, 143
accumulation, 97, 98, 157
Achaicus, 10
Achtemeier, Paul J., 130n12
adulterers, 139, 140
allegiance, Paul and Apollos as objects of, 116
allegorical hermeneutics, of Philo, 81
alliteration, 42, 68, 70, 157
alternation, contrasting Paul's feeling, 101
amplification. *See also* enumeratio
    figure of amplification
    defined, 157
    by enumeratio, 75
    of the grace of God, 31
    helping Paul sound emphatic, 72
    of Paul's feeling about his image, 101
    from Paul's sarcastic depiction of himself, 103
    to a prescribed course of action, 87
    to provide needed detail, 131
    providing procedure for executing Paul's judgment, 123
    between two imperatives, 147
    by way of commoratio, 92, 98, 104
    by way of enumeratio, 77
anadiplosis, 38, 84–85, 86, 157
analogy, 82
anaphora
    creating with repetition, 47
    defined, 157
    distinctio and enumeratio of the narratio involving, 36
    drawing attention to important parts of Paul's argument, 131
    employing to repeat for emphatic effect, 83
    ensuring sound effect for the enumeratio, 139
    list presented with, 88, 138–39
    Paul using, 107
    in Paul's concessional statement on wisdom, 60–61
    polysyndeton creating the effect of, 103
    for repetition and emphasis, 141
    of the repetition of a conjunction in the initial position of each phrase, 127
    in successive repetition, 43
    used by Paul, 100
"and I," as inferential and consequential, 54
angels, judging, 135
antistrophe, 100. *See also* epiphora/epistrophe/antistrophe
antithesis, 44, 61, 157
antithetical adjectival nouns, 87
antithetical statements, in parallel structures, 83
Anum, Eric, 14
aorist passive, 128
Aphrodite, temple of, 9
Apollos
    on baptism, 17

Index

Apollos *(continued)*
  baptizing converts with John's baptism, 16, 18, 37, 38, 40, 81
  behaving as a typical philosopher in Corinth, 96
  bibliographic information, 80–81
  blameworthy work of in Corinth, 154
  as builder upon the foundation laid by Paul, 78, 85, 154
  came to Corinth after Paul's departure, 21
  as a follower first of John, not Jesus, 17
  Hellenistic Jewish tradition of, 15
  influence of Philo on, 81
  as the intended object of Paul's judgment, 154
  on John the Baptist as the teacher of Jesus, 16
  more appealing to the Corinthians than Paul, 21
  motive for his work questionable, 95–96
  nature of his teaching in Corinth, 14–19
  not known to have worked with Paul in Corinth, 96
  Paul found fault with the work of, 95
  Paul narrowing the division (and strife) to, 74
  preaching with eloquent words or wisdom, 77
  role distinguished from Paul, 78–79
  roles assigned to, 3, 82
  on the Spirit coming upon Jesus at his baptism, 17
  spoken rhetoric superior to Paul's, 13
  taught a different gospel in Corinth, 80
  threat of another foundation other than Christ in the work of, 77
  who watered, 153
  as a wisdom teacher, 16
  wisdom theology of, 17
Apollos and Paul
  as God's fellow workers, 76
  place of in the climatic order, 91
  roles of, 2–3, 75, 79n10
apophasis, 108, 111, 152, 157
aporia, 110, 157
apostle of Christ Jesus, Paul as, 25, 25n6
Aquila, 16
arguments, of Paul, 106, 134
argumentum a maiore ad minus, 157
argumentum ad baculum, 110, 111, 157
arrogance, toward Paul, 22
asceticism, to control the body, 144
assessment, Paul setting a new standard for, 58
assonance, 42, 68, 70, 157
attitude
  of Paul versus that of the Corinthians, 104
  of pride, 124
authority, Paul's declining, 11, 21–23

background, connecting wisdom, knowledge, oratory, and inspired men, 13
baptism
  done in names other than Jesus, 16, 18, 37, 38, 40, 81
  as a factor in the schism, 38
  Paul's use of the sacramental language of, 40
baptism of John, by his followers, 17
Barrett, C. K., 148, 149
Barton, Stephen C.
  on the nature of the wisdom, 39
  on Paul's appeal to the temple metaphor, 85–86
  on Paul's lack of rhetorical prowess and personal presence, 58
  on the rhetorical practice of comparison (*synkrisis*), 104–5
  on settling disputes within a group, 135–36
  on the shift of architectural metaphors, 85n21–86n21
believers
  called, elected, or appointed as holy, 27

Index

claiming to belong to one of four figures (Paul, Apollos, Cephas, or Christ), 36
constituting the building and sanctuary of God, 85
core belief and shared value of, 50
importance of gifts to, 32
sanctified in Christ, 27
taking one another to unbelievers to have cases settled, 134
bending syllogism, 153, 158
benefits of Christ, 50
biblical standards, remaining within, 93n3
blameworthy state of the readers, Paul's attempt to deal with, 33
Blomberg, Craig L., 93, 93n3
boasting
 in the Lord, 50
 in men, 98
 against Paul, 105
 setting either Paul or Apollos against the other, 94
 on what they have which they also received, 97
bodily desires, indulging, 144
bodily presence, of Paul, 111
body
 not meant for sexual immorality but to the Lord, 143, 144
 as the temple of the Holy Spirit received from God, 147–49
 use in sexual immorality as evil, 145
 using as a term in both positive and negative senses, 130n12
body of leadership, overseeing the church, 129
the body-the Lord-the Lord-the body structure, of a chiasm, 144
Boring, M. Eugene, 95n7
Brookins, Timothy, 12
brother, taking to be judged before unbelievers, 137
builder's work, manner (how) of the quality of, 82

cacophony, 68, 70, 158

called apostle, Paul identifying himself as, 26
"called as holy" (GG), removing the notion of "not-yet-holy," 27–28, 27n7–28n7
"called as saints," by HSCB, 28
callings, 47, 50
cases among the saints, as lesser issues of this life, 135
catalogue of sufferings (*peristaseis*), 105
caveats, in antithetical clauses, 142
Cephas, 95n7
challenges, responding to, 1
Charles, Ronald, 22
chiasm
 in the body-the Lord-the Lord-the body structure, 144
 on the capacity of the spiritual person, 68
 on contrasts of joining oneself to a prostitute and oneself to the Lord, 146
 defined, 158
 forming another, 44
 highlighting the crucial role of the Spirit, 70
 of a maxim and Paul's caveat, 143
 presenting Isaiah 29:14 in a frame of, 42
 on the result of joining to a prostitute, 145–46
 revealing the nature of the builder's work, 82–83
 on the roles of the layer of the foundation and the builder upon the foundation, 81–82
 on the Spirit of God, 65
 used by Paul, 59–60, 102
chiastic structure
 of the argument of 1 Corinthians 2:1–4, 56
 of the contrast between Paul and the readers, 107
 placing emphasis on the appropriate act, 146
 on the power and wisdom of God, 45

Index

chiasm *(continued)*
  smaller built into a bigger chiasm, 147
children of Wisdom, 17
Christ. *See also* Jesus
  belonging to God, 89
  benefits of, 50
  Corinthians belonging to, 89
  deserving allegiance, 37
  as the foundation on which the building stands, 85
  Paul indicating who he is for the readers, 49
  as the power of God and the wisdom of God, 103
  proclaiming, 44
Christ group, as hypothetical, 74n4
church
  in Corinth, 13, 26, 30
  leaders and members, 1
  met in homes of prominent members in Corinth, 10
  stance on the problem of the immoral man, 129
  taking internal affairs to the public, 137
"church discipline," Fee on the "*ad hoc*" nature of, 124
"the church of God," occurrences of the phrase, 26–27
churches, identifying, 27
city, of Corinth, 8–10
classical rhetorical structure, 24
cleansing out, the old leaven, 125
Cleo's household, reported about division, 10
climatic order, 89, 158
coherence, of Paul's writings, 2
cohortatory
  defined, 158
  second-person subjunctive, 125
cohortatory injunctions, 131
Collins, Raymond F., 9
commoratio
  amplification by way of, 104
  amplifying "but is himself to be judged by no one," 117
  amplifying that believers are not their own, 149
  defined, 158
  describing bloated self-image of the readers, 100
  employed by Paul, 59–60
  enabling Paul to restate the same point in different words, 152
  Paul's use of describing the self-image of the readers, 107
  to a preceding question asking the same question in another way, 137
  presenting wisdom of God for our glory, 62–63
  reflecting Paul's treatment of his readers as infants, 63
  repeating divine activity among the readers, 47–48
  restating a rhetorical question, 141
  restating Paul's assessment of his readers, 72, 74
  restating the role of Apollos, 86
  of roles as "I planted" and "Apollos watered," 78
concluding statements, deriving from Paul's *exemplum*, 49
conclusion and practical implications of the argument, in 1 Corinthians 6:18–20, 147–50
conduplicatio, 37–38, 158
confirmatio, 41, 46, 73
contention, against Paul's apostleship, 26
contrast
  defined, 158
  distinguishing the spiritual person from the unspiritual person, 70
  establishing the readers' failure in actions as against their expected conduct, 140–41
  Paul returning to another series of, 104
Conzelmann, Hans
  on boasting in the Lord, 49–50
  on the destruction of the flesh meaning death, 130
  on groups in the Corinthian church, 36

Index

on judgment applying to Paul, 84
on maxims, 142
on the pneumatics as "a superior class," 69–70
on the relationship between the man and woman involved in the incestuous act, 121
on a Stoic maxim ("All things are yours"), 88n23
Corinth, city of, 8–10
Corinthians
  aligned themselves with favorite teachers, 11
  arrogance and judgmental attitude toward Paul, 129
  assessment of, 97
  assessment of the builder as not final, 83
  attitudes of, 1, 36, 99–100, 104
  belonging to Christ, 89
  boasting of their leaders, 116
  complained about Paul's unimpressive speech and bodily presence, 55
  conduct falling short, 138
  contesting teachings of Paul, 22
  describing in flawless words, 28
  dividing Christ himself, 85
  evaluating teachers by the same token as their secular counterparts, 12–13
  judging the in-group of the believers, 127
  judgment of Paul, 152
  lack of appreciation of the implications of their division, 37
  lacking sound knowledge, 19
  love for knowledge, wisdom, and oratory associated with spirituality, 19–21
  misconception of Paul's and Apollos's identities as indications of their being unspiritual, 115–16
  misinformed or misled on many matters, 6
  not appreciating Paul and Apollos as mere servants, 153
  not belonging to leaders, 89
  not spiritual, 116
  not understanding who Paul and Apollos are, 98
  overrating the leaders as worthy of allegiance, 115
  Paul and Apollos as servants to, 91
  Paul casting a slur on the wisdom and knowledge underlying the actions of, 21
  Paul describing as unspiritual, fleshly, and infants in Christ, 23
  rated as unspiritual, 72
  rating Apollos as more powerful or spiritual than Paul, 21
  regarding Paul's gospel as weakness, 153
  reminding of who they are in Christ, 29
  sarcastic depiction of the self-image of in 1 Corinthians 4:8–13, 99–107
  seen as wise, 102
  taking their internal cases before unbelievers for settlement, 134
  things God had freely given, 97
  unfavorable assessment and judgment of Paul by, 26
  unfavorable assessment of Paul, 6
  as unspiritual persons, 114
  wise in Christ, 102
correction, of the Corinthians' perceptions of Paul and Apollos in 1 Corinthians 3:5–9, 74–77
counter assessment, assessing the Corinthians in 1 Corinthians 3:1–4, 71–74
coworkers, 96, 115
Craddock, Fred B., 95n7
Crispus, 47
cross
  hiding the wisdom of God, 62
  message of as foolishness to those who are perishing, 87
  not emptying of its power, 38
  as the power of God, 41–42
  as a stumbling block and foolishness to the Jews and Greeks respectively, 44

Index

cross *(continued)*
  as worthy of proclamation for Paul, 44
crucified Christ, preaching of, 60
crucified Lord, rejection by the rulers of this age, 62
cumulative use, 158

Datiri, Dachollom
  on appointing judges, 136
  on Crispus, the ruler of a synagogue and Erastus, 47
  holding that the Christ group existed, 74n4
  on the "stomach and food" maxim, 144
dative expressing agency, 134
debaters, coming to nothing, 43
deductions, offered by Paul, 76
dehortatio
  defined, 158
  dissuading from boasting in men, 89
  dissuading readers from engaging in two courses of action, 98
  imperatives in the form of, 93
  "let no one boast in men" as an imperative, 88
  telling readers what not to do, 127, 131
deliberative expressions, seeking to persuade, 98
deliberative language and tone, of a rhetorical division, 39
deliberative oratory, not always requiring an exordium, 24
deliberative rhetoric, 49, 158
depth of God, Spirit searching, 65
destruction of the temple of God, resulting from division, 85
diaspora Jews, moved to Corinth, 9
dilemma (*aporia*), expressing with a rhetorical question, 111
discernment of the discerning, object of God's action, 42
disposition
  of the Corinthians in regard to incest, 121

  of Paul toward defending himself, 151
distinctio figure of speech
  clarifying a number of things, 152
  clarifying Paul's role and that of Apollos, 86
  clarifying roles and where the problem lies, 80
  defined, 158
  listing what things are theirs, 88–89
  removing ambiguity about roles, 82
"dividing Christ," 40, 111
divine action, 30, 44, 143
divine assessment, 44
divine calling, appeal to building *ethos*, 46
divine initiative, in God's choice of the readers, 48
divine presence, in the bodies of the readers, 149
division
  around personalities in the church, 36
  cause of traced to the number of converts a teacher baptized, 40
  in claims of allegiance to human leaders, 114
  as the destruction of God's temple, 85n21
  disastrous effects of, 111
  dividing Christ, 37
  having to do with Paul and Apollos, 95
  as an important factor in Paul's rating of the Corinthians, 74
  indications about the basis of, 35
  not harmless in the church, 85
  over favorite teachers, 11
  Paul introducing the problem of, 35
  Paul's lot in the, 58
  stemming from misconception about the leaders, 115
"Do you not know that...?" Paul's use of as a rhetorical device, 124–25
double conjunctions, use of, 43, 44
Drane, John, 9, 14
drunkards, 127, 139, 140

Index

economic and social hardships, Paul describing, 106
ecstatic utterances, common in pagan religions, 13
Ellis, E. Earle, 14, 20–21
enumeratio figure of amplification, 45, 76. *See also* amplification
  amplifying similes with additional detail, 72
  defined, 158
  detailing division and strife, 36
  details of the sexual act, 121
  emphasizing the unfavorable lot of Paul, 103–4
  establishing the cumulative effect of, 141
  giving details of the facts, 35
  giving further details of the preceding verse, 31
  listing of specific people who are the unrighteous, 138
  offering reasons why the spiritual person judges all things, 117
  of the one who builds on the foundation (Apollos), 115–16
  Paul using, 43, 47, 146
  portraying the spiritual state of the Corinthians, 71
  presenting qualities qualifying the Lord to judge, 98
  presenting reasons for a prescribed course of action, 87
  providing details of the people Paul considers inappropriate, 126
  providing details on the unspiritual person in contrast with the spiritual person, 66
  providing details to support points already clearly made, 152
  providing reasons why the readers should become wise by becoming fools, 89
  providing the needed details of Paul's condition, 107
  quotation acting as, 145
  specifying qualities about the Lord who judges, 92
  as a tool of amplification, 131

use of with anaphora, conduplicatio, and anadiplosis, 39
enumeration, 74
Epictetus, 144
Epicurus, 96
epideictic language, 49
epideictic rhetoric, 50, 63, 158
epiphora/epistrophe/antistrophe
  defined, 159
  effect of, 42
  Paul using, 107
  in repetition of various forms of a verb, 100
Erastus, 47
Erickson, Richard J., 4n1
ESV, Scriptures in English from, 25n5
ethnic diversity, of Corinth, 9
ethos mode of persuasion
  building as a mode of appeal, 35, 39, 41, 46, 52
  defined, 159
  incorporating by appeal to divine initiative, 50
  Paul building as the only father of the readers, 108, 111
  Paul building with a personal testimonial, 59
  Paul incorporating, 37
evidence, of the spiritual state of the Corinthians, 73
evil man, expelling from among them, 127
excommunication
  as being handed over to Satan, 130, 130n10
  as the clear verdict on the immoral man, 129
  meaning of, 123n3
  as the verdict, 131
exemplum, 46, 47, 49, 159
exhortation
  to become fools in order to be wise, 86–89
  for change in attitude and warning to the arrogant, 107–11
exordium, 24–25, 28, 35, 159
expert builder, Paul as, 78

Index

faithfulness, 33, 92
fallacious ad hominem argument, 160
famous persons, collecting the sayings of, 15
father
 of the believers, 108
 learning from Paul as, 112
Fee, Gordon D.
 on Apollos not being mentioned in 1 Corinthians 3:10, 79
 on believers judging angels reflecting an "apocalyptic motif," 135
 on boasting against Paul, 105, 105n15
 on Christ used as metonymy for the church, 85
 on a connection between Paul's personal weakness and his gospel, 55n6
 on the Corinthian view of spirituality, 144–45
 on Corinthians as less than enchanted with Paul's message, 73
 on crimes against one's own body, 148
 on "Everything is permissible for me," 21
 on the first maxim, "All things are lawful," 142n19
 giving a general application of the judgment to the Corinthians, 83–84
 on "To know nothing," 53
 on not inheriting the kingdom of God, 139
 on Paul calling for Apollos's visit, 80
 on Paul using the readers' language, 61
 on Paul's judgment as *ad hoc*, 129
 on Paul's usage for the "flesh/spirit" contrast, 124
 on Paul's usage of the expression "Do you not know that. . .?" 7–8
 on the roles of Paul and Apollos, 79n10
 on wisdom suggesting "superior spirituality," 13
fellowship in Christ, broken up by division, 37
fellowship of the believers, purpose of, 33
Finney, Mark T., 21–22
First Corinthians
 context of, 8–23
 Paul writing in response to reports of disturbing developments, 10
 rhetoric of in reference to its use of Old Testament Scriptures, 5
 rhetorical situation, 10–11
 rhetorical tone addressing those against Paul, 14
First Corinthians 1:1–3, 25
First Corinthians 1–4, 24, 112–13
First Corinthians 1:4–9, 30–31
First Corinthians 1–6, 151–55
First Corinthians 1:10–4:21, 111–12
First Corinthians 1:10–17, 34–35
First Corinthians 1:13–17, 38
First Corinthians 1:18–25, 41
First Corinthians 1:20, 43
First Corinthians 1:23–24, 45
First Corinthians 1:26–31, 46–47
First Corinthians 2:1–3, 2
First Corinthians 2:1–5, 52–53
First Corinthians 2:3, 2
First Corinthians 2:6–9, 60
First Corinthians 2:10–16, 63–64
First Corinthians 2:14–16, 113
First Corinthians 3:1–4, 71–72
First Corinthians 3:5–9, 74–75
First Corinthians 3:5–15, 2
First Corinthians 3:10–14, 77–78
First Corinthians 3:18–23, 86–87
First Corinthians 4:1–7, 90–91
First Corinthians 4:8–13, 99
First Corinthians 4:12:b–13, 104
First Corinthians 4:14–21, 107–8
First Corinthians 5:1–2, 119
First Corinthians 5:1–3, 119–20
First Corinthians 5:4–13, 122
First Corinthians 5–6, 119
First Corinthians 5:8, 126
First Corinthians 6:1–11, 132–33
First Corinthians 6:12–19, 141–42
First Corinthians 6:16b, 145

Index

First Corinthians 6:18–20, 147
first-person plural
  as an indirect reference, 64n16
  Paul speaking about himself in, 104
  Paul speaking of his lot as an apostle, 101
first-person singular, depersonalizing the sin of sexual immorality for the readers, 146–47
"flesh," using as a term, 130n12
fleshly person, 114
"fleshly" rating, as opposed to "spiritual," 73
flexible rhetorical approach, 4, 5–8
"food for the stomach and the stomach for food" maxim, 143
food offered to idols, 11n25, 19, 32
fool for Christ, Paul content with his image as, 118
foolishness and weakness, Paul sticking to a message of, 54
foolishness of God, wiser than men, 87, 103, 114–15, 154
fools, becoming in order to become wise, 102
fools (to the world), becoming, 115
fool-wise contrast, by Paul, 102
forensic, as accusing and judgmental tone, 140
forensic expression, implying that the readers are fools, 89
forensic language
  defending the wisdom of God against human wisdom, 46
  due to judgmental tone, 131
  employed by Paul, 74
  finding serious fault with use of maxims, 142
  of God nullifying the wisdom of this world, 50
  implying the Corinthians are actually fools, 87
  Paul using, 43
  in Paul's defense of himself, 98
forensic rhetoric, passing judgment on the readers, 71
forensic/legal/judicial rhetoric, defined, 159

Fortunatus, 10
foundation
  of Christ laid by a wise builder, 95
  exclusive nature of Paul's, 80
  of God's building (the readers), 78
  laid as Jesus Christ, 80
  Paul's role as the sole layer of, 154
  in the tradition of John and his baptism, 18
free gifts of God, Paul and Apollos as, 116

Galatians, Paul insulting the readers in his perplexity, 6
gentiles, perceived to have a loose moral life, 121
geographical location, of Corinth, 9
gifts, 32, 33
"glorify God," with bodies, 147
Gnosticism, Paul's appeal to expressions typical of, 61
gnostics, 13–14
God
  action against the wisdom of the wise and the discernment of the discerning, 42
  building of, receiving greater attention, 78
  catching the wise in their craftiness, 87, 87n22
  foolishness of as wiser than human wisdom, 45, 153
  freely giving what Paul teaches, 66
  glorifying in your body, 149
  granting growth, 76, 116, 153
  judging outsiders, 127
  made foolish the wisdom of this world, 43
  objects of the giving of, 116
  Paul and Apollos as fellow workers of, 80
  role in contradistinction to the roles played by Apollos and Paul, 75–76
  saving people through the folly of what Paul preaches, 50
  setting aside the wisdom of this age, 50
  temple of, 84, 85

Index

God *(continued)*
  weakness of as stronger than human strength, 45, 153
  working out perfection in recipients, 33
God's Spirit. *See* Holy Spirit; Spirit of God
God-the Spirit-the Spirit-God chiasm pattern, 65
good news, Paul sent to preach, 38
gospel, 41–46, 59
Gospel of Thomas, discovery of, 15
grace, 31
Greco-Roman rhetoric, not limiting rhetorical criticism to, 5
greedy, 127, 139, 140
Greek text, attention to clarifying issues, 2–3
Greek view of the world, placing little or no value on the material order, 144
Greek words, meanings of, xi
Greeks
  inclined to despise the human body, 144
  seeking wisdom, 44
Green, Joel B., 130n12

"Hand him over to Satan," 131
Hardison, O. B., Jr., 4n1
Harmening, William M., 9
Hartin, Patrick J., 76–77
Hays, Richard, 138
Heil, John Paul, 5, 24n2
Hellenistic rhetoric, 4
Hogeterp, Albert Livinus Augustinus, 24n2
Holladay, Carl R., 10
Holy Spirit. *See also* Spirit of God
  necessary to understand the message of the cross, 114
homosexual acts, 139n14
homosexuals, 139, 140
hope, for the blamelessness of the readers, 33
household of Chloe, 10, 36
"how," of the preaching assuming great importance, 39

human body, Greeks inclined to despise, 144
human leaders, boasting in, 86–89
human person, as comprising the flesh (*sarx*), the soul (*psychē*), and spirit (*pneuma*), 16
human wisdom, 44, 112
Hyatt, Darlene, 34
hyperbole, 57n12
hypophora
  clarifying the identity of Apollos and Paul, 77
  defined, 159
  highlighting the horrible nature of sexual immorality, 145
  Paul using, 65, 75, 130
  providing the answer, 75, 152–53
  treating readers as children, 131
  by which the right answer is given, 147
hypothetical items, creating the effect of accumulation, 98

idolaters, 127, 139, 140
if clause, establishing that the saints will judge the world, 134
ignorance, accounting for taking matters to unbelievers for settlement, 134
image of the preacher, shaped by the nature of the message, 57
imagery, of the procession of a victor returning from war, 101
imitators, appeal for the readers to become, 108
immoral life, Corinth noted for, 10
immoral man
  failure to judge, 127–28
  gave his body to Satan for destruction, 130–31
  as old leaven, 126
  Paul presenting a case for the guilt of, 119
  problem of as embarrassing for Paul, 129
  sarcastic depiction of, 3
  separation of the flesh and the Spirit of, 124

Index

immoral persons, not associating with, 127
immoral sexual act, spiritual risk involved, 153
immortality of the soul, idea of, 144–45
imperative
  defined, 159
  in the form of dehortatio, 93
  as the intended result of the indicative, 125
  Paul's use of, 28–29
  series of statements in amplification of, 147
"in favor of one," "against the other" creating rivalry, 94–95
incest
  danger of the sin of, 125
  issue of in the church, 10
  Paul's condemnation of, 121
  right picture of, 123
  widespread news of, 120
inclusio
  answering the question, "Who are the unrighteous who will not inherit the kingdom of God?" 139
  enclosing clauses of, 98
  First Corinthians 2:12 and 2:16 forming, 67
  giving meaning to the list referring to anything they have, 88–89
  presenting Paul and Apollos as the men of whom they boast, 98
  for the purpose of distinctio clarifying in detail what Paul meant by "all things are yours," 89
  rhetorical style lying between 1 Corinthians 2:13–15 and 1 Corinthians 2:12–16, 68
indicative, 28–29, 30, 125, 159
infants, Corinthians as, 72
insiders, judging, 127
inspiration, misconception about "gifts," 20
instrumental dative, 140
ironic contrasts, 107
ironic nexus, between gifts and conduct, 33

irony
  of becoming fools to become wise, 87
  defined, 159
  of foolish things shaming the wise and weak things shaming the strong, 48–49
  heightening the folly, 134, 141
  of lack of knowledge and understanding, 33
  Paul confronting readers with the overwhelming wisdom and power of God, 46
  by Paul in calling on the readers to become fools to become wise, 89
  Paul using to shame the readers, 130
  shaming the Corinthians for lack of sound judgment, 131
Isaiah 29:14, 42
issues, deliberate overelaboration and emphasis on, 152

jealousy and strife, attitude of, 59, 153
Jeremiah 9:23–24, 49
Jeremiah 9:24, 50n28
Jesus. *See also* Christ
  collection of the sayings of, 15
  considered along with John as messengers sent by God, 18
  death of as less important than his sayings, 15
  as the foundation, 81
Jewish idea, of the lofty being brought low as the lowly is lifted high, 47
Jewish Platonism of Alexandria, 16
Jewish rhetorical criticism, 5
Jews
  asking for signs, 44
  wilderness experiences of, 59
Jews and Greeks, Christ as the power of God for believing, 45
Johannine prologue, insistence that Jesus, and not John, was the Logos sent by God, 18
John the Baptist, 16
judging others, accounting for the problem of division and boasting, 94

Index

judgment
- of all things, 118
- belonging to the Lord, 92
- of the one who builds on the foundation in 1 Corinthians 3:10–14, 77–86
- procedure for executing Paul's, 123
- revealing the nature of the builder's work, 82
- for the role of only one of the two leaders, 154
- of the world, 134

judgmental attitude, toward Paul, 6
judgmental language, of the argument of 1 Corinthians 5 as forensic, 119
judicial rhetoric. *See* forensic/legal/judicial rhetoric
Julius Caesar, rebuilt Corinth, 8

Keener, Craig S.
- on believers judging the world, 135
- on Corinthians "evaluating" or "examining" Paul, 13
- on divisions over favorite teachers and styles, 11
- on God's people constituting his temple, 84
- hypothetical view of the Christ group, 74n4
- on opposing views in terms of absurdity (*reductio ad absurdum*), 37
- on Paul putting more rhetoric in his letter, 14
- on Paul's hardship list, 105
- on Paul's manual labor in support of his ministry, 55
- on Paul's unimpressive speech, 54–55
- on political parties bearing the names of the founders, 73
- on politicians, philosophers and orators competing for attention, 12
- on the practice of incest, 142
- on settling matters within a group, 136
- on sexual immorality and food dedicated to idols, 10

king, ridiculed in expectation of a shameful and painful death, 105
kingdom of God, 17, 111
klētos apostolos (GG), 25n6
knowledge
- as the guiding principle for Corinthians, 19
- misuse of, in relation to eating food offered to idols, 32
- obtaining consistent with nature and living by it, 39
- possessors of, 11n25

Kwon, Oh-Young, 9

lack of understanding, of Paul's message, 115
lawsuits, as a sign of spiritual degeneracy, 132–50
layer of the foundation, as a "wise" builder, 82
leaders, as part of the "possession" of the Corinthians, 89
leaven, of malice and evil, 126
legal rhetoric. *See* forensic/legal/judicial rhetoric
lessons, from Paul and Apollos, 93
"let no one boast in men," as a prescribed course of action, 88
letters, of Paul as weighty and strong, 58–59, 111
Lietzmann, Hans, 148
limited good, concept of in Mediterranean society, 94
local church, phrases qualifying in the New Testament, 27
logos mode of appeal
- advancing reasons for which the Corinthians are misguided and guilty in their actions, 131
- building as the mode of appeal, 89
- defined, 159
- incorporating *pathos* with appeal to shame, 140
- as the mode of appeal, 99
- offering up of reasons for rating of the Corinthians, 74

providing logical support clarifying the identity of Apollos and Paul, 77
supporting an argument, 46
"the Lord," Paul using as a metonymy for himself, 117
Lord
　as the only one qualified to judge, 92
　result of joining oneself to, 146
love and gentleness, opting for a spirit of, 110

MacArthur, John F., 57
MacBride, Tim, 105
maiore ad minus, 141
Malcolm, Matthew R., 4, 13, 24n2
man, having his father's wife, 121
Marsh, Paul W., 137
mature, able to discern God's wisdom, 61
maxims
　caveats against, 142
　enslaving effect of the use of, 142
　repetition of as significant, 142
members of Christ, 145, 146
members of the church, Paul dividing, 61
message, nature of determined by the manner in which it is proclaimed, 57
message of the cross
　as God's power unto salvation, 114
　as the power of God unto salvation, 118
　preached without human wisdom, 106
　representing God's wisdom and power, 109
　as the weakness of God, 106
messengers of God, Jesus and John as, 18
metanoia
　clarifying issues, 152
　clarifying what the sin of sexual immorality is against, 147, 149
　defined, 159

qualifying Paul's statement that he knows nothing against himself, 92, 98
saying the readers are not their own, 149
metonymy
　for Apollos to be judged for his work as a builder upon the foundation of Christ, 82
　defined, 159
　enabling Paul to use the first-person plural and "the Lord" referring to himself, 70
　of "God's temple" for "God's building," 84
　for Paul, 44
　Paul using to describe himself, 101
　Paul using to point indirectly to himself, 64
　temple of God as for the readers, 86
Mihaila, Corin, 24n2, 56
"milk"
　for learners failing to live up to their training, 73n1
　in terms of the teaching given to the readers, 72
Miller, Mark Heber, 79, 79n8
mind of Christ, having, 67, 69, 92, 117
mind of God, no one knowing except the Spirit of God, 65
minds, having different, 35
ministry, preparing for unfortunate realities of, 1
minore ad maius argument, 65
miracles, Paul's avoidance of appeal to, 59
"motive," Paul's emphasis on, 95
mystery of God, Paul proclaiming not with eloquent word or wisdom, 53
mystery of God's wisdom, as incomparable to anything ever experienced, 62–63

name of a deity, appealing to people in, 35
narratio part of the argument, 36, 39, 160
nature, behaving according to one's, 29

Index

Naylor, Peter, 33, 56–57
negative image, assigned to Paul, 22
Nestle-Aland Greek New Testament, 28th edition, 25n4
nexus, between one "in weakness and in fear and much trembling" and Paul's resolution to preach nothing but Christ and him crucified, 2
Nguyen, V. Henry T., 12
nonfallacious argumentum ad hominem, 74, 153, 160
"nothing beyond what is written," 93–94
noun phrases, describing Paul's state, 53–54

objective, stated in the form of an appeal, 35
obvious answers, provision of, 152–53
old leaven, 125, 126
Old Testament
    interpreting in the light of Greek philosophy, 81
    Paul's use of scriptures from, 5
one flesh, result of becoming, 146
opponents, Paul's tone of one addressing, 20n63
orator, not preaching the gospel as an, 55
"our glory," as the purpose for wisdom proclaimed in hidden mystery, 62
outsiders, judging, 127

pagan religions, spirit possession in, 13
Papias, sayings of Jesus by, 15
parallel structures, employed in enumeratio to achieve amplification, 141
parallelism
    defined, 160
    enabling Paul to set out the roles of Apollos, himself, and God, 77
    in the imagery of the Passover feast, 128
    presenting the judgment of the builder upon the foundation, 86
    presenting the maxim and the two caveats, 142
    repeating similar structures for emphatic effect, 46
    in the repetition of the same structure, 48
    setting the focus on God's actions and their outcome, 43–44
    stating important points deserving attention, 131
    used by Paul, 76
parentheses, Greek words in, xi
parent's way of life, demanding from children of Paul in Christ, 108
partitio, 35, 160
Passover
    imagery of, 124, 125
    preparation of, 126
pastoral letters, rhetorical structure complex in, 25
pathos mode of persuasion
    with appeal to shame, 140
    building, 38
    defined, 160
    incorporating into the argument, 39
    incorporating into the *logos* mode of appeal, 63
    indirect appeal to shame building, 108, 111
    Paul incorporating with an appeal to shame, 137
Patterson, Stephen J., 15–18, 38, 80
Paul
    on Apolos's style of presentation, 77
    assessing and evaluating his readers, 6, 6n12–7n12
    authority declining, 22, 26
    baptized Apollos's converts in the name of Jesus, 81
    baptized "disciples" of Christ in the name of Jesus, 16
    behaving as a fool for Christ's sake, 106
    as blameless in the test of faithfulness expected of a servant, 92
    called by God and made an apostle, 25n6

challenged readers to accept being wronged or defrauded instead of taking one another to the law court, 138
clear instructions on how his judgment of the immoral man should be carried out, 121
coherence of his writings, 2
combining both the greeting of peace from his Jewish tradition, and grace from his Christian tradition, 30
dealing with issues specific to the Corinthian church, 30
declining authority of, 21–23
deliberate isolation of the one who builds on the foundation, 95
difficulties in understanding, 2–3
displeased with envy, strife, and division, 28
evaluating and rating believers, 22–23
feeling judged, 6, 6n11
finding fault with those who preach the cross with eloquent words of wisdom, 38
finding fault with wisdom and knowledge of the Corinthians, 6–7, 7n13
as a fool because of Christ, 102
on his ministry in the Corinthian church, 38
identifying himself, 25
image among the Corinthians, 52–60
ironic presentation of himself as a more spiritual person, 104
judging the Corinthians with the very judgment with which they have judged him, 102
knowledge of those behaving as though he was not coming to them, 109
as the layer of the foundation, 85
not baptizing many people, 38
not known to have worked with Apollos in Corinth, 96
not referring to any insignificant members of the church, 136
not shying away from defending himself, 21
not treating the Corinthians as they treated him, 118
obsessed with evaluating and rating the Corinthians, 6
pitching himself against the hero of the Corinthians, 154
placing himself higher in spiritual understanding, 117
pointing accusing fingers at Apollos, 154
pointing out even the obvious answer, 145
pointing out the destructive effect of division, 85n21
preoccupied with evaluating and rating his readers, 8
preoccupied with his unfavorable image, 105–6
presenting division in a ridiculous way, 73–74
pronouncing judgment even before meeting, 129
proving blameless in relation to the wisdom and power of his gospel and his spirituality, 153–54
proving that the Corinthian believers were babes in Christ, 5–6
raising caveats against the words of wisdom, 20
recognition of a teaching other than Christ, 80
refraining from reviling back, 106–7
resolution and focus on the gospel, 53
resolution to know nothing except Jesus Christ and him crucified, 55–56, 57, 57n12
role as the one who preaches the mysteries of God, 64
role as the sole layer of the foundation, 80
rolling back the effects of Apollos's teachings, 16

Index

Paul *(continued)*
   speaking as a father addressing his children, 20n63
   as a spiritual person who judges all things with the mind of Christ, 118
   threatening to come to the Corinthians with a rod, 20n63
   treating his readers as infants having all solid foods turned into liquid, 135
   use of pronouns other than first-person singular to refer to himself, 64n16
   using different verbs to distinguish his role from that of Apollos, 78–79
Paul and Apollos
   as freely given gifts of servants to the Corinthians, 97–98
   not accepting as things freely given, 153
   roles of, 2–3, 75, 79n10
people with no standing in the church, as not "despised people" within the church, 136
perception
   affecting the attitude of members toward groups of leaders, 155
   Paul dealing with a problem of, 91
   as the problem of the recipients, 39–40
peroratio
   bringing out the essence of the argument, 147
   concluding Paul's argument, 149–50
   defined, 160
   giving the conclusion, 131
   representing how Paul wants the believers to live, 128
   summing up the action to take on the immoral man, 128
persuasion, association with wisdom and spirituality, 14
persuasive words, Paul's failure to use, 151
Phillips, John, 77n6, 80–81
Philo, 77n6, 81

philosophers, have come to nothing, 43
philosophical concepts, accounting for why Corinthians were indifferent to the sin of incest, 142
philosophical schools, collected sayings and anecdotes of great teachers, 15n45
planting, role of for Paul, 75
pneumatics
   association of wisdom and knowledge with in the Corinthian church, 14, 14n40
   cherished gifts of utterance, wisdom, and knowledge, 58
   testing, 20n63
polysyndeton
   in the abundant use of a conjunction, 127
   creating the effect of anaphora, 103
   defined, 160
   drawing attention to important parts of Paul's argument, 131
   giving cumulative effect to benefits from Christ, 49
   giving divine acts cumulative effect, 139
   increasing the cumulative impact of two lists, 107
   as Paul's way of highlighting the totality of his feeling of reproach, 101
   for repetition and emphasis, 141
   used in stating noun phrases, 54
   using to stress the Corinthians' low perception of Paul, 60
population, of Corinth, 9
possessors of knowledge, not caring about how their actions affected members, 11n25
Powell, Mark Allan, 30
power, 109, 111
power of God
   equated to "weakness" (of God), 45
   faith resting on, 59
   as the folly of the message of the cross, 110
   Paul unparalleled in demonstrating, 109

power-wisdom-wiser-stronger chiasm, 45
preaching, 45, 95
premises, Paul establishing, 53
Priscilla, 16
probatio, 5
problem of division, and resulting strife, 36
problems, addressed by Paul, 32
pronouns, Paul's creative and rhetorical use of, 145
prophets of wisdom, John the Baptist and Jesus as equal, 17
propositio, 1 Corinthians 1:10 as, 4
prostitute, 145, 146
prostitution, as part of the pagan religion, 9–10
psychikoi, in the Corinthian church, 83n16
punishment, pronouncing on the immoral man, 119
purpose, for writing biblical text, 3

Q source, 15, 17
quality, of Paul's work as a major defense, 32
question, establishing readers' failure of dealing with ordinary matters, 135
question tag, presenting the task of judging the world as a greater task, 134
question-and-answer (hypophora), use of the rhetorical device of, 130
question-and-answer response, Paul employing, 65
quotations, supporting a course of action, 87

rapport, establishing with an expression of gratitude, 31
rating, Paul defending his as given by the Corinthians, 53
readers
  acting out of folly and ignorance, 134
  admonishing as beloved children, 108
  appeal to the calling of, 46–51
  becoming wise by becoming fools, 89
  blameworthy state of, 33
  bloated self-image of, 100
  bodies as members of Christ, 145
  calling of, 46, 47
  challenged by Paul, 51
  cheating and defrauding their own brothers, 137
  choice of the greater evil, 137
  confirming the testimony of Christ among, 34
  confronting with the overwhelming wisdom and power of God, 46
  constituting the temple of God, 84
  depersonalizing the sin of sexual immorality for, 146–47
  dissuading from engaging in two courses of action, 98
  divine activity among, 47–48
  divine presence emphasising the bodies of, 149
  expected conduct of, 140–41
  failing to understand the mysteries of God, 103
  failing woefully in their assessment, 152
  failure in dealing with ordinary matters, 135
  false self-image of, 107
  as the foundation of God's building, 78
  God's choice of, 48
  as God's field and building, 76
  God's Spirit dwelling in, 84
  hope for the blamelessness of, 33
  as infants, 3, 63, 135, 153
  instructing on how they ought to live, 150
  inviting to join in what is right for their current situation, 131
  involved in acts belonging to the realm of the condemned, 139
  lack of wisdom and knowledge, 152
  "milk" used for teaching, 72
  misconception about Paul and Apollos, 91
  as not spiritual, 74

Index

readers *(continued)*
  as not their own, 149
  passing judgment on, 71
  Paul as the only father of, 111
  Paul assessing and evaluating, 6, 6n12–7n12, 8
  Paul not depicting as builders, 84
  Paul using the language of, 61
  Paul virtually insulting in Galatians, 6
  Paul's assessment of, 72, 74, 107
  Paul's clear references to the views of, 21
  as people "washed," "sanctified," and "justified," 140
  persuading to boast in the Lord, 49
  as proud in spite of contemptible acts, 143
  relying on wisdom of this age, 87
  shaming, 108, 111, 130
  spirituality of, 72, 74
  taking one another to the law court, 138
  telling what not to do, 127, 131
  as temples of God, 86
  treated as people who cannot be trusted, 147
  treating as children, 131
  as unrighteous, 138
refuse of all things, Paul as, 107
refutatio, rhetorical division as, 142
refutation, 144, 146, 160
reigning kings, behaving as, 100
religious diversity, of Corinth, 9
religious leaders, some weak in delivery, 55
remorse, in the face of the sin as correct, 121
repeated emphasis, on going before unbelievers with little cases, 135
repetition
  defined, 160
  for a deliberate emphatic effect, 121
  use of in parallelism, 146
repetitive depiction, of wisdom in a negative light, 152
repetitive emphasis, on Paul's image, 54

repetitive parallels, giving overelaborations and overemphases, 6
resurrection, 17, 20, 145
rhetoric
  defined, 160
  language of all three forms of, 112
  limiting, 4
rhetoric language, combination of all three forms of, 50
rhetorical analysis, approaches to, 4
rhetorical critical approach, 2
rhetorical criticism, 3–5
rhetorical devices
  in 1 Corinthians 1–4, 112–13
  Paul resorting to sarcasm, 100
  Paul using in order to achieve persuasion, 112
  revealing Paul's intent of demonstrating his readers as infants in Christ, 3
  uniqueness of, 3
rhetorical division, of 1 Corinthians 1–6, 24–25
rhetorical exegetical approach, to interpreting Scripture, xii
rhetorical function, of the salutation, 30
rhetorical models, applying, 4
rhetorical question(s)
  addressing the Corinthians' self-image, 96–97
  calling attention to important points, 146
  clarifying the identity of Apollos and Paul, 77
  confronting the readers with who they are as the temple of God, 86
  defined, 160
  excessive use of revealing Paul's astonishment and perplexity, 133–34, 141
  on the identity of Apollos and Paul, 115
  Paul employing, 131, 152
  Paul engaging to build *logos* as a mode of appeal, 36–37
  pointing to the rod-deserving attitude of the Corinthians, 110

Index

providing support for the claim that the readers are not spiritual, 74
    with respect to the Corinthians' perceptions of Paul and Apollos, 75
rhetorical situation, of First Corinthians, 10–11
rhetorical strategies, 152, 153
rhetorical structure, forcing Paul's letters to fit some particular ancient, 4
rhetorical studies, 2, 5
rhetorical terms, glossary of, xii
rhetorical unit, 24n1
rhetoricians, granting fame to, 12
rhyme, and assonance in words calling attention to contrasts, 104
"ridiculing," use of, 123n3
rivalries, putting an end to, 93
rod, Paul coming with, 110, 151
Roman and Greek gods, worship of in Corinth, 9
rulers of this age, contrasted with Paul, 65

saints, 29, 135
salutation, of 1 Corinthians 1:1–3, 25–30
salvation, of the immoral man's spirit in isolation from his body, 130
Sampley, Paul
    on Paul being like Moses unskilled in speech, 55
    on Paul making a call to maturity, 93
    on Paul using "indirect" or "figured speech," 94
    on Paul's message of weakness, 57, 57n12–58n12
    on the preference for indirect speech, 79
    role of *pater familias* ("head of the household"), 108
sanctification, 27, 29–30
sarcasm
    defined, 160
    as a judgment, 123
    mocking bloated self-image, 107
    of Paul, 100, 107, 151
    recognizing the Corinthians' capacities, 33
    use of, 123n3
sarcastic contrast, establishing, 101
Satan, 123, 129–30
schism and its cause, described in 1 Corinthians 1:10–17, 34–40
"schools," formed around Paul and Apollos, 13
Scripture, in Ghanaian and African contexts, xi
scum of the world, Paul as, 104, 107
self-defense, 1 Corinthians 1–6 as Paul's, 154
self-image
    playing back to the Corinthians, 99–107
    rhetorical questions addressing the Corinthians,' 96–97
self-perception, of the Corinthians, 100
Seneca, 149
sententia
    capturing the main sense of argument, 49
    defined, 160
    inquiring if one could know the mind of the Lord, 67
    instructing readers on how they ought to live, 150
    summing up Paul's polemic on sexual immorality, 149
servants, Paul and Apollos as, 93, 93n3, 115
"services" and "works," by people lacking inspiration, 20
sex, as inimical to spiritual development, 19
sexual immorality
    Corinthians' failure to appreciate the dangers of, 122–31
    as evidence of lack of sound knowledge and spirituality, 119–31
    fleeing from, 147
    giving one's body to, 123
    gravity of, 146
    horrible nature of, 145
    repetition of as emphatic, 120–21

Index

sexual immorality *(continued)*
  as sin against one's own physical body, 148
sexual immorality and lawsuits against fellow believers, as a single rhetorical unit for Paul, 142
sexually immoral man. *See* immoral man
sexually immoral persons
  calling for mourning rather than pride, 103
  not associating with, 127
  not inheriting the kingdom of God, 139
  relating to the incident of incest, 140
signs (GG), demanded by the Jews, 44
simile, 72, 74, 86
Simutowe, Alice Nyirenda, 5
sin, against one's body, 148
slanderers, 127, 139
Snyman, Andries H., 4, 5
social scientific criticism, as a useful approach, xii
social script, expecting children to behave like their parents, 108
Socrates, 137–38
"solid food," Hellenistic use of, 72n1–73n1
sophists, 95, 96
Sosthenes, 26
sound, enhancing the emphatic effect of various arguments, 112
speakers, expected to speak persuasively, 13
"spectators," Corinthians as, 105
Spirit
  demonstration of accompanied Paul's words, 56
  demonstration of in terms of gifts and miraculous acts, 59
  Paul appealing to the activity of, 58
  role in aiding understanding and communication of the message of the cross, 111
  role of searching and revealing the things of God, 64
spirit (the divine), association of with wisdom and knowledge (revealed knowledge), 58
Spirit and power, demonstration of, 58
Spirit of God. *See also* Holy Spirit
  comprehending the thoughts of God, 64
  Corinthians not having, 153
  dwelling in readers, 84
  possessing necessary to understand Paul's message, 103
  purpose for having as also the purpose for having the mind of Christ, 67
  purpose for receiving, 65–66
  unspiritual person not accepting the things of, 113
spiritual "credentials," exhibiting by displaying gifts during meetings, 20
spiritual exaltation, of the Corinthians, 105
spiritual experiences, Corinthians' overreliance on, 59
spiritual person
  defined in 1 Corinthians 2:14–16, 116–18
  freedom from the judgment of all others, 117
  having the mind of Christ, 69
  interpreting things by means of the Spirit, 67
  judged by no one, 68–69, 116–17
  principles defining, 69, 70
  qualities of a, 63–70
  teaching things freely given in spiritual terms, 66
  understanding the mystery of God's wisdom, 63
spiritual state, given away by amplification in repetitive descriptions, 73
spiritual status, of children with unbelieving spouses, 19
spiritual things, 66, 114
spiritual truth, Corinthians unable to appreciate mature, 6
spiritual understanding, Corinthians' lack of, 114

spirituality, wisdom and knowledge associated with, 13
sports, 10, 10n22
Stephanas, 10
stewards, faithfulness sought in, 91
Stoic maxim, "All things are yours," 88n23
stomach, sandwiched by food, 143
"stomach and food" maxim, 144
strife, between groups built around personalities, 36
students, of Apollos cursing Jesus, 18
subunits, of 1 Corinthians 1–6, 24
super apostles, who came to Corinth after Paul, 22
supporting arguments, of an author, 3
swindlers, 127, 139, 140
syllogism, 66–67, 70

talk, futility of, 109
teachers
  attempts to win loyalty and patronage, 12
  claims of allegiance to respective, 73
  competition among, 14
  emotional attachment to, 96
  evaluation and alignment to favorite, 11–19
  of knowledge, 39
  of wisdom, 103, 151
teaching
  of Christ, 107
  inability to understand Paul's, 114
temple of the Holy Spirit, sinning against, 149
testimony of Christ, confirming among the readers, 34
thanksgiving
  of 1 Corinthians 1:4–9, 30–34
  concluding words of forward looking, 33
  functioning as part of the exordium in a letter, 31
  as part of the exordium, 34
  speech and knowledge pointed out for, 31–32
thieves, 139, 140
Thiselton, Anthony C., 12, 92, 96

Thompson, Marianne Meye, 130n12
thoughts of the wise, as futile, 88
Timothy, 109
Tomlison, F. Alan, 79
topical statement, 35, 63
tradition of John, not ended by the Gospels, 17–18

unbelievers, as "the unrighteous," 134
uniqueness, of the wisdom Paul preached in 1 Corinthians 2:6–9, 60–63
unity, appeal for building *ethos*, 39
unleavened bread, of sincerity and of truth, 126
unmarried, contemplating remaining as, 19
unrighteous people, 138, 140
unspiritual people, 124
unspiritual person
  contrasting with the spiritual person, 66
  described in 1 Corinthians 2:14–16, 113–16
  not discerning things spiritually, 67
unspiritual state, 114–15
utterance, misuse of the gifts of, 32

verdict, process for carrying out, 123–24

watering, role of for Apollos, 75
weakness, of the gospel as really the power of God, 57
weakness of God
  carrier of appearing weak to the Corinthians, 106
  Paul's message as, 55n6
  stronger than men, 59, 103, 115, 154
weapons of Paul's warfare, having divine power, 110
we-you-you-we chiasm, affording Paul the chance to end sarcastic contrasts, 102
"what is written," 93, 94
wisdom
  hierarchical and discriminatory nature of, 39

Index

wisdom *(continued)*
    of the rulers of this age, 61
    sought by the Greeks, 44
    sources of, 39
wisdom and knowledge, 13–14, 152
wisdom of God
    equating "foolishness" (of God), 45–46
    as good, 60
    Paul establishing the superior and unique nature of, 63
    qualifications of, 62
    rulers of this age not knowing, 62
    spiritual person understanding, 63
wisdom of the wise, as an object of God's action, 42
wisdom of this world, 87, 111
wisdom of words. *See also* words of wisdom
    Paul having an aversion to, 4
    Paul preaching without, 38
    Paul's avoidance of, 43
    Paul's style without, 95
    preaching the gospel with, 112
    preaching without, 38
    reliance on, 35
wisdom sayings, prior to the writing of the canonical Gospels, 15
wise in Christ, becoming, 115
wise person, failure to appoint to settle lawsuit cases, 153
Witherington, Ben, 34
women, customs and traditions, 19, 20
words of wisdom
    Paul identifying, 19n61
    Paul not preaching with, 43
    Paul raising caveats against, 20
world, not knowing God through wisdom, 43, 44

www.ingramcontent.com/pod-product-compliance
Lightning Source LLC
Chambersburg PA
CBHW062040220426
43662CB00010B/1585